FEAR

FEAR
A Dark Shadow Across
Our Life Span

Edited by
Salman Akhtar

First published in 2014 by
Karnac Books Ltd
118 Finchley Road
London NW3 5HT

British Library Cataloguing in Publication Data

A C.I.P. for this book is available from the British Library

ISBN-13: 978-1-78220-068-0

Typeset by V Publishing Solutions Pvt Ltd., Chennai, India

Printed in Great Britain

www.karnacbooks.com

To
Dilip & Parvati Ramchandani
in friendship

CONTENTS

ACKNOWLEDGEMENTS

Seven distinguished colleagues devoted their time and effort to writing original papers, upon my request, for inclusion in this book. They abided by the deadlines I set and responded to my editorial suggestions with utmost grace. My assistant, Jan Wright, prepared the manuscript of this book with diligence and good humour. My colleagues in the Department of Psychiatry at Jefferson Medical College, especially Drs Jonathan Beatty, Solange Margery-Bertoglia, Shawn Blue, Rajnish Mago, Deanna Nobleza, Stephen Weinstein, and Stephen Schwartz kept me in good humour while I delved in the dark realm of dread and terror which this book is all about. To all these individuals, my sincere thanks, indeed.

Salman Akhtar
Philadelphia, PA

ABOUT THE EDITOR AND CONTRIBUTORS

Salman Akhtar, MD, is professor of psychiatry at Jefferson Medical College and a training and supervising analyst at the Psychoanalytic Center of Philadelphia. He has served on the editorial boards of the *International Journal of Psychoanalysis* and the *Journal of the American Psychoanalytic Association*. His more than 300 publications include fourteen books—*Broken Structures* (1992), *Quest for Answers* (1995), *Inner Torment* (1999), *Immigration and Identity* (1999), *New Clinical Realms* (2003), *Objects of Our Desire* (2005), *Regarding Others* (2007), *Turning Points in Dynamic Psychotherapy* (2009), *The Damaged Core* (2009), *Comprehensive Dictionary of Psychoanalysis* (2009), *Immigration and Acculturation* (2011), *Matters of Life and Death* (2011), *Psychoanalytic Listening* (2013), and *Good Stuff* (2013)—as well as forty-one edited or co-edited volumes in psychiatry and psychoanalysis. Dr Akhtar has delivered many prestigious addresses and lectures including, most recently, the inaugural address at the first IPA-Asia Congress in Beijing, China (2010). Dr Akhtar is the recipient of the *Journal of the American Psychoanalytic Association*'s Best Paper of the Year Award (1995), the Margaret Mahler Literature Prize (1996), the American Society of Psychoanalytic Physicians' Sigmund Freud Award (2000), the American College of Psychoanalysts' Laughlin Award (2003), the American

Psychoanalytic Association's Edith Sabshin Award (2000), Columbia University's Robert Liebert Award for Distinguished Contributions to Applied Psychoanalysis (2004), the American Psychiatric Association's Kun Po Soo Award (2004), the Irma Bland Award for being the Outstanding Teacher of Psychiatric Residents in the country (2005), and the Nancy Roeske Award (2012). Most recently, he received the Sigourney Award (2013), which is the most prestigious honour in the field of psychoanalysis. Dr Akhtar is an internationally sought speaker and teacher, and his books have been translated in many languages, including German, Turkish, and Romanian. His interests are wide and he has served as the film review editor for the *International Journal of Psychoanalysis*, and is currently serving as the book review editor for the *International Journal of Applied Psychoanalytic Studies*. He has published seven collections of poetry and serves as a scholar-in-residence at the Inter-Act Theatre Company in Philadelphia.

Jerome S. Blackman, MD, DFAPA, FIPA, FACPsa, is clinical professor of psychiatry at Eastern Virginia Medical School, Norfolk, VA; training and supervising analyst with the Contemporary Freudian Society in Washington, DC; past Designated Sexual Abuse Treatment Resource for the State of Louisiana. He has been visiting lecturer at Beijing University, Fu Dan Medical University (Shanghai), and Zhe Jiang Medical School in Hangzhou, China. The Psychiatry Teaching Award at Naval Medical Center, Portsmouth, VA was named in his honour in 1992. He is the author of *101 Defenses: How the Mind Shields Itself* (2003), *Get the Diagnosis Right: Assessment and Treatment Selection for Mental Disorders* (2010), and *The Therapist's Answer Book: Solutions to 101 Tricky Problems in Psychotherapy* (2013). The first of these books has been translated into Romanian, Chinese, and Turkish.

Calvin Colarusso, MD, is a clinical professor of psychiatry at the University of California at San Diego and a training and supervising analyst in adult and child psychoanalysis at the San Diego Psychoanalytic Institute. He is the author of more than fifty peer-reviewed articles and book chapters. An expert witness in more than 100 cases of child sexual abuse, he has treated both victims and perpetrators. Dr Colarusso has co-authored two major texts on adult psychological development: *Adult Development: A New Dimension in Psychodynamic Theory and Practice* (1981), and *New Dimensions in Adult Development* (1990). In addition, he has authored many books of his own, including: *Child and Adult Development: A Psychoanalytic Introduction for Clinicians* (1992), and *The Long Shadow of Sexual Abuse: Developmental Effects Across the Life Cycle* (2010).

M. Hossein Etezady, MD, is a board certified child and adult psychiatrist and psychoanalyst in private practice. He has worked in multiple settings of inpatient, outpatient, and consultation services in child and adolescent, as well as adult psychiatry. For over thirty years, he has served as the moderator, coordinator, contributor, and is currently serving as the senior co-chair of the Vulnerable Child Discussion Group of the American Psychoanalytic Association and the Association for Child Psychoanalysis. Dr Etezady has written numerous articles on clinical, theoretical, and research work in child and adult psychoanalysis. His recent writings include updated psychoanalytic perspectives on topics such as development of the self, narcissism in pathology and normality, faith and transformation, and creativity and play. In addition, he has edited several books, including *The Neurotic Child and Adolescent* (1990), *Psychoanalytic Treatment of the Young* (1993), *The Vulnerable Child, vol. I* (1993), *The Vulnerable Child, vol. II* (1995), *The Vulnerable Child, vol. III* (1996), and *Clinical Perspectives on Reflective Parenting* (2012). He is the co-editor of three additional volumes of *The Vulnerable Child* series including *From Chaos to Organization*, in press. Since 2007, Dr Etezady has served as the head of the faculty and the chair of the Education Committee of the newly established Tehran Psychoanalytic Institute, where he has been actively involved in the construction and implementation of the training programme in psychoanalytic psychotherapy. Dr Etezady is a board member of Margaret Mahler Psychiatric Research Foundation and a faculty member of the Psychoanalytic Center of Philadelphia, PA.

Peggy B. Hutson, MD, is a training and supervising analyst at the Florida Psychoanalytic Institute and the past president of the Florida Psychoanalytic Society and Foundation. She is on the volunteer faculty of the Department of Psychiatry at the University of Miami's Miller School of Medicine where she holds the rank of clinical professor. A graduate of Temple University School of Medicine in Philadelphia, she obtained her psychoanalytic training from the Baltimore-Washington Psychoanalytic Institute. She has served on many important committees of the American Psychoanalytic Association and has been a member of the editorial board of the *Journal of the American Psychoanalytic Association*. Dr Hutson has made numerous presentations to psychoanalytic groups in the United States; her topics have included body image disturbance, self-esteem disorders, envy, fear of success, shame, love, and hate. Her papers have appeared in *Psychoanalytic Inquiry* and her book reviews in that journal as well as in *Psychoanalytic Quarterly*. She is a member of the International Women's Forum, a global organisation of professional women who contribute to the socio-economic growth of regional communities.

Susan Kavaler-Adler, PhD, ABPP, NPsyA, DLitt, is in a psychologist and psychoanalyst in private practice, working with individuals and groups. She is the founder of the Object Relations Institute for Psychotherapy and Psychoanalysis in New York City, where she has served as executive director, training analyst, senior supervisor, and faculty member. She is also a prolific author who has published five books and more than sixty articles, and has eleven awards for her writing. Her books are: *The Compulsion to Create: Women Writers and Their Demon Lovers* (Routledge, 1993; Other Press, 2000); *The Creative Mystique: From Red Shoes Frenzy to Love and Creativity* (Routledge, 1996); *Mourning, Spirituality and Psychic Change: A New Object Relations View of Psychoanalysis* (Routledge, 2003, winner of the National Gradiva Award from NAAP); *The Anatomy of Regret: From Death Instinct to Reparation and Symbolization in Vivid Case Studies* (Karnac, 2013); and *Klein-Winnicott Dialectic: New Transformative Metapsychology and Interactive Clinical Theory* (Karnac, 2013, in press). Dr Kavaler-Adler integrates psychoanalytic work on creativity, spiritual self-evolution, and erotic transference with mourning as a developmental process, and addresses the addictions to bad/traumatic eroticised objects that forestall mourning.

Andrew Klafter, MD, grew up in upstate New York, where he also attended college and medical school. He trained as a psychiatrist and served as chief resident at Thomas Jefferson University in Philadelphia, PA. In 2000, he was recruited to the faculty of the University of Cincinnati Department of Psychiatry, where he continues to teach psychodynamic psychotherapy theory and technique to psychiatric residents. Dr Klafter did his analytic training at the Cincinnati Psychoanalytic Institute, and is now a member of the teaching faculty for the analytic training and the advanced psychodynamic psychotherapy training programmes. He maintains a private practice in psychoanalysis, psychotherapy, and psychotherapy supervision. Dr Klafter has been invited to speak and lead workshops nationally and internationally on psychoanalytic theory and technique, psychoanalysis and religion, boundaries and boundary violations, and ethical dilemmas over confidentiality and mandatory reporting. He has won numerous awards for his teaching and supervision, including the University of Cincinnati Golden Apple Award in 2008, 2009, 2010, and 2011. Dr Klafter also serves on the executive committee of the Jewish Board of Advocates for Children, an international organisation devoted to the prevention of physical and sexual abuse of children. In his personal life, he is an accomplished musician and photographer. He resides in Cincinnati, OH with his wife and four daughters.

Elaine Zickler received her PhD in English literature from Bryn Mawr College and her MSW from Rutgers University. She did her psychoanalytic training at the Psychoanalytic Center of Philadelphia. She has written reviews and essays on theoretical issues in gender and sexuality, contemporary French theory, the intersections of literature and psychoanalysis, and is currently engaging with the work of W. G. Sebald. She has also created and organised a biennial conference on children's literature and psychoanalysis, co-sponsored by the Psychoanalytic Center of Philadelphia and the University of Pennsylvania. Dr Zickler is on the faculty of the Psychoanalytic Center of Philadelphia, where she teaches courses on gender and sexuality to analytic candidates and psychotherapy students, and maintains a private practice in psychoanalysis and psychotherapy in Moorestown, New Jersey.

INTRODUCTION

The concept of anxiety is central to psychoanalytic theorising. Viewed as an ego-inhibiting agent and a motivator of defences, anxiety has been meticulously studied and catalogued. Its myriad forms include automatic anxiety, signal anxiety, annihilation anxiety, psychotic anxiety, neurotic anxiety, separation anxiety, castration anxiety, and so on. Add developmental origins, concurrent fantasies, and the accompanying ego alteration to each form and you get the idea of how extensive is the presence of anxiety in psychoanalytic literature. We cannot stop talking about anxiety, it seems.

Our patients, however, rarely use the word. Instead, they talk of fear. One implores that we cure him of his fear of dogs. Another offers the fear of aloneness as the rationale of her staying in a bad marriage. Yet another avoids all athletic activity due to the fear of physical injury. And a fourth one lives in utter denial of passing time to avoid facing his fear of death. The list can be extended endlessly but the point, I think, is made. Anxiety is an experience-distant theoretical construct. Fear is what our patients feel. It curdles their blood, stops them in their tracks, keeps them awake at night. Or, at least, it is what our patients define as "fear". The truth, as this collection of essays demonstrates, is that the concepts of anxiety and fear have considerable overlap.

My introductory chapter deals with this very issue, while extending the phenomenological and psychodynamic terrain to include phobia and characterological cowardice. It sets the ground for six main fears of life that, to a large extent, are arranged on the basis of developmental chronology of their first appearance. These include the (i) fear of breakdown, (ii) fear of aloneness, (iii) fear of intimacy, (iv) fear of injury, (v) fear of success, and (vi) fear of death. Each of these fears is addressed by a distinguished psychoanalyst in a contribution written specifically for this volume. Though each contributor uses a phenomenological and metapsychological perspective, each brings his or her own voice to it. As a result, some essays are more theoretically nuanced while others are more technically inclined. Some are developmentally oriented while others are descriptively rich. Such shifting of vantage points adds texture to the conceptualisations offered and enhances the reading pleasure. The entire material is brought into a harmonious gestalt by the concluding chapter of the book. This chapter takes all preceding contributions, examines them afresh, and weaves them deftly into a thoughtful composite of empathy and insight. We feel closer to our patients' subjective experiences, understand them better, and find ourselves more prepared to help with their fears.

PROLOGUE

CHAPTER ONE

Fear, phobia, and cowardice

Salman Akhtar

Fear is ubiquitous. All of us experience it at one time or another. The sound of footsteps approaching us from behind in a dark alley, an unexpected visit to the city morgue, eye contact with a large alligator in the zoo, and a precipitous "fall" of a rollercoaster can all give us goose bumps of terror. We shriek, scream, or simply become paralysed with fear. We readily recognise its dark arrival at the threshold of our hearts and feel its movement in our blood.

But do we understand the actual nature of fear? Do we know the purpose it serves? Do we agree upon the circumstances under which it is "normal" to be afraid? And, when does fear become abnormal or morbid? Is fear to be avoided at all costs or can this bitter gourd of emotion be transformed into a sweet mango of cultural delight? Questions like these suggest that fear is simple and self-evident only on the surface. Examined carefully, it turns out to be a complex and nuanced phenomenon.

Fear

Webster's Dictionary defines fear as "an unpleasant, often strong emotion caused by anticipation or awareness of danger" (Mish, 1998,

p. 425). While the source of the threat is not identified, the tone makes it clear that the danger referred to resides in external reality. Fear, in other words, is a dysphoric reaction to an actual object (e.g., a wild animal, a knife-wielding drunkard), event (e.g., an earthquake, a stampede), or situation (e.g., watching a horror movie, losing control of a car on an icy road) that is felt to be threatening. The extent of dysphoria in the face of approaching danger varies and four levels of fear's severity are identified in the English language: (a) *apprehension*, which refers to a mild anticipation of a bad occurrence; (b) *dread*, which blends the conviction that one is facing danger with a powerful reluctance to encounter the scary object or situation; (c) *panic*, which denotes an overwhelming sense of being scared, coupled with alarmed hyperactivity (e.g., pacing, running away) and physiological arousal (e.g., increased heartbeat, laboured breathing); and (d) *terror*, which signifies an extreme degree of consternation, a feeling of doom, "catastrophic aloneness" (Grand, 2002), and psychomotor paralysis.

The fact that fear is ubiquitous in the animal kingdom suggests that it is a "needed emotion", that is, one that is important for the organism's survival and functioning. For all living beings, including humans, the emotion of fear serves as a protective device; it warns them that some danger is approaching and they had better undertake measures to avoid it. This could be in the form of actively combating the "enemy" or rapidly escaping from it—the well-known "fight-or-flight" response to threats.

Some fears are widespread over the animal kingdom and seem "hard-wired". Others are the result of developmentally unfolding, epigenetic sequence of fantasies that are specific to human beings. Among the former are fear of loud noises, sudden and jerky movements, looking down from heights, and animals that have fangs, claws, sharp teeth and can jump or move at great speed (Abraham, 1913a; Akhtar & Brown, 2005). Present from birth onwards and persistent throughout life (even if in attenuated forms and at a preconscious level), these fears give testimony to man's essential kinship with animals since their function is self-protective and oriented towards survival. Among the latter are the developmentally derived fears of loss of love objects, loss of love, and castration (Freud, 1926d); fear of death joins this list somewhat later during the course of psychic development. These "hardwired" and developmentally derived fears exist in both sexes though there is some evidence (Horner, 1968; Miller, 1994; Symonds, 1985) that, owing to socialisation patterns and internalised cultural biases, fear of becoming alone and fear of success are somewhat more prevalent among women.

Another point needs mention here. The experience of fear is mediated through two different routes: a shorter, rapid, and subcortical route which goes directly through the amygdala and a longer, slower, and more complex route that includes hippocampal and cortical participation (Damasio, 1999; Emanuel, 2004; Pally, 2000). Each route has an identical output: a fear response. However, the shorter route lacks the benefit of contextual information that the longer route provides. As a result, the shorter route produces a direct and simple fear response which can be tempered or even entirely inhibited by the longer route. The profound implications of this for psychic development and for therapeutic intervention are nowhere better illustrated than in the "visual cliff" experiment devised by Gibson and Walk (1960).

This experiment consists of having the glass floor of a room papered, from below, with a chequerboard design up to its midpoint. As a result, the first half of the floor does not appear any different from ordinary floors but, as the paper affixed from below runs out, the floor suddenly appears threatening due to the depth perception through the transparent glass. The point at which the transparent glass begins is the "visual cliff". Now, a toddler is placed on the papered end of the floor and his or her mother is asked to watch him from across the room. The toddler begins to make his way towards her but abruptly stops at encountering the "visual cliff". If the mother remains impassive, the child does not move forward. However, if the mother smiles, spreads her arms, and vocally encourages the child to come to her, the child crawls or walks over the transparent glass. Mother's loving support activates the hippocampal-cortical system that dampens the fear aroused by the amygdala-sponsored pathway mentioned above.

While this is a salutary consequence of environmental modulation of "hard-wired" childhood fears, adverse and even sinister interplays of childhood vulnerability and carer input also exist. Children (more so than adults) need company and

> ... their needs for attachment experiences and even moments of intimacy will lead them to shadow, seek out, and submissively engage the parents who, for the most part, cause them pain and disappointment. Their avidity for exploration and assertion will

lead them to follow a ball out into a dangerous street, climb up an unstable support, or put fingers in electric plugs. Their love of sensual enjoyment from fondling, kissing, and rocking will result in their participating in sexually over-exciting play or overt seductions by older children and adults. The pleasure of social contact will expose older children to the smiling-faced inducements of a kidnapper, and the same desire coupled with greed leaves adults exposed to psychopathic salesmen and con men. Thus, parents must inculcate a sense of danger as an active educative effort. (Lichtenberg, 1991, pp. 396–397)

Such nuanced interplay of "nature versus nurture" variables in the genesis and modulation of fear undergirds the epigenetic unfolding of phase-specific fears throughout childhood development. "Natural" fears of starvation and physical injury are given specific "human" colouring via the potential danger of anaclitic betrayal and loss during infancy, castration and genital mutilation during early childhood, and moral anxiety (the internalised consequence of the preceding fear) during later childhood and adolescence (Freud, 1926d). Still later, in the course of adult life, fear of death appears on the psychic horizon; multiply determined and culturally variable, this fear combines fears of physical infirmity, separation from love objects, and loss of self (Akhtar, 2010; Chadwick, 1929; Freud, 1923b; Hoffman, Johnson, Foster, & Wright, 2010; Natterson & Knudson, 1965; Zilboorg, 1943).

Anxiety

Fear and anxiety share some characteristics. Both evoke a sense that something bad is about to happen. Both are unpleasant and undesirable experiences. Both can serve as alarms and thus protect us from danger. However, in other ways, the two experiences are different. Fear is a response to external danger; anxiety to dangers emanating from the internal world. As early as 1895, Freud noted the relationship between "unpleasure" (not yet delineated as anxiety) to earlier painful experiences. He wrote:

> If the memory image of the hostile object is in any manner freshly cathected (e.g., by fresh perceptions), a condition arises which is not pain but has a similarity to pain. It includes unpleasure and the

inclination to discharge corresponding to the experience of pain. Unpleasure is released from the interior of the body—is freshly provoked—by the cathexis of memories. (1950a, p. 320)

Thirty years later, Freud (1926d) published his major work on the problem of anxiety and restated this thesis. However, this time, he linked the cathexis of previous traumata and their memories to the specific affect of anxiety. He stated:

> Anxiety is not newly created in repression; it is reproduced as an affective state, in accordance with an already existing mnemic image. If we go further and enquire into the origin of that anxiety—and of affects in general—we shall be leaving the realm of pure psychology and entering the borderland of physiology. Affective states have become incorporated in the mind as precipitates of primeval traumatic experiences and when a similar situation occurs, they are revived like mnemic symbols. (p. 93)

In the same contribution, Freud also delineated the seminal "danger situations" causing anxiety. These included threats of (a) loss of a love object, (b) loss of the love object's love, (c) castration, and (d) moral condemnation from within oneself. "Each situation or danger corresponds to a particular period of life or a particular developmental phase of the mental apparatus and appears to be justifiable to it" (p. 146). Some "danger situations" lose their evocative power as the individual matures while others survive by acquiring more up-to-date forms. Still others (e.g., superego's attack) accompany people throughout their lives. "Danger situations" mobilise anxiety and set ego defences in motion. This is "signal anxiety". It contrasts with "automatic anxiety" which results from the ego being overwhelmed by threats from within. The feeling in anxiety that something bad is about to happen is due to the ego's sense that one might give in to id impulses that would lead to physical harm, others' disapproval, or rebuke from one's own conscience. However, since the impulse in question is almost always repressed, the nature of danger felt remains vague. This explanatory model, however, applies only to what is generally called "neurotic anxiety". It does not address anxiety that presumably arises during the infantile era where a coherent ego and hence a wishful intentionality is not yet in place. In such anxiety, the dread is not of an instinctual breakthrough but that of psychic "breakdown" (Winnicott, 1974). Variously termed "psychotic anxiety" (Klein, 1932), "unthinkable anxiety" (Winnicott, 1962), and "annihilation anxiety" (Hurvich, 2003), such dysphoria threatens to disorganise mental functioning altogether. Elsewhere, I have noted the main characteristics of this anxiety.

> ... (i) it originates in early infancy; (ii) it can, however, be reactivated by later phase-specific anxieties; (iii) a combination of excessive constitutional aggression and severe traumatic experiences leads to ego weakness which, in turn, increases the vulnerability to such anxiety; (iv) it might exist in preverbal forms or might acquire retrospective fantasy content from later developmental phases; (v) it is generally associated with propensity towards psychosis but might also underlie non-psychotic conditions especially those of addictive, psychosomatic, and perverse varieties; and, (vi) it mobilizes defenses that are particularly recalcitrant. (Akhtar, 2009a, p. 22)

Regardless of whether it is "neurotic" or "psychotic" in nature, the intrapsychic origin of anxiety also precludes its control by physical flight; one can run away from fear, not from anxiety. Fear and anxiety are thus both similar and dissimilar. The phenomenological terrain is further muddled by the fact that the two often coexist. External threats are played up by internal vulnerabilities and intrapsychic threats can readily be externalised. Some admixtures of fear and anxiety are commonplace, others curious.

Phobia

By itself, fear is a rational response and therefore poses few problems. When it gets fuelled by anxiety in a regressive blurring of external and internal realities, difficulties of clinical proportions begin to arise. The most well-known among these conditions is phobia. A term derived from the Greek word *phobos* (meaning flight, dread, and panic), phobia stands for "marked and persistent fear that is excessive or unreasonable, cued by the presence or anticipation of a specific object or situation" (DSM-IV-TR, 2000, p. 449). In effect, both anxiety (internal danger) and fear (external danger) coexist within phobia, although in their pure forms, anxiety and fear are quite different (see Table I). Phobia is distinct from

Table I. Fear, anxiety, and phobia.

Variables	Fear	Anxiety	Phobia
Source	External	Internal	Externalised
Risk	Actual	Unknown	Imagined
Threat	Clear	Vague	Clear
Danger	Plausible	Implausible	Exaggerated
Avoidance	Helpful	Futile	Helpful
Prevalence	Universal	Limited	Limited

fear because it is out of proportion to the situation in reality. Indeed, a fear must meet the following criteria in order to qualify as a phobia: (i) it should not be age-specific, (ii) it should not be widely accepted as normal within a culture or subculture, (iii) it should be noticeably out of proportion to the plausible danger from the object or the situation, (iv) it should result in impairment of psychosocial functioning, (v) it should be associated with active avoidance of the dreaded stimulus, and (vi) such avoidance should provide symptomatic relief.

Phobia also needs to be distinguished from the paranoid fear insofar as there is no motive assigned in phobia to the frightening object; the statement "I am afraid of pigeons" represents phobia and the statement "Pigeons are out to get me" represents paranoia. The former is the result of displacement, the latter that of projection.

Phobias can be of many types, as is attested by the profusion of specific phobias with Greek prefixes,[1] and many classifications exist. While a bit older, the classification by the British psychiatrist, Isaac Marks (1970a), seems not only to be valid today but perhaps most sensible. According to him, phobias can be grouped into the following categories:

- *Agoraphobic syndrome*: is the commonest variety, constituting about sixty per cent of all phobias. The agoraphobic patients have fears not only of open spaces but also of shopping, crowds, travelling, and even of closed spaces. Other neurotic symptoms including panic attacks and dizziness, and compulsive rituals and feelings of depersonalisation are also often present. Most agoraphobics are women and the majority develop their symptoms after puberty.
- *Animal phobia*: constitutes the most clear-cut variety of phobia but, in its pure form, is infrequently encountered in clinical practice. The symptom usually develops at the onset of latency, or around six to

eight years of age. There is little tendency for its "generalisation" and there is little tension in the absence of the phobic object.

- *Social phobia*: involves fear of public speaking, blushing, shaking, writing, eating, drinking, vomiting, or becoming incontinent in public. It occurs with equal frequency among men and women and usually starts after puberty, with a peak of incidence in the late teens.
- *Miscellaneous specific phobias*: start any time in life and persist fairly consistently. The phobic situations vary from one case to another but remain fairly specific for a given individual. The dreaded situations include travel, heights, wind, thunderstorms, darkness, bridges, and large bodies of water.

Of these four types, animal phobias and miscellaneous specific phobias have received the most attention from psychoanalysis. Beginning with Freud's (1909b) widely known study of Little Hans, to numerous subsequent contributions (e.g., Campbell & Pile, 2011; Kulish, 1996; Lewin, 1952; Rangell, 1952; Sandler, 1989; Tyson, 1978; Wangh, 1959), psychoanalysts have sought to discern what underlies such focal reigns of terror upon the ego. Freud traced Little Hans's fear of being bitten by a horse to his dread of castration by his father; this, in turn, was the talion punishment for the boy's incestuous longings for his mother. Freud's early followers (Abraham, 1913a; Deutsch, 1929; Fenichel, 1945) fervently subscribed to this explanation and began to view all phobias as derived from castration anxiety. However, as psychoanalytic theory advanced and attention shifted towards the vicissitudes of pre-Oedipal development, the "danger situation" (Freud, 1926d) of loss of love gained explanatory ascendance,[2] The centrality of castration anxiety came under question and anxiety over good internal objects getting drowned by the aggression within (in a newer rendition of the "loss of love" hypothesis) became an equally, if not more, important motivating force for symptom formation.

Regardless of their source, till such anxieties remained repressed, one simply failed to see, hear, or otherwise attend to threatening internal (wishes, impulses) or external (triggers, temptations) stimuli. Nonetheless, the repressed material continued to seek expression. In Freud's (1915e) words, "The repressed exercises a continuous pressure in the direction of consciousness" (p. 51). This tendency becomes stronger in the face of a reactive increase in the intensity of drives. Many "simple phobias" (Fenichel, 1945) can thus be explained.

In certain cases there is not much displacement; anxiety is simply felt in situations where an uninhibited person would experience either sexual excitement or rage ... For such cases, a formula is valid which would be an oversimplification in more complicated cases: what a person fears, he unconsciously wishes for ... In other and still simple phobias, the feared situation does not represent a feared temptation; rather, it is the threat that causes the temptation to be feared: castration or loss of love. There are knife and scissor phobias, the implication of which is that the touch or even the sight of these instruments awakens the feared thought of a possible castration (and, it is true, in most cases, also an unconscious temptation for a repressed hostility). Certain persons are afraid of seeing cripples or of witnessing accidents, which means: "I do not want to be reminded of what might happen to me" (and again, the fear may also arise from such sights being a temptation for unconscious hostile wishes). (pp. 195–196)

The psychodynamics of most phobias is, in practice, far more complicated. However, before going into these details, it should be noted that many non-analytic aetiological models of phobia also exist. Modelling, vicarious learning, and observational conditioning are alternative pathways by which animals acquire their phobic potential (Cook & Mineka, 1987; Emde, 1983; Eysenck, 1965, 1976; Marks, 1987; Mineka, Davidson, Cook, & Keir, 1984; Solyom, Beck, Solyom, & Hugel, 1974; Wolpe & Rachman, 1960). This perspective supports cases of phobias arising after a child observes a parent responding fearfully to an animal (Solyom, Beck, Solyom, & Hugel, 1974), or, as in Mineka, Davidson, Cook, & Keir's (1984) experiments, after laboratory-reared rhesus monkeys view wild-caught monkeys reacting fearfully to snakes. More recently, learning theory has been challenged and broadened by biological research in animal phobias (Bennett-Levy & Marteau, 1984; Davey, 1992; Davey, Forster, & Mayhew, 1993; McNally & Steketee, 1985; Mineka, Davidson, Cook, & Keir, 1984). This view suggests that learning is "biologically prepared" in that there are anatomic portions of the brain preprogrammed to perceive specific, fear-evoking animal movements much like the non-dominant parietal lobe perceives faces. Sudden movement and speed are "chosen" as fearful. Some of these authors have pointed to the fact that most animal phobias involve harmless (spider, cockroach, maggot, snake, and rat) rather than predatory animals (lions, tigers, sharks); they postulate that animal phobias correlate more with contamination and disgust rather than with fear. Together, these three aetiological perspectives, namely modelling, vicarious learning, and observational conditioning, along with consideration of potential hereditary determinants of fear and phobias (Delprato, 1980), might explain why specific animals have remained both "chosen" phobia objects and symbols in mythology in almost every culture.

Returning to the psychoanalytic perspective on phobias, one notes that the complexity of their dynamics is due to the fact that repression alone becomes incapable of keeping the threat sufficiently removed from awareness. As a result, displacement, symbolism, and regression come into play. Displacement, the process by which an affect or attitude is unconsciously transferred from one object to a more acceptable substitute, is then added to repression. Now, it is not the *sexual* situations but the *sexualised* situations that are feared. The diffuse anxiety becomes bound to a specific object/situation. This makes life easier, since the specificity of the fear now makes matters manageable through the active process of avoidance. The advantage offered by displacement is that the original offensive idea/affect does not become conscious. Also, by binding the hostile vector of ambivalence towards one's father, for instance, into a fear of horses, the displacement tends to resolve conflicts of ambivalence. Also, as Freud (1909b) pointed out, displacement by itself renders avoidance easier.

The feared object/situation often represents an exquisitely unique and symbolic crystallisation of all the important determinants of the phobia, including the predominant impulse of threat against which the phobia is a defence. Jones (1948) emphasised the role of symbolism in phobia, noting that there is a certain affinity between the individual and the icons he chooses to express his instrapsychic concerns. Lewin (1952) likened the process determining the specific phobia to the dream work, sharing the same overdetermination and other parallel phenomena, including traces of early experiences. Although universally symbolic meanings for various phobias may be suggested, these are not invariably valid. It is therefore better not to approach the patient's phobia with preconceived ideas about its meaning. The true meaning of any symbol to an individual patient can be determined only by listening to his/her associations.

A certain amount of regression is also central to all phobias. The phobic's cognition, in the restricted area of his neurotic symptom, is strikingly similar to the child's animistic perception of the world as threatening and overwhelming. Regression also is evident insofar as

> ... all phobics behave like children, whose anxieties are soothed if the mother sits by the bedside and holds their hand. Such a demand for reassuring measures on the part of parent substitutes is especially evident in those agoraphobics who feel protected in the presence of a companion ... in phobias in which the companion is essential, the relationship to this companion is of basic importance. The companion not only represents the protecting parent but also the unconsciously-hated parent; his presence serves the purpose of diverting the patient's mind from unconscious fantasies to reality, that is, of reassuring him that he has not killed this person who is walking safely at his side. In such cases, the fear that something may happen to the patient is often preceded by a fear for the safety of the same person who, later on in the agoraphobia, is used as a companion. (Fenichel, 1945, pp. 206–207)

Agoraphobia, the roots of which were traced to a repressed prostitution fantasy by Freud (1897, cited in Masson, 1985, p. 253), is actually more often the result of conflicts pertaining to "optimal distance" (Akhtar, 1992; Escoll, 1992; Mahler, Pine, & Bergman, 1975). In an early paper on "locomotor anxiety", Abraham (1913b) noted that neurotic inhibitions of motility emanate not only from defences against constitutionally strong pleasure in movement and unconscious sexual concerns but also from difficulty in separating from love objects. They fear going out but also are unhappy at being left alone indoors. Speaking of such "topo-phobia", Abraham said that in patients with this malady:

> ... anxiety prevents them from becoming free from themselves and from the objects upon which their love was fixed in childhood, and from finding the way to objects belonging to the external world. Every path which leads them away from the charmed circle of those people upon whom they are fixated, is closed to them. (p. 241)

Some years later, Deutsch (1929) declared the involvement of a partner to be the crucial determinant of the agoraphobic's malady. However, she felt that hostile and controlling fantasies were frequently hidden underneath the consciously experienced need for libidinal attach-ment. Following this, Mittelmann (1957) observed the confinement of the agoraphobic to a "limited circumference" (p. 289) and Weiss (1964) noted that such patients grow more anxious the farther they go from their home. This led him to define agoraphobia as an anxiety reaction to abandoning a fixed point of support. More recently, Kohut (1980) concluded that the agoraphobic's consciously felt need for a reassuring companion is the key to what lies in a psychic depth, namely, the continued search for a maternal self object.

Clearly, all these authors regard agoraphobia as a malady of distance. My own elucidation of the ubiquitous, though unconscious, fantasy of a "psychic tether" (Akhtar, 1992) lends support to such a formulation. How far can one go away from one's objects without endangering the cohesion of one's self, seems to be the question.[3] The opposite question, that is, how close can one get to another person without risking one's autonomy, applies to claustrophobia. And, just like in agoraphobia, in claustrophobia, too, anxieties regarding optimal distance (from love objects) are intermingled with psychosexual anxieties and other dreads pertaining to Oedipal conflicts. B. D. Lewin's (1935) declaration that there is a close connection between claustrophobia and being inside the mother, and the fear of being buried alive is a transformed wish to return to the womb, can be interpreted in both Oedipal and pre-Oedipal ways. The fact is that almost all psychopathology comes from both sources. It is rarely an "either-or" matter. A phobic symptom is derived from diverse sources and contains tributaries from multiple phases of development. This statement applies to monosymptomatic phobia as well as to the diffuse agoraphobic syndrome. It is even more true when phobic concerns pervade the entire character.

Introduced by Fenichel (1945), the designation "phobic character" is reserved for individuals "whose reactive behavior limits itself to the avoidance of situations originally wished-for" (p. 527). Those with severe inhibitions of sexuality and aggressiveness also display a similar picture of generalised apprehension and social withdrawal. Elaborating on Fenichel's proposal, Mackinnon and Michels (1971) emphasised that more common than ego-dystonic, monosymptomatic phobia is the use of fearful avoidance as a character defence, adding that such an individual is "constantly imaging himself in situations of danger while pursuing the course of greatest safety" (p. 49). More recently, Stone (1980) recognised a "phobic-anxious" personality type that displays extremes of "fearfulness and avoidance of the most harmless objects and situations" (p. 332). While resembling schizoid individuals in their restricted lifestyle, phobic characters are different in significant ways. They are not "shy" and idiosyncratic like schizoid people. They avoid situations (and physical objects), not people. Their avoidance of certain situations (e.g., visiting an amusement park, watching a pornographic movie, going to a new restaurant), can lead to the false appearance of discomfort with people in general. The fact is that when not in the dreaded situations, they can have empathic and meaningful affective interchanges with others. Phobic characters are not associated with "identity diffusion" (Akhtar, 1984; Kernberg, 1975) and extensive reliance upon splitting mechanisms. They do not therefore represent a borderline personality organisation (Kernberg, 1967); they are organised at a higher level with fears emanating from the externalisation and symbolic reification of their internal conflicts. Their fears are imaginary. Cowardice, in contrast, involves a recoil from plausible, if not actual, threats. Symbolism lies at the heart of phobic character, and anxiety about object loss forms the bedrock of cowardice.

Cowardice

A habitual reaction to threat and danger, cowardice—at least on the surface—is a response to fear of actual harm. It involves a "crippling of the will" (Menaker, 1979, p. 93); one succumbs to fear and withdraws from the "combat".[4] Cowardice can be evident in physical, intellectual, and moral realms. Physical cowardice involves an inordinate fear of injury and the resulting restriction of exploratory and playful motor activity; one avoids athletics, amusement park rides, and any possibility of physical altercation. Intellectual cowardice results in inhibition of mental activity; one cannot think "outside the box" and gets scared if new insights do pop up in the mind. Moral cowardice manifests as the inability to uphold ethical standards and speak the truth under difficult circumstances; one lies, suddenly seems to lack words, and adopts the "silence of the complicit" (Akhtar, 2013).

The coward reacts to confrontation with distress. In part, this is due to "automatic anxiety" (Freud, 1926d), that is, the spontaneous reaction of helpless dread in the face of a massively traumatic situation. And, in part, this is due to projection of the coward's own anger. Unable to express his resentment directly, the coward attributes vicious intent to his opponent and gets terrified. Consequently, he postpones the "debate", falsely concurs with his adversary, or, worse, flees the situation in reality. Recognition of his timidity fills him with shame and self-disgust; these are often drowned in drink or covered over by the narcissistic fantasy of having deliberately engineered his defeat. The spineless combatant of yesterday thus transforms himself into the lofty bestower of victory to others.

But there is more to cowardice than its narcissistic dynamic. The base of cowardice is formed by a "thin-skinned" (Rosenfeld, 1971) psyche which is the consequence of weak maternal containment of early infantile anxieties (Bick, 1968). The cowardly individual tends to get affectively overwhelmed while facing a narcissistic threat; withdrawal from a full encounter with it follows. Deficient identification with the same-sex parent also contributes to such psychic vulnerability. The most important aetiological factor in cowardice, however, is a condensation of body mutilation anxieties (including, of course, castration anxiety) and a dread of separation and aloneness. An "ocnophile" (Balint, 1968) par excellence, the coward clings to his objects and is willing to sacrifice dignity at the altar of relatedness. All cowardice, at the bottom, is the fear of being disliked and being alone. Meltzer (1973) notes:

> Where dependence on good internal objects is rendered infeasible by damaging masturbatory attacks and where dependence on a good external object in unavailable or not acknowledged, an addictive relationship to a bad part of the self—the submission to tyranny takes place. An illusion of safety is promulgated by the omniscience of the destructive part ... Where a dread of loss of an addictive relation to a tyrant is found in psychic structure, the problem of terror will be found at its core, as the force behind the dread and the submission. (p. 78)

Meltzer's proposal has implications for the technical handling of individuals trapped in relationships with narcissistic-sadistic partners. However, before discussing them, it is pertinent to take a few steps back and consider the myriad ways in which fear is exploited, used, marketed, and enjoyed by societal institutions created by man.

A cultural digression

Although fear is ubiquitous in human existence, it does have a deep and complex relationship with culture. Their relationship is often dialectical in nature. Fear can disturb a culture's slumber and mobilise adaptive and maladaptive responses. Cultural narratives can embellish existing fears, create new ones, and offer rich iconography for both. All this becomes evident in the realms of regional concerns, prejudice, politics, literature, and even entertainment. The following passages address these matters in brief.

Some fears (e.g., looking down from a great height, fast-moving animals) seem so widely spread across the globe as to appear independent of cultural influences. Like "universal dreams" (Freud, 1900a),[5] such "universal fears" combine phylogenetic predisposition, evolutionary advantages, and precipitates of early childhood experiences. Other fears are idiosyncratic, limited to some people, and, at times, restricted to regions and eras. Fear of ghosts and evil spirits, for instance, has largely gone from modernised societies while persisting in less educated, less industrialised, rural and sub-rural communities of the world. Fears of earthquakes, floods, and tornadoes are generally restricted to areas with vulnerability to such disasters. Similarly, animal phobias are regionally anchored; it is hardly conceivable for one living in Saudi Arabia to be afraid of polar bears.

The phenomenology of "culture-bound psychiatric syndromes" (Guarnaccia & Rogler, 1999; Meth, 1974; Yap, 1969) is replete with observations that support this line of thought. Not only animals that populate a specific region are chosen as phobic objects by people living there, they can also become the suitable containers of projections of the attributes of bravery and cowardice. In colloquial English, for instance, a coward is referred to as "chicken-hearted" or merely "chicken", and in Spanish as *gallina* (hen). In Arabic, a brave man is called an *assag* (lion), while in Urdu such a person is called *sher-dil* (one with a lion's heart); in contrast, a coward is called *buz-dil* (one with a goat's heart). What all this demonstrates is that not only are the objects of fear but even the metaphors of bravery and cowardice often regionally determined.

Fear plays in important role in prejudice as well. The "unmentalized xenophobia" (Akhtar, 2007) that results in bland indifference to and avoidance of those different from oneself is merely the tip of the proverbial iceberg here. The relentless need to externalise aggression and the deployment of paranoia as a "psychic vitamin for threatened identity and a powerful anodyne against the pain that results from genuine self-reflection" (ibid., p. 17) results in the creation of frightening outside figures. Since minorities are often "suitable reservoirs for projection"

(Volkan, 1988), all sorts of dread and danger are seen as emanating from them. Blacks, homosexuals, and Muslims are frequent targets of hostile projection and therefore objects of fear, which, in turn, is utilised as a rationalisation for discrimination and prejudice. Mesmerising oratory of hatred by charismatic though paranoid leaders fuels the imaginary dangers posed by the Other and sanctions acts of cruelty and violence. No wonder fear and politics are often intertwined with each other.

Monarchies and totalitarian regimes are customarily prone to create a "culture of fear" for their citizens. The term "terrorism"—used these days mostly to designate the political violence of small groups— actually originated in the context of state-sponsored intimidation. First used in 1795, "terrorism" denoted the French Revolutionary statesman Maximilien de Robespierre's Reign of Terror (1785–1794). Robespierre defended his fear-mongering, iron-fisted control, and terrorising of the masses by claiming that the Revolution enacted the despotism of liberty against tyranny. He was, however, not an exception. More recent times have witnessed Adolph Hitler's Holocaust, Joseph Stalin's gulags and purges, and Pol Pot's killing fields. Government, turned mercenary, can be a source of great fear, indeed.

Unfortunately, even democratic nations can regress and make people tremble while expressing their opinions or, worse, become altogether mute. The so-called "emergency rule" enforced by India's prime minister, Indira Gandhi (1917–1984), before she was assassinated, and the unauthorised wire-tapping and "extraordinary renditions" by the CIA during the post-9/11 era of George W. Bush's presidency were no less terrorising to the people of their respective nations.[6] Within psychoanalysis itself, there have been prominent individuals and organisations that have inculcated a "culture of fear". This ranges from Freud's authoritarian suppression of dissent (Rudnytsky, 2012) to the pervasive sense in the field that openly expressing a pro-Palestinian stance is risky if not tantamount to professional suicide. Needless to add that when such dread pervades the tissue of an organisation, its advance is seriously compromised.

Evoking and fuelling large group fears is a favourite strategy of political leaders with narcissistic and paranoid tendencies (Volkan, 1997). Hitler's pronouncement that Jews were a threat to the European economy, Slobodan Milosevic's poisonous reminder to the Serbs that some of their fellow citizens were actually Turks, and the constant evocation of mortal danger from Arabs by Israelis and vice versa, are some prominent illustrations of fear-mongering as a tactic for strengthening one's political hand. Fear then becomes a ploy for oppression, disenfranchisement, and even genocide of hated others.

A dramatically different interaction between fear and culture occurs when judiciously titrated and aesthetically cleansed fear forms the basis of literature. The oral tradition of telling scary tales dates back to antiquity and the written genre of fear-laced fiction has seen steady output over centuries. Essentially such sagas belong to two categories, namely those of supernatural horror (e.g., ghost stories, tales from beyond the grave, satanic machinations, attacks by aliens and zombies), and of evil lying within the human heart itself (e.g., murder stories, sadomasochistic cliffhangers). Reading such novels and short stories stirs up psychic terror; this is often accompanied by a sense of helplessness (a result of identification with the victimised protagonist). There is also a feeling of being immersed in the goings-on and yet experiencing a bit of uncanniness. Freud's (1919h) discussion of *unheimlich*, or the uncanny, clearly stated that it derives its terror not from something externally alien or unknown but—on the contrary—from something strangely familiar which defeats our effort to separate ourselves from it. There is a quality of something "fateful and inescapable" (p. 237) being forced upon one. Freud goes on to state that:

> An uncanny effect is often easily produced when the distinction between imagination and reality is effaced, as when something that we have hitherto regarded as imaginary appears before us in reality, or when a symbol takes over the full functions of the thing it symbolizes, and so on. It is this factor which contributes not a little to the uncanny effect attaching to magical practices. (p. 244)

Writers of terrifying fiction, ranging from Clara Reeves (1729–1807) and Ann Radcliffe (1764–1823) through Edgar Allan Poe (1809–1849) and Bram Stoker (1847–1912) to Ann Rice (b. 1941) and Stephen King (b. 1947) are deft in evoking an uncanny response by straddling the line between reality and unreality within the plot and the details of its characters. They succeed in collapsing the boundary between mind and matter, ordinary and strange, and natural and diabolical.

However, for some individuals menace in print is not sufficient. They require visual images and sound effects to experience fear. Enter, horror movies. A genre which emerged at almost the inception of commercial cinema (circa 1910), horror movies exploit many ubiquitous human tendencies, even if these are ordinarily banished from conscious awareness. Among these are the need for excitement, novelty-seeking, the pleasure of an adrenaline rush, counterphobic pressure to master fear, and the vicarious gratification of repressed perverse fantasies and impulses to defy social norms (Goldstein, 1998).[7] Especially appealing to young men, such movies become an engrossing topic of conversation and a glue for peer bonding. It must, however, be added that horror movies are not uniform and many sub-genres exist. Some include themes pertaining to: ,d—a

- Demon-child, such as *The Exorcist* (1973), and *The Omen* (1976).
- Alien invasion—*War of the Worlds* (1953), and *Puppet Masters* (1994).
- Dangerous animals—*The Birds* (1963), and *Jaws* (1975).
- Gory violence—*The Texas Chain Saw Massacre* (1974), and *A Clockwork Orange* (1971).
- Perverse and psychotic ruthlessness—*Psycho* (1960), and *The Shining* (1980).

The common element in all such movies is the evocation of fear, often to an unsettling and near-traumatic extent.[8] They provide an encounter with the "uncanny" (Freud, 1919h) by disrupting routine and by transforming the all-too-familiar into the bizarre and unpredictable. While gratuitous throat-slitting violence can elicit tormented joy from filmgoers, it is the helpless anticipation that truly terrifies them. The great maestro of fear, Alfred Hitchcock (1899–1980), recognised this and declared: "There is no excitement in the bang, only in the anticipation of it." Hitchcock knew that while fear is unpleasant, playing with fear, if done artistically, can yield pleasure.

Back to the clinical realm

Having discussed the differential diagnoses in the realm of fear (i.e., fear, anxiety, phobia, cowardice), I wish now comment upon the management of fear and fear-related phenomena in the clinical situation.[9] That such work involves a great deal of countertransference vigilance and can be taxing for the analyst's ego goes without saying. Indeed, all interventions in such work require patience, tact, and forbearance from the analyst (besides, of course, his or her interpretive skill) and the categorisation of such interventions here is largely for didactic ease. That being said, three main tasks in working with those afflicted with fear and those capable of inducing fear in the analyst are (i) sensing fear, assessing dangerousness, and setting limits, (ii) bearing and containing the patient's fear, and (iii) managing one's own fear and learning from it. My selecting these three areas to focus upon is by no means dismissive of the customary interpretive and reconstructive work that forms the basic material of all psychoanalyses. Defence and resistance analysis, confrontation with the repudiated preconscious material, linking-up of derivatives, and helping decipher what underlies the symbolic and displaced forms of fear constitute the bread and butter of psychoanalytic work. Such work is needed regardless of whether the patient's fears are neurotic, paranoid, or self-annihilatory. The three areas chosen to be addressed are additive and not alternative to the customary work of psychoanalysis.

Sensing fear, addressing dangerousness, and setting limits

Since most analysts and psychoanalytically oriented therapists screen their patients for possessing "a fairly reliable character" (Freud, 1905d, p. 263) and only take into treatment those individuals who are not sociopathic and are not suicidal or homicidal, assessment of the patient's dangerousness does not figure in their usual repertoire of concerns. Nonetheless, situations can—and do—evolve where the analyst has to decide whether it is safe to continue working in the usual and customary manner. The following declaration by Hoffer (1985) is pertinent in this context.

> The analyst's neutrality with respect to conflict may be suspended in situations the analyst feels are (a) emergencies for the patient— e.g. suicidality, psychosis, toxic state, etc.; (b) emergencies for someone potentially vulnerable to the patient's destructiveness—e.g. the analysand's children; and (c) emergencies for the analyst—physical or psychological threats. (p. 786)

Under such circumstances, the analyst might feel afraid and rationally worry about the safety of himself, others, or the patient. This might happen in the course of an ongoing treatment or, at times, in the very first encounter between the patient and the analyst.[10]

Clinical vignette: 1

> Sarah Green, a forty-five-year-old librarian made an appointment to see me upon her sister's insistence. She appeared overwhelmed with pain at the break-up of a romantic relationship. Having lived alone most of her life, she found this belated attachment profoundly significant. The man she was involved with was married. He abruptly left her saying that he could no longer continue cheating on his wife. She was destroyed. Heartbroken, she came to see me.
>
> We began the first hour of consultation in a customary history-taking way. However, within twenty minutes of the session, she announced that she had decided to blow her head off with a gun which she had bought earlier that day. Alarmed by the earnestness of her tone, I suggested that we take immediate steps to get the gun removed from her apartment, obtain some collateral information regarding the extent of her depression, and consider beginning our work on an inpatient basis. The patient reacted sharply to my suggestion and, refusing to let me contact her sister who could remove the gun, got up to leave the office. At this point, I said to her, "Look, everybody gets about ten candles' worth of life and inside you eight have already gone off. The wind is blowing hard and to protect the remaining two candles, you came here and put them in my heart. Now, since you have enlisted me for this purpose, it is my duty to keep these two candles protected from the wind. When the storm settles, I will return them to you so that you can light the other eight candles back with their help." The patient broke down in tears and after some thinking gave me the permission to contact her sister who subsequently removed the gun from the patient's apartment and encouraged the patient to stay at her house for the next few days.

Such admixture of limit-setting, supportive measures, environmental interventions, and interpretive approach might tilt in favour of one or the other component given the seriousness and/or urgency of threatened violence (towards self or others). Generally speaking, in psychoanalytic practices, supportive and interpretive measures carry the day while in psychiatric clinics (especially in the emergency room settings), limit-setting, hospitalisation, and medications might become necessary to manage the patient's aggression and the fear induced into others by such aggression.[11] Kernberg's (1984) guidelines for the management of hatred in severely borderline patients allow for assuring safely by strict limit-setting. Frightening outbursts of rage in such patients have to be met not only by holding and containment but also by explicitly informing the patient of what he or she can and cannot do within the clinical setting.

Clinical vignette: 2

> Bob Dolinski, a borderline young man in twice weekly psychother-apy, exploded with rage when I refused to comply with his demand for painkillers. In a menacing tone, he threatened to take my eye-balls out and crush them under his feet. Alarmed by his emotional flooding and rapidly disintegrating reality-testing, I firmly told him to stay put in his chair. I added that if he as much as laid a finger on me I would terminate the treatment and never see him again. I told him that he needed someone who could listen to him peacefully, not someone who was afraid of him and that I would be afraid of him if he acted even once on his impulse to hurt me. Noticing that he was settling down, I added that the idea that he could take my eyeballs out was both unrealistic and intriguing. He could not do it; I would not let him. And, why did he think of eyeballs in the first place? Could it have something to do with the memory of his mother looking contemptuously at him? Interventions along these lines calmed him down and soon the session was progressing in a more mutually related manner.

Similar to the technical interventions in the preceding vignette, my stance during this frightening episode, with imminent risk of physi-cal violence, included firm limit-setting coupled with comments to improve reality-testing. In addition, I also made an attempt to link the content of his threat with certain memories he had reported during an earlier phase of our work. While such active efforts were needed here, in cases where the threat is subtle and slow, one can maintain relative neutrality and just by bearing the fear induced by the patient, prepare the ground for customary interpretive work.

Bearing and containing the patient's fear

Prominent among the analyst's tasks is to hold and contain the fears that the patient can feel and verbalise as well as those fears that remain unspeakable for the patient. Discerning such "beta elements" (Bion, 1967) through his reverie, his resonance with the patient's projective identification, and his empathy-driven "trial identifications" (Fliess, 1942) with the patient, the analyst senses the patient's fears but does not hurriedly unmask them. Instead, he allows himself to be the depository of such affects, waiting for the process of defence analysis and for the patient's resulting ego-growth to permit the verbalisation of hitherto repudiated anxieties. Stated in the language of contemporary relational psychoanalysis, fear is an intersubjective response which, like any other countertransference reaction, helps the analyst understand himself, his patient, and the nature of their interaction. Moreover, since the patient and the analyst need to feel safe, a modicum of mutual regulation is important for the dyad in "setting and re-calibrating the danger-safety balance in their analytic work" (Kafka, 1998, p. 102).

Such is the process in most ongoing analyses. However, there are occasions when the dreaded fragments of the patient's psyche burst through the rational mind of the ego and result in a state of "emotional flooding" (Volkan, 1976). Under such circumstances, the analyst's containing capacity acquires a greater importance; this capacity then prepares the ground for an interpretive demonstration of what just took place.

Clinical vignette: 3

Rebecca Cohen, twenty-six-year-old daughter of a Holocaust survivor father, was in analysis with me. The course of early treatment was filled with anxiety-laden fantasies about her father's experience in the Nazi concentration camp. Dreaded scenarios of ethnic hatred and violence preoccupied Rebecca and this readily spread to the transference. She feared and hated me, regarded me as a Jew-hating Muslim or Arab, and suspected that I supported anti-Israeli violence by Palestinians. Projections of her own transgenerationally given post-traumatic Jew-Nazi split of the self were constantly active in her relatedness with me. One day, I was hated and viciously attacked. Next day, I was deeply feared.

During one session while talking of the Holocaust, she suddenly jumped up from the couch and ran to the corner of the office that was farthest from me, trembling and obviously shaken by something she had just experienced internally. Rebecca stood there crying. I remained silent. Then she found a box of tissues on the desk nearby, cleaned her face and began to look a bit composed. I did not say anything and waited patiently for things to unfold. Rebecca jumped up, sat on my desk, and asked me if I knew what had happened. I shook my head, telling her that I did not. She then revealed that she had felt that I was going to take out a knife and stab her while she was on the couch and that's why she had to get away from me. As she was narrating this, I noted that she had become much calmer. I remained quiet. Rebecca went on to say, "You know, I have never seen your office from this end. It looks so strange … You know, what it looks like … It looks so still. Everything is unmoved, quiet. It is like a dust cover jacket of a best-seller murder mystery. And you know what, sometimes when you read the whole book, you find out that all the clues were already shown in the photograph on the cover of the book. Yes, your office, from this side, looks like a photograph of just that sort, with all the clues intact." Now I spoke. I said, "And, I guess I would be the corpse in this murder scene." Rebecca smiled, stretched her arms, and aiming her clasped hands at me, made a noise indicating that she was shooting me with a gun. I responded by saying, "You know what, a little while ago you thought that I was going to kill you and now that you have taken some distance from that position, you find yourself killing me. Look, this murder and murderer are both parts of your own self and, for the work we have mutually undertaken, it is my hope that we hold on to both these views and see how they are related to each other, where they came from, and what purposes do they serve." Rebecca got off the desk, walked back to the couch, and lay down. The session continued in the "usual" way.

This clinical exchange illustrates a number of interventions, including the interpretation of splitting and projective identification. However, what I wish to emphasise here is how my unperturbed and non-intrusive stance facilitated the unfolding of the clinical material. My verbal interventions were important but these became possible only because of the material that became available due to my containing her terror by an unshaken and quiet stance.

Managing one's own fear and learning from it

During the course of his clinical work, the psychoanalyst experiences a vast array of emotions, and fear figures prominently in that list.

Warren Poland (cited in Mathias, 2008) has described four different ways in which fear arises within the analyst: (i) elicited by the patient, (ii) originating within the analyst himself, (iii) pertaining to the analytic process, and (iv) from the realities of the human condition. Finding these categories to be overlapping, I classify the analyst's fear into (i) his fear of the patient, (ii) his fear of acting out and making mistakes, (iii) his fear that the analysis will fail, and (iv) his fear of making unusual interventions. Acknowledging that such things cannot be neatly catalogued and one classification might clarify some things and muddle some others, in the following passages I will follow my scheme.

First is the analyst's fear of the patient. This is most marked when he is working with paranoid or borderline individuals, especially if they are given to outbursts of rage (see clinical vignette 2). Those who are chronically on the verge of committing suicide can also induce fear in the analyst. Fears of being sued and of damage to one's professional reputation can become quite powerful under such circumstances. These concerns might constitute rational responses to the patient's self-destructiveness and be accentuated by the projection of the analyst's own unconscious hatred of the patient (Maltsberger & Buie, 1974). At times the analyst is successful in bearing such fears for long periods of time and can continue working with the patient in a holding-interpretive mode. His decision to not set limits but allow the process to unfold is based upon a sense that the patient needs him to tolerate being afraid and that this transference demand is going to become amenable to interpretive resolution. Then something happens and the whole edifice falls apart.

Clinical vignette: 4

> As the treatment proceeded, Sarah Green (the patient mentioned in clinical vignette 1) recounted details of her long-term suicidal wishes and her constant sense, while growing up, that her mother hated her and wanted her dead. She also talked about the harsh criticism her mother directed at her: she had repeatedly called Sarah a "monster" and an "evil one". Not surprisingly, Sarah was terrified of her mother and made few demands on her time and attention.
>
> As these details unfolded, Sarah stole a revolver from her sister's house and started sleeping with it—fully loaded—in her

hand. I was terrified and yet felt prompted to stay away, this time, from insisting that she get rid of the gun immediately. I had a vague sense that the fear I was experiencing was the consequence of projective identification with her frightened child-self, as well as a direct result of her revenge-seeking fantasies. In other words, I had become scared little Sarah and she, her terrifying mother. And, at the same time, she had transformed herself from poor little Sarah to intimidating Sarah and I, as the mother, had to be tormented for what I had done to her as a child.

The very fact that I could conceptualise the enactment and put what was, most likely, going on into mental words, told me that there was something containable and, ultimately, interpretable here. The risk (for her) was high and the fear (in me) palpable, but session after session we talked about the potential underlying what was taking place—feelings, somewhere deep in our hearts, that we did not need to rupture the enactment by behavioural limit-setting, that she needed me to bear the anxiety. We felt that all that was happening was in the "pretend mode" (Fonagy & Target, 1997).

Then one afternoon, Sarah called me, saying that she was feeling truly suicidal again. I had another patient in the waiting room and asked her if she could assure me that she would not do anything impulsive and self-destructive for the next hour. She promised and we agreed that I would call her as soon as the patient I was about to see left. However, when I called, the phone kept ringing and ringing and Sarah did not pick it up. I was horrified, and thought that she had killed herself. Trembling with fear and cursing myself for being unduly heroic and adventuresome in my clinical work, I called her sister, who immediately departed for Sarah's apartment. The next thirty minutes were the longest thirty minutes I have ever lived. Then, I got a call from her sister that she had found Sarah fast asleep and that everything was fine and under control. Sarah came on the phone and profusely apologised for what had happened. I accepted her apology but feeling that a certain line had been crossed (and, that from a containing mother, I was becoming an ignoring and destructive mother), I insisted that the sister not only take the gun away but immediately dispose of it in a manner that Sarah would never be able to get her hands on it again. This intervention and its subsequent discussion in the clinical setting paved the way for the deepening of our therapeutic work.

Second is the fear of the analyst's own impulses to act out. If the analyst is under great personal stress (e.g., bereavement, divorce, serious illness), his fear of acting out with his patients, using his patients to diminish his loneliness, and venting sexual or aggressive affects (even if in a mild and aim-inhibited manner) is plausible and worthy of attention; consultation with a trusted colleague or return to some treatment must be considered under such circumstances. However, there are other times when the analyst is functioning optimally and yet develops a fear of doing something odd or strange with his patient. This is the stuff of countertransference, and restraint coupled with self-reflection often reveals the nature of transference that is putting such pressure on the analyst. Here is a clinical example of such an occurrence.

Clinical vignette: 5

Melanie Wright, a boyish young woman had sought treatment owing to feelings of anxiety and some marital tension. She had panicked when her husband was laid off from his job and, even though he was able to find gainful employment soon afterwards, remained anxious; in fact, she feared that they would become destitute. She and her husband frequently argued over this fear of hers and the friction between them was growing.

What struck me most when I first met her, however, was not this undue anxiety but the fact that she—a young woman in her mid-twenties—looked like a teenage boy. Making a mental note of it, I proceeded with gathering some background history. It turned out that her parents were divorced when she was six years old and that she had been raised by a loving but industrious and busy professional mother. Two other important facts were that the divorce had been precipitated by her father's announcement that he was gay and that young Melanie had to grow up with a very difficult older brother who constantly and, at times, physically hurt her. All sorts of factors, it seemed, worked in unison and led to the compromise of her femininity. The fact that she had been married for three years and seemed to love her husband appeared a little out of place.

As we began an analysis, I found myself experiencing something I had never felt during a clinical hour before. With Melanie talking—sometimes haltingly and at other times freely—about this or that issue, I experienced a peculiar discomfort in my ribcage and upper abdominal area. It is as if someone was tickling me very hard (my mind went to some childhood memories that involved my older brother). I repeatedly wanted to change my position in the chair, as if to evade this tickling. Alongside such physical unease, I also felt impulses to interrupt her by saying something absurd and totally unrelated to what Melanie was talking about. If, for instance, she was talking about her parents' divorce, I felt like asking her if she knew the capital of Iowa and if she ruminated on her financial future, or I had the urge to tell her about the intricacies of Urdu poetry.

While I kept such impulses in check, the experience was nonetheless unnerving. I kept wondering what it was about. What would be the impact upon her were I to utter my passing thoughts? To be sure, she would be shocked. She might experience me as bizarre, if not outright mad.

A few weeks of sitting upon such impulses, waiting, allowing the material to evolve further, and conducting piecemeal defence analysis, led to her revealing that her father had not only become gay but quite "crazy": he had painted the living and dining room ceilings purple, had started inviting his gay lovers to their home and would have sex in front of Melanie and her brother (when the mother was out working). Once or twice, he invited the children to join him and his lover in the bed while they were making love. As this material emerged—amid much distress and crying—I found a sudden reduction in my impulses to "act crazy"!

With the countertransference tension more in control, I became better able to think about what had transpired between the patient and myself. My "conjecture" (Brenner, 1976) was that the patient had been shocked by her father's perverse behaviour and had internalised this traumatic object relations scenario. It remained "unmetabolised", however, and needed to be deposited into me, like Bion's (1962) beta elements, for my containing and processing. She could retrieve it only after her capacity to bear the trauma and to "mentalise" (Fonagy & Target, 1997) grew. Meanwhile, I had to bear the noxious experience alternately as the victim (e.g., my feeling mercilessly tickled) and the perpetrator (e.g., my wishing to shock her by uttering absurdities) of the psychic violence.

A *third* fear experienced by the analyst is that of analytic failure. While exceptions exist, generally this fear reflects that the patient was not really suitable for analysis (e.g., too concrete, too paranoid, too lonely), and was taken into treatment by misjudgment or for the wrong reasons (e.g., analyst's need for money, patient's seductiveness). Generally this becomes evident via the concreteness of thought, the unrelenting inability or refusal to free associate, and/or the poverty of affective life displayed by the patient. A different sort of scenario unfolds with patients who flood their clinical situation with their "militant hopelessness" (Poland, cited in Jordan, 2002, p. 989). Session after session they complain about how futile their lives are, how the analyst is not helping them, and how they are certain that the analysis will fail. They might pay lip service to recognising that the analyst is devoted and doing his best but their way of relating remains dismissive of all his interventions. Possessed by a sort of "daemonic force" which Freud (1920g, p. 35) talked about in his elucidation of the death instinct, such patients suffer greatly while making the analyst suffer as well. Anticipating their suicide (which seems imminent each day), the analyst feels a bone-chilling fear at the destruction of his professional reputation and his personal well-being. Judith Chused also mentions the fear generated by feeling utterly helpless as an analyst and acknowledges being haunted by memories of failed analyses which "make [her] afraid not of these patients but of the limited value of what we do" (cited in Jordan, 2002, p. 992). Yet another situation where the fear of failed analysis appears is when the patient carries a tenacious "someday ..." fantasy (Akhtar, 1996). The patient keeps hoping, reflecting a state of pathological optimism, that his or her longed-for wish (e.g., a deceased parent to come back alive, for the analyst to marry the patient) will "someday" come true. And, having worked interpretively for a very long time, the analyst begins to feel the terror that this hope will not be renounced by the patient and the analysis will either go on forever or be abruptly ended; in either case, it will be a failure. Under such circumstances, consultation with a colleague or supervisor is indicated. And, it might become necessary to convert psychoanalysis to psychotherapy (see Akhtar, 2009a, pp. 57–58).

Finally, the analyst (especially the novice analyst) fears making what for the lack of a better term might be designated as "unusual interventions" (Akhtar, 2011). Here, the fear is one of attitude from supervisors, mentors, and analytic heroes internalised into the analyst's superego, rather than his "working self" (Bolognini, 2011). "What will they say?" becomes the driving injunction rather than what the truth of a particular clinical moment demands. Clearly, this is a murky area and the inexperienced analyst is safe in erring on the side of caution but the fear of acting in an "unusual" manner has to be put aside sooner or later if the analyst has to work with a "free-floating responsiveness" (Sandler & Sandler, 1998) and authenticity of participation. In an edited volume (Akhtar, 2011), I have collated nine so-called unusual interventions, including (i) making extraordinary monetary arrangements, (ii) conducting treatment outside the office, (iii) changing the frequency, length, and timing of sessions, (iv) refusing to listen to certain kinds of material, (v) giving advice, (vi) interpreting in the form of action, (vii) talking about oneself, (viii) touching the patient, and (ix) giving mementos and gifts to the patient. The volume also elucidates the pros and cons of their deployment and the reader might benefit by looking up that material.

Concluding remarks

In this contribution, I have described fear, categorised its intensities, and traced its developmental origins. I have delineated the similarities and differences between fear and anxiety while showing how the two coexist in the state of phobia. Following this, I have made a brief foray into the cultural realm and attempted to demonstrate how the unpleasant emotion of fear can be turned into the excitement of horror movies, gothic literature, and thrill-seeking games while, on the negative side of things, forming a part of ethno-racial prejudice and political oppression. Returning to the clinical realm, I have discussed the presence of fear in the transference-countertransference matrix and outlined the strategies to deal with the resulting problems.

Before concluding, however, it seems only fair to make some comments about psychic states that seem to be the opposite of fear. There are three such conditions: (i) fearlessness, (ii) counterphobia, and (iii) courage. Fearlessness is of two varieties. Primary fearlessness exists in infants and young children who are not aware of the dangers that surround them; they can put potentially poisonous items in their mouths and insert fingers in electric sockets. Getting hurt a few times and being repeatedly instructed by parents gradually curtails such "un-fear". Secondary fearlessness is seen among low-level operatives in a criminal ring; they carry out nefarious and risky acts under the protection of a powerful boss and feel that nothing can and will happen to them.

The state of counterphobia refers to that unconscious attitude of the ego which propels the individual to undertake, and even enjoy, the very activities that arouse fear and anxiety in him. However, there is a rigid and exaggerated quality to such behaviour. According to Fenichel (1945),

> The obsessive manner of the search for the once-feared situations shows that the anxiety has not been completely overcome. The patients continuously try to repeat the way in which in childhood other anxieties gradually had been mastered by active repetitions of exciting situations. The counterphobic pleasure is a repetition of the child's "functional" pleasure of "I do not need to be afraid anymore" (Silberer, 1909). And, as in the child, the type of pleasure achieved proves that the person is by no means really convinced of his mastery, and that before engaging in any such activity, he passes through an anxious tension of expectation, the overcoming of which is enjoyed. (p. 480)

A common example of counterphobic attitude is the social and motoric daredevilry of adolescents (e.g., driving at high speeds, experimenting with drugs, defying social etiquette, confronting the high school principal). Another illustration is the strikingly rapid assimilation into the host culture on the part of some immigrants (Akhtar, 1999). They adopt the new local customs in a magical way in order to deflect the social anxiety of being "different". More examples can be given. An individual who accepts the recommendation of a major surgery in the blink of an eye is most likely showing a counterphobic attitude. The grotesque youthfulness of some aging narcissists (Kernberg, 1980) and the "gallows humour" of some terminally ill individuals also belies a defensive avoidance of approaching threats. In all these situations, there is a suspicious absence of expectable fear. The fact is that fear exists but is kept in abeyance by forceful self-assurances to the contrary.

Finally, there is courage. Hardly synonymous with fearlessness, courage implies that the person knows that his stance (physical, intellectual, or moral) and his actions can have adverse consequences: financial loss, social isolation, personal ridicule, physical punishment, and so on. And yet, he braces himself to encounter their impending onslaught. Only then can he face destruction and death and not betray the meaningful core of his existence. John Wayne, the movie actor who personified boldness in his roles, quipped that "Courage is being scared to death and saddling up anyway" (downloaded from *www.Thinkexist.com*). General William T. Sherman (after whom the Sherman tank is named) declared courage to be "a perfect sensibility of the measure of danger and a mental willingness to endure it" (cited in Kidder, 2006, p. 9).

The courageous man accords great weight to his own thoughts and perceptions. He needs no consensus and does not depend upon others' approval. He can stand on his own even when others do not agree with him or oppose him. Courage becomes for him "an exceptional state of mind allowing and producing an extraordinary form of behavior" (Coles, 1965, p. 85).

In essence, courage is a particular variety of response to fear, as are counterphobia and cowardice. And the fact is that we—all of us—are capable of reacting to fear in all three ways. Which one predominates, when, and with what consequences ultimately gives shape to our adaptation to inner and outer reality, our overall character, and the direction our life takes.

Notes

1. An admittedly incomplete list includes *ablutophobia* (fear of washing), *acrophobia* (fear of heights), *agoraphobia* (fear of open spaces), *arachnophobia* (fear of spiders), *batrachophobia* (fear of frogs), *claustrophobia* (fear of enclosed spaces), *homophobia* (fear of homosexuals), *Islamophobia* (fear of Muslims), *photophobia* (fear of lights), and so on. The list, frankly, can be endless; one internet site contains 530 entries!

2. This affected the later reconstructions of Little Hans's childhood as well (Joseph, 1990; Silverman, 1980), which gave more attention to his pre-Oedipal development.

3. The childhood disorder commonly known as "school phobia" has little to do with school per se; the anxiety aroused by separating from parents (usually the mother) and from the familiar environment of home mostly contributes to such fear.

4. A curious overlap seems to exist between cowardice and procrastination. Biswas-Diener (2012) observes that not finishing a task that one undertook is associated with a kind of "minor cowardice" (p. 7) in many people's minds.

5. According to Freud (1900a), the following dreams were so widely prevalent as to be considered "universal": the dreams of (i) flying, (ii) falling, (iii) being chased, (iv) being inoptimally dressed or naked in

public, (v) the death of a loved one, (vi) having difficulty performing in an examination or test, and (vii) teeth falling out.

6. The colour-coded alert system devised by the US Homeland Security Administration in 2003 was intended to keep the public informed about the potential threat of terroristic attacks. At the same time, one wonders about the extent to which the shifts from Red (for severe) through Orange (for high), to Yellow (elevated), etc., were utilised for keeping people afraid and hence hesitant to question governmental surveillance of private lives.

7. Amusement park rides, especially roller coasters with sudden and sharp drops and turns, also gratify some of these impulses.

8. The fact is that some people do get traumatised by seeing horror movies. Relatively widespread traumatisation after the release of the movie, *Jaws*, was evident in a large number of people's avoiding swimming at the shores.

9. My observations are limited to working with adults. Not having experience of working with children, I am not comfortable commenting upon the vicissitudes of clinical praxis in that realm.

10. The first three of the four clinical vignettes provided in this chapter have also appeared elsewhere (Akhtar, 2013) with a somewhat different slant.

11. Assessment of the risk of violence becomes a truly important measure in such work. For details on this, see Otto (2000), and Gellerman and Suddath (2005).

SIX MAIN FEARS OF OUR LIVES

CHAPTER TWO

Fear of breakdown*

Elaine Zickler

Since the posthumous publication of Winnicott's (1974) "Fear of Breakdown", the phrase has entered into common parlance in the psychoanalytic literature, mainly in object relational writings, and construed loosely to indicate what, for more classical analysts, would be termed the "infantile anxieties" (Abram, 1996; Blum & Ross, 1993; Faimberg, 2007; Friedman, 1983; Mitrani, 1998; Phillips, 1988; C. Winnicott, 1980). In fact, its use has become a shorthand for a significant departure from Freud's theories of anxiety, based as they are on an edifice that has as its foundation the human infant's basic condition of helplessness and, in ascending developmental order, fear of castration, fear of loss of the object and the object's love, and fear of the superego and of loss of the superego's approval and love. By contrast, "fear of breakdown" is used to connote a "primitive agony" of disintegration of the ego and descent into a state of mind both pre-Oedipal and opaquely resistant to memory and subjective historicisation. It has come to connote fears of loss of ego organisation or fears of becoming psychotic

---

*I wish to thank Vincent Hausmann, Jonathan House, and the Friday Society for generous and helpful reading and suggestions in the preparation of this chapter.

(Bollas, 2013). It has, as a shorthand for both theory and practice, come to valorise and at times, reify, a notion of trauma that is always located in historical reality (as opposed to the Lacanian Real) and opposed to internal, or neurotic suffering rather than related to it by the complexities of time, memory, and fantasy. Winnicott emphasises the priority of this fear to castration anxiety, thereby foreclosing on the role of infantile sexuality and conceptualising the existence of an infantile state without even the retrospective organisation of Oedipal sexuality, such as Freud posits, and certainly without the notion of "general seduction" that Laplanche (2011) posits. Winnicott's essay, however, is tantalisingly ambiguous on a variety of important theoretical and clinical questions and exposes fault lines specifically in the areas of temporality, infantile sexuality, the possibility of trauma conceived as a universal "humanising" experience, and the question of psychoanalytic intervention as interpretation, construction, or re-translation. The fate of the concept of infantile sexuality will be an object of particular attention, as its theoretical foregrounding or neglect affects our understanding of all the other concepts—temporality, trauma, and the role of interpretation. This chapter aims to stage a conversation between Winnicott, Freud, Lacan, and Laplanche, using Winnicott's "Fear of Breakdown" as a point of departure for looking at these psychoanalytic problems and the directions they have taken with these important analytic figures and their heirs.

Winnicott's "fear of breakdown": a rereading with questions

Winnicott begins his article with what seems clearly to be a discussion of psychotic phenomena and psychotic, as distinct from psychoneurotic, patients. He is very clear that "Whereas there is value in thinking that in the area of psycho-neurosis it is castration anxiety that lies behind the defences, in the more psychotic phenomena that we are examining it is a breakdown of the establishment of the unit self that is indicated" (1974, p. 88). He enumerates the essentially non-neurotic, early infantile "primitive agonies" that can constitute this fear, one he relates to failures in the "facilitating environment" against which the individual cannot defend herself, being dependent upon that very environment to provide auxiliary ego support in the form of the mother. His list then, a preliminary and incomplete one, includes "a return to an unintegrated state" the defence against which is "disintegration" (p. 89). It is Winnicott's contention that disintegration, or breakdown, is a defence against the fear of breakdown which is a fear of "the unthinkable state of affairs that underlies the defence organization" (p. 88). This somewhat tautological reasoning seems a restatement of Freud's observation that psychosis is an attempt at self-cure. Indeed, Winnicott goes on to assert that psychotic illness is not a breakdown, but a "defence organization relative to a primitive agony, and it is usually successful" (p. 90). In sum, a psychotic breakdown can provide the cure for the fear of breakdown, in the form of a defence organised against the primitive agony.

Winnicott goes on to the most cited, because most intriguing, proposition of his article, namely his contention that "… clinical fear of breakdown is *the fear of a breakdown that has already been experienced*. It is a fear of the original agony which caused the defence organization which the patient displays as an illness syndrome" (p. 90, italics in original). Here, he reintroduces the Freudian temporal schema of overwhelming traumatic anxiety, in which the anxiety emerges some time after the original trauma which overwhelmed the ego's defences, in an ex-post facto attempt to prevent the trauma, which had already happened, from happening for the first time. However, it is in this "Statement of the Main Theme" that Winnicott introduces crucial, and to my mind, somewhat confusing distinctions between the phenomena he is attempting to define and theorise and what Freud has already introduced. He defines a special state of the unconscious prior to the requisite ego integration needed to "gather all the phenomena into the area of personal omnipotence" (p. 91). He writes that the "unconscious here is not exactly the repressed unconscious of psycho-neurosis, nor is it the unconscious of Freud's formulation of the part of the psyche that is very close to neuro-physiological functioning" (p. 90). Winnicott proposes that it is not a question of bringing a trauma out of repression in the treatment that is at stake, but it is a question of allowing it to happen for the first time in analysis "assuming the auxiliary ego-supporting function of the mother" (p. 91) can be successfully performed by the analyst. What began as a fear of a primitive state of defencelessness, the condition of every helpless human infant, has shifted subtly to a fear of a repetition of a particular environmental failure.

In this shift of perspective, we are now in the position as analysts of assisting the patient in a search for what Winnicott calls "this detail" which is "already a fact". He admits it is a "queer kind of truth, that what is not yet experienced did nevertheless happen in the past", and if the patient can be convinced of this, "then the way is open for the agony to be experienced in the transference, in reaction to the analyst's failures and mistakes" (p. 91). There are two kinds of confusions by now. One is about the nature of psychosis and psychotic breakdown in Winnicott's uses of the terms, and the other is about the nature of and recuperability of the original traumata. If this trauma can be experienced in the transference, then are we not, by definition, in the realm of the psychoneuroses? If the breakdown that is feared is the return to a pre-ego state of disintegration, would this not constitute at some level, a universal human trauma, the trauma of infantile helplessness? Rather, the language shifts to one of "failure" in the facilitating environment, introducing a shift, or a profound instability, in the definition of trauma that Winnicott is using, and a concomitant shift in his location of the trauma, relative to infantile sexuality (as we shall see) and to the role of the analyst. At this juncture in his thesis, Winnicott conceives of the analyst in the maternal role of assuming auxiliary ego-supporting functions. As well, he conceives of the breakdown as a symmetrical failure of the original maternal function of holding and support of the incipient infantile ego.

Winnicott indicts what he terms the "futility" of an analysis conducted as if the patient were a psychoneurotic when she is, in fact, psychotic and asserts that even if the analysis is going well, there is a collusive denial in place between analyst and analysand. He writes of this "futile" analytic endeavour that it "… was valid, it was clever, it was cosy because of the collusion. But each so-called advance ends in destruction" (p. 91). The analysis is not only futile, but endless, interminable: "But alas, there is no end unless the bottom of the trough has been reached, unless *the thing feared has been experienced*. And indeed one way out is for the patient to have a breakdown (physical or mental) and this can work very well" (p. 92, italics in original). Again, the confusion occurs in the definition of breakdown. If Winnicott is referring to a condition of ego-less disintegration or pre-integration, then this is not a breakdown that has already happened (that would require an existing ego structure), but a potentiality, a pre-symbolic state, the memory of which might represent itself as a fall into space, for instance. The ambiguity of his logic seems to express itself at times in his positing of a first breakdown due to environmental failure which affects an already somewhat organised ego-state, as when he writes:

> The purpose of this paper is to draw attention to the possibility
> that the breakdown has already happened, near the beginning of the
> individual's life. The patient needs to "remember" this but it is not

possible to remember something that has not yet happened, and this thing of the past has not yet happened yet because the patient was not there for it to happen to. The only way to "remember" in this case is for the patient to experience this past thing for the first time in the present, that is to say, in the transference. This past and future thing then becomes a matter of the here and now, and becomes experienced by the patient for the first time. This is the equivalent of remembering, and this outcome is the equivalent of the lifting of repression that occurs in the analysis of the psycho-neurotic patient [classical Freudian analysis]. (1974, p. 92)

The psychosis to which he refers seems occulted within a psychoneurotic personality, in fact, as in his notion of the false-self, created in response to maternal impingement, that occults or protects the true-self. This idea seems borne out by Clare Winnicott's (1980) presentation of a case based on this article. The problematics of this kind of theorising are challenging and provocative. With what assumptions does one begin an analysis? How does one conceive of the neurotic/psychotic divide? As a continuum? Or as a regularly occurring phase in any analysis? All these possibilities seem at least suggested by Winnicott's efforts in this article (and seem more of a piece with the later Lacan in this respect as discussed by Kalaidjian (2012)). He seems at times to be describing a parallel universe to the Freudian, and at other times to be suggesting that this area of breakdown, if not experienced in an analysis, will persist like something uncanny, to repeat and haunt the person. What begins as a cautionary tale against analysing a psychosis as if it were a neurosis seems to come to a clear fork in the road, or possibly a dead end. How could an analyst, faced with the possibilities Winnicott describes, somehow take both roads at once? It seems as if this article presents a set of clinical circumstances that clearly require specific clinical choices without, at the same time, being very clear itself about its theoretical position. It is a marvel of instability and ambiguity; its appeal to experiential truth, however, is unmistakable.

Winnicott gives a very brief clinical example by way of illustrating "emptiness" in analysis as embodying this proleptic breakdown. A young woman "lay uselessly on the couch" and complained that "nothing is happening in this analysis!". Winnicott writes that:

> She had been feeling feelings, and she had been experiencing these gradually fading, according to her pattern, a pattern which made

her despair. *The feelings were sexual and female. They did not show clinically.* Here in the transference was myself (nearly) being the cause now of her female sexuality fizzling out; *when this was properly stated* we had an example in the present of what had happened to her innumerable times. In her case (to simplify for the sake of description) *there was a father who at first was scarcely ever present,* and then when he came to her home when she was a little girl *he did not want his daughter's female self, and had nothing to give by way of male stimulus.* (1974, p. 94; italics mine)

Having dismissed sexuality as playing any role in the primitive agonies that he is describing, Winnicott presents a case of a woman whose sexual desire fades or fizzles in the transference situation and he does two things with this piece of analytic evidence. He displaces it immediately onto the reality of her father's absence in her early life and his refusal of her incipient feminine sexuality; then, this fact is "properly stated" to her by way of interpretation of her dilemma. What is at stake in such a clinical moment? What is the effect of this interpretation of the transference, one not remarkable in its own right except that it is not characteristic of Winnicott's practice (Phillips, 1988), and recognisable by most of us for its quotidian nature, referring her back to her earlier impossible sexual desire for her father? We cannot be sure that Winnicott interpreted her desire for her father, or only her father's unavailability to her as another need-satisfying object. There is a notable lack of any connection on Winnicott's part between the theory he brings to this moment and its effect (and his effect as analyst) on repeating the father's contribution to her dilemma, namely that he "had nothing to give by way of male stimulus" (Winnicott, 1974, p. 94). We might properly ask at this juncture if we are not seeing a return of the repressed in this late work of Winnicott's, a return of infantile sexuality, a return of the father, a return of interpretation proper, and all in contrast to the theoretical and clinical premises from which Winnicott's views proceed.

The times of trauma, anxiety, and of breakdown: what does sexuality have to do with it?

By the time he writes *Inhibitions, Symptoms and Anxiety* in 1926, Freud has pondered the question of temporality in numerous works (1899a, 1914g, 1915a, 1918b). In this work, he exhibits an integration of both temporal and spatial dynamics to the problems of trauma, danger situations, and anxiety, as well as human development. It is the passage of time along with the maturation of the ego (and implicitly the biological sexual body) that turns trauma into anxiety; external danger into internal; reality into fantasy or expectation. In this schema, which antedates Winnicott's by more than forty years, the play of temporality is spatialised (as it is in *Beyond the Pleasure Principle*) and we are presented with a complexity more like a Moebius strip than a timeline or a developmental *telos*. *Nachtraglichkeit*, or *après-coup*, takes on two meanings in Freud's writings. There is a retroactive conferral of meaning whereby a current danger situation becomes one by virtue of projection backwards to a previous one; there is a deferred action, whereby the situation that occurred in infancy or early childhood only acquires meaning after maturation, like a time bomb. Here is Freud (1907) in an early passage on his thoughts about *Nachtraglichkeit* in a letter to Karl Abraham: "The child is not equipped to cope mentally with stronger sexual impressions, and hence reacts to them compulsively, as if unconsciously—that is the first deficiency in the mechanism; as a consequence of the somatic intensification of the releasing of sexuality, these impressions later exercise more powerful effects as a retrospective reaction [*nachträglich*] and as *memories* than they did when they were real impressions, and that is the second psychological deficiency, because this constellation of retrospectively strengthened *unpleasure released by memories* [*Erinnerungsunlust*] makes repression possible, which would not succeed against *perceptions*" (p. 3, italics in original). Note here the fine distinction between the impossibility of repressing a perception and the possibility of repressing a memory, itself already in the realm of reconstruction or *Nachtraglichkeit*.

There is a persistent play between reality and fantasy or construction after the fact, both in the analysand's narrative history and in the work of the analysis. Freud writes that while a "real danger" is a threat from "an external object, and a neurotic danger is one which threatens … from an instinctual demand" (1926d, pp. 167–168), the distinction is necessarily not clear because an instinctual demand, or a drive pressure, is also a reality. Furthermore, it is a reality that can constitute a real danger or threat to the individual "because its satisfaction would bring on an external danger—that is, because the internal danger represents an external one" (Freud, 1926d, pp. 167–168). In Freud, then, it is the drive that is situated on the divide of external and internal, as well as past and future, in determining an anxiety situation. In his familiar hierarchy of typical danger situations it is the developing sexuality as well as the developing ego and superego that continually rework the original condition of helplessness into more complex and sexualised scenes of anxiety. Thus, castration anxiety will retroactively subsume earlier scenes of separation like weaning or toilet-training; and Oedipal-level fears of loss of the love of the superego will recast earlier fears again with moral and punitive significance.

Laplanche's critique and reformulation of *Nachtraglichkeit* is in the context of his project to recast Freud's abandoned general theory of seduction and in so doing, to recoup the role of the real[1] into a psychoa-nalysis that had seemed to abandon it in favour of endogenous fantasy. Laplanche posits that infantile sexuality is involved in any compulsion to repeat a trauma and in any formulation of deferred action precisely because there is a universal, humanising trauma involved in the sexual-ising of the human infant, which includes, but is not limited to, cases of actual sexual molestation or abuse.

Laplanche's *après-coup* is neither the projection back of the present onto the past, nor the realisation belatedly of the meaning of the past. It is specifically in the area of *the sexual* that *après-coup* has any mean-ing at all. Consider, for instance, Laplanche's interpretation of this Freudian anecdote from *The Interpretation of Dreams*: "Love and hunger, I reflected, meet at a woman's breast. A young man who was a great admirer of feminine beauty was talking once—so the story went—of the good-looking wet-nurse who had suckled him when he was a baby: 'I'm sorry', he remarked, 'that I didn't make a better use of my opportu-nity'" (Caruth, 2001, p. 3). For Laplanche, this anecdote is an example of both kinds of temporality in Freud. That is, there is the innate sexuality of the infant at the breast; there is also the adult sexuality of the man ruing his lost opportunity. Laplanche proposes a third possibility, a syn-thesis to "… take into account what he [Freud] doesn't take into account, that is, the wet nurse. If you don't take into account the wet nurse her-self, and what she contributes when she gives the breast to the child—if you don't have in mind the external person, that is, the stranger, and the strangeness of the other—you cannot grasp both directions implicit in *afterwardsness*" (p. 4, italics in original). It is neither the determinism of an innately, biologically sexual infant at birth nor the sexualisation of an infantile scene after the fact by the sexualised adult but the specifically sexual messages from the unconscious of that wet nurse, unrecognised by her, yet received by the child who can never fully translate them, not only because of developmental immaturity, but because these messages are enigmatic both to the adult who transmits them and to the helpless, receptive child. So the scene is always/already a sexual scene, a scene of sexual seduction and translation. There is the baby who grows into an adult and the adult whose communications to the baby are compromised and rendered unstable by the sexual unconscious, so that the child experiences the communication as an enigma, one that is overdetermined and polysemic, like parapraxes, and subject to successive translations as he grows. We might infer that in the scene cited in Freud's joke, there are at least three present: besides the baby and the mother are her desires for the (perhaps absent) father; her own father; and perhaps a revivification of her own infantile situation that makes a *mise en abyme*, an infinite regress, of this seemingly simple scene of suckling and nurture.

Laplanche's work on the sexual message and on translation is significant in this area of temporality because it refuses a hermeneutic based on the recuperation of an originary trauma, such as we saw in Winnicott's interpretation of his patient's emptiness. Laplanche puts forward a sexual version of Winnicott's enigmatic thing that happened but cannot be remembered because it did not happen and at the same time rejects Winnicott's idea that a clear statement of the repetition is all that is required:

> Even if we concentrate all our attention on the retroactive temporal direction, in the sense that someone reinterprets their past, this past cannot be a purely factual one, an unprocessed or raw "given". It contains rather in an immanent fashion something that comes before—a message from the other. It is impossible therefore to put forward a purely hermeneutic position on this—that is to say, that everyone interprets their past according to their present—because the past already has something deposited in it that demands to be deciphered, which is the message of the other person. (Laplanche, 2011, p. 265)

Laplanche proposes a "hermeneutic of the message" and specifically, the enigmatic sexual message that is first implanted in the infant and later translated by the child and much later, perhaps, de-translated in the analysis, provided the analyst understands that he/she now holds the place of the original seducer and the analysis is another primal scene. This is a significant commentary on the status of constructions in analysis, one which actively enlists the analyst as the recipient of enigmatic messages and as holding the place of the enigmatic other for the analysand, but not in a symmetrical way, as in the intersubjective and relational theories. For Laplanche, the asymmetrical situation of the primal scene of seduction is the one reproduced in the analytic scene. "I felt that the analytic situation could not be understood just as reviving a factual situation, but as reviving the situation of being confronted with the enigma of the other" (Caruth, 2001, p. 17). As I understand this conceptualisation of the analytic scene, what the analyst must bear in mind, what puts her out of symmetry with the analysand, is that messages addressed to her will be addressed to this seductive, enigmatic other and her communications will be received as if coming from this same other.

Laplanche is staking out a position against hermeneutics or interpretation in the sense of refusing the possibility of recuperating an originary situation from the language of the analysand. This is a problem that has plagued psychoanalysis from the start, one that Freud grappled with in the Wolf Man case of 1914 (1918b) and left off in famous (and courageous) ambiguity.

Christopher Bollas, in his recent book on the psychoanalysis of "breakdown", attempts to tease apart the categories of patient that might or might not break down in the way that would require his heroic therapeutics; in doing so he, necessarily, makes a distinction in the *après-coup* itself, defining it not so much by its temporal movement, but by its *origins* in either "parental or other early environmental failure" so that the trauma is located either in the realm of the "real" or in a "predominantly internal war going on between the drives and the self's mind" (2013, p. 119). In making his clinical determinations, it is the former group of patients—who have suffered some event in the "real", who break down in the particular way that he ascribes to Winnicott's description. It is important to note that in neither of these cases that Bollas is trying to tease apart from one another, is the sexual desire of the person playing any role in their experience of *après-coup*. There is neither the possibility of both an internal and an external playing out of conflict nor the possibility that infantile sexuality might be positioned in both.

Is a separation of the kind Bollas and Winnicott make entirely possible or useful? What they seem to be grasping after is an originary moment of trauma, and theorising that if that moment is sufficiently early in the infant's life, it will repeat as "fear of breakdown", and if it is later, at some undefined Oedipal moment or the moment of castration anxiety, then it will repeat in some more garden-variety neurotic way. This seems problematic in multi-layered ways, from theory-making to clinical decision-making. For now, staying at the theoretical level, we can point at least to the likelihood that both kinds of trauma will be present in all patients to one degree or other. Even in egregiously traumatised patients or those with histories of multiple or cumulative trauma (Khan, 1963, 1974), is it ever true that the Oedipal level anxieties will be absent as a factor in their fears of breakdown? The play of temporality implicit in *Nachtraglichkeit* makes this proposition impossible and Bollas's and Winnicott's psychical "triage" impossible to carry out without some decision to foreclose on infantile sexuality on the part of the analyst, even if only with some selected patients. It seems more compelling to theorise that the enigmatic thing in the "real" that both Bollas and Winnicott (and earlier, Ferenczi) were helping their patients to remember, is by way of a foundational moment in infantile life, both real and out of the reach of memory; both unique to each subject and subject to repetition.

Another way around the either/or dilemma of the *après-coup* as conceived by Winnicott is proposed by Haydee Faimberg (2007; Markman, 2010) in her recent paper on *Nachtraglichkeit*. Faimberg cites Winnicott's article as key in her "broader concept of *Nachtraglichkeit*" which focuses primarily on the role of assigning or creating meaning in the analytic context as a way of affecting unconscious temporality, that is, of specifically converting the fear of future breakdown into a past event and thus freeing the future from this kind of determinism. Faimberg's article is significant in several ways. It is almost alone in the literature in making use of Winnicott's article to address an important theoretical and related clinical concept. It attempts to get at the problematics of analytic interpretation in the case of a trauma that will not and cannot speak its name. In a post-structuralist move reminiscent of Spence (1982) and others (Fonagy, 1999; Friedman, 1983) she affirms that a construction in analysis need not be historically true in order to serve the therapeutic function of dissolving the anxiety rooted in an unrecoverable past. But, just as significant is her neglect of the part played by infantile sexuality in *Nachtraglichkeit*, or the *après-coup*. In Freud and later in Laplanche, the two ideas are inseparable; it is a mark of the de-sexualisation of theory that they become separated and Winnicott's article emblematises this conceptual divide. Just as he asked the question about the "fizzling" of his patient's sexuality in the transference, we may ask the question about the fizzling or fading of infantile sexuality from psychoanalytic discourse.

Aphanisis or castration?

Winnicott was, apparently, intrigued by Jones's concept of "aphanisis" or the fading of desire (Jones, 1927; Winnicott, 1974). One senses, in fact, that his use of the words "fizzling" and "fading" in his article were allusions to aphanisis and Jones's article, as well as refusals to use "castration anxiety" in the context of fear of breakdown. Jones proposed that the threat of castration was not the whole story, as it were, but that the:

> ... fundamental fear which lies at the basis of all neuroses ... is this aphanisis, the total, and of course permanent, extinction of the capacity (including opportunity) for sexual enjoyment .... The nearest approach to the idea of aphanisis that we meet with clinically is that of castration and of death thoughts (conscious dread of death and unconscious death wishes) .... The male dread of being castrated may or may not have a precise female counterpart, but what is more important is to realize that this dread is only a special case and that both sexes ultimately dread exactly the same thing, aphanisis. (pp. 461–462)

It is Lacan (1982) who takes after Jones on this concept of aphanisis and specifically on the following counts: that Jones conceives of castration as an unmediated concept, in the real as opposed to in the symbolic register; that Jones slips in his usage from anxiety to fear, therefore (this is the same "sliding" that Winnicott performs in his article); that desire is indestructible, though subject to repression; that we cannot therefore imagine someone experiencing fear of a repression while it is in operation. Lacan's critique of Jones's article resonates with Winnicott's "fear of breakdown" in several key ways. He writes:

> Doubtless aphanisis of desire corresponds to a recognizable stage in the clinical treatment of neurosis; but this should not stop us from seeing that the neurotic, far from fearing it, seeks refuge in it,

and pretends to give up his or her desire in order to safeguard that which is more precious than desire itself—its symbol, the phallus. Which means that by entering into the discourse on aphanisis, the analyst becomes equally complicit in the attempt to avoid what is unbearable in the castration complex. (pp. 109–110)

The immediate consequence of the failure or refusal to tolerate the "unbearable" implications of castration in the psychic field, is to witness its return in theory, that is, in a castrated theory, as well as in a clinical practice that has as its hallmarks a diminishment of the symbolic nature of psychic reality and a privileging of the real; an insistence on the primacy of the primitive and maternal over the neurotic and the Oedipal/paternal in an attempt to locate an area of development completely cut off from the sexual; and the repetitive enactment of this "fizzling" of sexual desire without acknowledgement of the resistance of the analyst in the playing out of this anticlimactic drama. A similar set of tendencies were in evidence in Ferenczi's theoretical and clinical writings, of course (1930–1931, 1933). The importance of Lacan's extensive critique of Jones for our consideration of Winnicott's article and its afterlife is in the way he situates the problematic of object relations in relation to the question of the sexual in Jones's article on aphanisis. Lacan faults Jones on three important issues: first, that Jones reverts to the biological and retreats from the psychic, thereby conflating desire with need, in contradiction to Freud's problematising of sexual desire as repetitive and "beyond" the pleasure principle; second, that Jones reduces and conflates notions of "privation, frustration and castration" to "frustration and gratification" again eliding the realm of the symbolic; and finally, and most significantly, for our reading of Winnicott,

> … a foregrounding of the criterion of adaptation to reality in which the very issue in dispute is taken for granted—namely, the moment of castration, as the moment which should be located as the very instigation of the subject in the confrontation with the real of sexual difference. (Lacan, 1982, p. 110)

If we can accept that desire does not fade, but gets repressed, we begin to see the dimensions of a sexual desire that is excessive and disturbing, even traumatic in its effects on the immature psyche. Winnicott had this view of the instinctual drives, that they were experienced by the infant as "an overwhelming assault" and he viewed the role of the mother as assisting the infant, in her role as auxiliary ego, in metabolising these disturbing and foreign intruders from within (Phillips, 1988, p. 100). Both Lacan and Laplanche address, in their different theoretical approaches, this traumatic, excessive aspect of desire, as did Freud in conflating the sexual drive with the death drive, as insisting beyond the pleasure principle, in a realm of pure repetition and disturbing uncanniness (1920g). Once the sexual has been de-linked from any biological imperatives, as Freud does in his *Three Essays* (1905d), it cannot be confined to developmental *telos*, nor to normative moral or romantic allegories without raising suspicion as to what repression may be at work (Fonagy, 2008; Mitchell, 1997; Stein, 1998).

Blevis and Feher-Gurewich (2003) describe *jouissance* as distinct from both desire and enjoyment, as a "not symbolized" condition and one indicative of the gulf of unknowing between one subject and another, as "enigmatic" and "able to threaten the very core of the subject's being" (p. 243). In their account of the infant/mother dyad at the first moments of the initiation of the infant into his subjectivity, its "subjectivation", they make reference to Lacan's mirror stage and note that the mother is the first or prototypical enigmatic Other for the child, whose subsequent fantasies will be determined by the way he "situates him or herself in relation to the jouissance and desire of the Other" (p. 243). In their account of the first structuration of the ego in the mirror phase, it is interesting to note that the burden of seduction is on the infant, who is in the position of working "to capture the mother's attention" and to deciphering "what it is that the mother lacks" that he, the infant, can provide. So that, in this account of the Lacanian schema, the castration complex is initiated in this formative structural moment simultaneous with the ecstatic, proleptic sense of phallic sufficiency that the infant experiences in the mirror, with the mother. Castration, in this structure, is the horror of the lack, both in the mother or Other and in the infant himself (or herself). It is captured in the enigma of "What is demanded of me?", "What does she want of me?" And also in the gap between the experienced body of the infant and the body reflected and mediated by the mirror. In this structuring moment, according to Lacan, the ego ideal, as well as the basic lack of correspondence it exposes, originates. The language that Blevis and Gurewich use is evocative of Winnicott's here as they describe the situation of the child as one of "fundamental anguish"; but, unlike Winnicott, who cannot ascribe this anguish or agony to castration, rightly intuiting that it is prior to Freud's Oedipal stage, they identify it as precisely the anguish of castration and in the language of translation that Laplanche uses to define the advent of the sexual in the life of the human subject. This definition of castration situates it:

> ... at the moment when the child is able to give a translation of the mother's incomprehensible demand: *There is something or someone other than me that she wants, and so I must relinquish the position of being the exclusive object of her desire.* (p. 245, italics in original)

The Lacanian baby makes a translation that is mortifying and terrifying: she is not enough or everything for her mother and furthermore, her mother lacks something essential that cannot be satisfied, so she will never be able to satisfy her mother. The Laplanchian baby seems more particular and phenomenological, forming her unique fantasy of seduction and the *sexual* from her own partial translations of the enigma of her mother's *sexual* unconscious; in this schema, the unconscious is communicated through conscious and preconscious words and behaviours, the language of ordinary infant care. The Winnicottian baby suffers a "primitive agony" that is likely universal, but may not be; she is fused with her mother's ego and it is her mother's job to protect her from the assaults of her own drives; this mother is not sexual herself and seems not to be troubled by her own drives or desires, especially not for the baby's father. The father is as absent from Winnicott's writings as he seems to be from his patient's sexuality.[2]

In Lacanian terms, the act of signifying already enacts the separation from the maternal that is both necessary to save the infant from the engulfing maternal *jouissance* and is narcissistically mortifying because it confirms the castration, the insufficiency of the infant for the mother. For Lacan, castration is a psychic fact for both sexes and instantiates a law against incest that protects the emerging subject from being overwhelmed by the *jouissance* of the mother. In his account, castration emerges as the subjective limit that propels sexual desire and safeguards it; it secures the subject's ability to persist in desiring. Lacan rejects the notion of the possibility of desire ever "fizzling" or fading. Instead he interprets the fading on the side of the subject, withdrawing from the threat of *jouissance*. Some translation into language is at stake in all three of these accounts. For both Lacan and Laplanche, in their different approaches, the work of analysis consists in discovering by association and by language, the sexual fantasy, the infantile translation if you will, and then subjecting it to "de-translation" in Laplanche's terms; in Lacanian psychoanalysis, it is to deconstruct the unconscious fantasy that has been erected to neurotically (or psychotically) prevent the elaboration of desire in language. Here, the task of the analyst is to direct treatment away from the "pull of such a *jouissance*" (Blevis & Feher-Gurewich, 2003, p. 259) and towards the establishment of a neurotic structure in which desire is attempting to fulfil an Oedipal wish. In Winnicott's terms, it appears that the direction of treatment is regressive in the putative service of the rebuilding of the ego; in the direction of the site of an illusory but real and nameable, originary trauma, in the failure of the parental environment.

Here are the unities and distinctions we can draw between these various theorists striving, in their own ways, to come to terms with an early, foundational experience, a universal experience of infancy, that could explain the formation of sexual fantasy, the sense of a lack in being, and the inability to translate into language these originary enigmatic messages received in infancy. The "fear of breakdown" is itself an enigmatic concept, implying the undoing of a structure, a return to fragmentation and internal chaos. It is interesting that only Lacan seems to theorise the possibility of this moment with any elegance in the *mirror stage*, in the sense that the feeling of inner fragmentation arises at the moment when the infant is presented with a mirror image that is whole, that presents a gestalt, in Lacan's words (1949, p. 95). In that specular moment, both the ego-ideal, a proleptic wholeness, and a concomitant sense of inner fragmentation or lack, form a binary system, an *imaginary* system that, nonetheless, is formative, is seductive towards development and, significantly, is erotogenic, that is, it arouses sexual desire, however primitive. It is understandable then, that the sexual is implicated in all theories of the formation of the unconscious. Winnicott's efforts to predate the "fear of breakdown" to a time previous to the sexuality of the child, return in his case example as the "fizzling" of his patient's sexual desire. I find myself curious about this in technical ways as well as theoretical ways. Is the invitation to regression, for instance, itself a provocateur of this "fear of breakdown" because, in Lacanian terms, it threatens the analysand with the excessive demand, the *jouissance*, of the analyst? Further, if the analyst believes that there is an analytic "thing" that can be retrieved from the regression in the form of a specific trauma, does the production of this sexual trauma become the only way out of the maternal analyst's *jouissance* for the analysand?[3]

In trying to decipher what may be at stake for the analysand in these different theoretic and clinical perspectives, the importance of the Oedipal direction of the interpretation has less to do with fixing the Oedipal at a particular developmental age or deciding whether the analysand's pathology is pre-Oedipal or Oedipal in nature, than with the Oedipal orientation of the analyst. Consider that if the primary narcissism of the mirror stage is undercut by castration, by a sense of lack, it is simultaneously marked by the presence of an unseen other, possibly the father, possibly the future of the child. The mirror mediates the gaze of both the mother and the infant. If the infant looks towards the mother's face, she will see her gaze averted towards the mirror; if the infant looks into the mirror, their two gazes will meet somewhere in that reflected image, already in the future. This moment then, is already Oedipal or at least not dyadic, as it is in Winnicott's iteration of Lacan's theory in the "Mirror-Role of the Mother" (1971). It is rather a moment of profound, formative estrangement in which both the infant and the mother are perceived as others. So, in the scene of analysis, what Laplanche calls the new primal scene, the resurgence of the transference makes it possible to "de-translate" in his terms, or "to both retrieve and to fabricate [the] oedipal fantasy" in Lacanian terms (Blevis & Fehrer-Gurewich, 2003, p. 260; Laplanche, 2011).

The notion of the *sexual* as articulated by Laplanche essentially dissolves the pre-Oedipal/Oedipal boundary, instead conceptualising all drive activity as existing apart from instinctual sexuality which aims for orgasm and relaxation; the drive, by contrast, what he terms the *sexual*,[4] aims for excitation and is infantile in nature. It persists, never completely bound by the Oedipal or by sexual relationships, or by sublimatory activities. A residue in excess always remains. Therefore, with the restoration in full of the concept of infantile sexuality as *the* unconscious realm with which psychoanalysis constitutes itself, Laplanche rejects notions of the pre-Oedipal which might equate it as a distinct developmental period that predates the sexual. Rather, in Laplanche's work, as in Freud's, the *sexual* predates sex. It is sex, as such, as instinctual activity, that partially binds the *sexual*—what Freud called the genital organisation. But, it has to be emphasised that, for Laplanche's reading of Freud, inasmuch as the *sexual* comes first, comes before sex, and has an opposing vector, seeking excitement rather than relaxation, it is the *sexual* that comprises the unconscious of psychoanalysis.

Interpretation, construction, and re-translation

Laplanche does not privilege the notions of castration or the Oedipus complex, except as categories of translation, as distinct from interpretation or hermeneutics:

> You may also have a translation into a type of code which is internal to language, for instance, the castration code or the Oedipus myth, which is a type of code into which you can translate something. So why do I speak of translation and not of interpretation? Interpretation may mean that you interpret some factual situation. Translation means that there is no factual situation that can be translated. If something is translated, it's already a message. That means, you can only translate what has already been put in communication, or made as a communication. That's why I speak of translation rather than of understanding or interpretation. (Caruth, 2001, p. 15)

I do not understand (or translate) this passage as eliminating notions of any originary sexual traumata or founding anxieties in a manner that would seem to put psychoanalysis into a more post-structural universe, one that depends upon the endless circulation of language and signification, of a writing that is always and already circumscribing the *lack* of fixed origin or of an original text. In practice, one is hard put to find this kind of psychoanalysis, one that would endlessly defer a statement of meaning, a construction, an interpretation. But Laplanche is simply underscoring the role of the communication or the message as already a translation, a writing, in much the same vein as Freud's comment in his letter to Abraham, cited earlier.

It is in the relational and object relational theorists that one finds both the postmodern questioning of origins and the imperative to speak with the analysand, to co-construct or co-create meaning and not necessarily to uncover or discover it (Blum, 2003; Fonagy, 1999). However, as notions of infantile sexuality and its corollary of castration anxiety get jettisoned, there is an inevitable emphasis on the significance of specific trauma, or of a "breakdown" at once non-specific in origin and discoverable that propels the analytic process towards what Adam Phillips termed "the locating of legitimate grievances" (1988, p. 125; see also Mitrani, 1998).

Winnicott prescribes the maternal role for the analyst in the transference. What form does language and interpretation assume in this dyadic situation? Is it background music that avoids signification? Bollas (2013), for instance, refers to a certain type of interpretation, or "spoken reveries" made to patients who are experiencing breakdown, as creating a "verbal matrix within which the patient can imagine something completely different", a Winnicottian potential space, as it were (p. 122). Is it in its supportive and "ego-auxiliary" function, a supplier of language, of words and meanings? It is hard to know. Winnicott is enigmatic. He takes up both sides: the analyst must "properly state" what is going on, but the analyst must not offer up interpretations that impinge on the privacy of the true self. The clinical direction and the theoretical direction moved always towards containment and dyadic mirroring, seeing any excess or failure as bad and traumatic for the infant and for the analysand, while allowing that the analyst's failure, like the good enough mother's failure, is inevitable and necessary. In this context, what Winnicott interpreted as the fading or fizzling of sexual desire, his patient's anaphisis, can be seen, perhaps more fruitfully, as the patient's and the analyst's rejection of this excess of the *sexual*. Yet the *sexual* will always escape such containment, whether by the parents or by the analyst, for all the reasons Laplanche theorises. Finding the language for sexual excess in the transference would seem to be a challenge, as the inclination of the analyst, like the parent, is to avoid both the Scylla of sharing in the sexual excess or excitement and the Charybdis of inhibition and suppression. The "basic incompatibility of child and adult in matters of sexuality" that Stein notes would seem to transfer to the analytic pair in the asymmetrical arrangement of the transferential primal scene (Fonagy, 2008; Stein, 2008). To the extent that the analyst, as mother, insinuates herself within and beneath the discourse of the analysand, there is a distinct danger of the most unbearable kinds of invasion of privacy. This is the paradox of Winnicott's psychoanalytic vision, that it tends towards the revolt against this excessive maternal environment and towards the return of the father and of sexuality.

Can it be that in this postmodern psychoanalytic universe, there is, nonetheless, a need for castration anxiety? For a stronger paternal presence to contain the limitless and engulfing world of maternal holding and *jouissance*? Theory contains within itself a blindness and a compulsion to repeat and an inevitable return of the repressed. Certainly, we have seen this in the turn away from drive theory towards a reified theory of object relations; away from the Oedipal father and towards the pre-Oedipal mother; away from language itself towards the preverbal or even non-verbal realms in psychoanalysis. Is it at least a possibility that the fading of desire in Winnicott's patient was part of a *mise en abyme* of symbolic collapse, of breakdown in the symbolic order that finds its foundational moment in castration? Is it possible that the emphasis on breakdown in the analytic setting emerges from a foreclosure on the paternal function, on castration anxiety, on infantile sexuality which then make their return in the form of a demand for the intervention of the law, a demand for castration that enables symbolisation and speech, a demand that something be, in Winnicott's words, "properly stated"?

Notes

1. Laplanche's notion of the "real" is phenomenological and distinct from Lacan's definition of the Real as one of the three registers of mental life.

2. From Rodman's biography (2003), this note: "In the 'Use' papers, 'Moses and Monotheism' makes an appearance in connection with the idea of the father as the first person who is whole from the start. This unprecedented appearance of the father occurred, for Winnicott, in the shadow of death" (p. 352).

3. For examples of this phenomenon, see Ferenczi's *Clinical Diary* (Dupont, ed. 1988); also Rodman's biography of Winnicott (2003) in which he tells the story of Winnicott's patient who committed suicide in a rageful and vengeful reaction to Winnicott's own critical illness; Winnicott seems to accept the responsibility in a show of omnipotent masochism; he puts her in the "category of patients who are an actual physical threat to the survival of the analyst" (p. 333). Also, see Mitrani (1998).

4. In Laplanche's use of "the *sexual*" the term is apposite to "infantile sexuality", and comprises the Freudian unconscious.

CHAPTER THREE

Fear of aloneness

Peggy B. Hutson

Throughout life, fear of aloneness is an intermittent feeling in all people. It spells out the first and always present need in everyone, a need for safety and security. Symptoms due to fear of aloneness may occur with or without being attached to thoughts. In the early period of life, it presents as high anxiety and fear upon separation. When the infant is basically helpless, this alarming feeling of aloneness occurs upon even short separation from the mother (carer). From the toddler stage, a defining view of the early normal fear of aloneness is the scene of a lost child frantically crying in a department store. The feeling of safety and security is gone. The connection has been broken. Adults close by move quickly towards that child until one reaches him or her and connects. The others begin to look for the mother. And the mother, once aware that the child is not there, is frantically looking for her child. From their unconscious and conscious memory banks from their own early days, most adults know they are seeing a desperate need for safety and security. This was precipitated by a severe fear of aloneness in this little one. The best solution at that moment was through reconnection with a warm, reassuring and mature mother or mother figure.

Developmental background

Each individual who has experienced a "good enough mother" (Winnicott, 1965) will, in adulthood, be able to be alone, but also be able to couple and have good friends. He or she will have freedom to differ and feel comfortable, in terms of self-esteem, next to others. There will be comfort in sublimations such as meaningful connections in various organisations. The positive experience in receiving comfort in connection during times of aloneness will remain as a guiding light. Unfortunately, sometimes certain types of early parenting leave that child uncertain of safety and security throughout life. Thus, that child remains concerned about the early fears of aloneness. The unconscious worries and young solutions to the early fears of aloneness continue into adulthood from this pre-Oedipal in origin time. In this case, the object is used as a selfobject for support. This may be disguised in many ways. Often this goes unnoticed by the owner, for the solutions are lived out so smoothly. They can include presenting as a very agreeable person. But under that is inhibition of aggression. Also, the self-esteem problems have a multitude of presentations after the shame has signalled defence activity. This is called hidden shame. The use of the selfobject to reassure the self and feel secure may have been missed until a very strong reaction to a new episode of fear of aloneness appears.

Both resolved and unresolved early concerns about fear of aloneness will remain within on the road to adulthood. The unresolved concerns will often automatically be added to the new episodes of fear of aloneness throughout life. There are two very common contributions to this fear of aloneness which may remain unresolved in early childhood and thus continue into adulthood. The first is early mothering coming from a carer who is unable to empathically connect well enough to provide "good enough mothering" to the infant and/or later the little child. This may be due to not wanting to be in that position of mothering, or due to repeating the poor parenting received by her, or due to physical or emotional problems in the carer, or due to many other reasons. Also, frequently the carer has little patience for the child's early expressions of differing or anger and withdraws loving connection and understanding too much. In these cases, the early unconscious understanding in the child—and later that adult—is that differing or aggression equals abandonment and thus, lack of safety and security. In these cases, the adult unconsciously continues to need to receive reassurance from the object that he or she will not be alone.

Aggression from without or within usually prompts defensive activity. The very feeling that ordinarily calls one to attention to protect the self has been disabled. The object is used as selfobject for safety and security for the self. Usually, the earlier the development of the problem, the stronger the symptoms. The second contribution comes at some point after the development of the self representation and object representation has evolved in this pre-Oedipal period, when the child's sense of self and then ideals begin to be defined. They are passed on verbally and non-verbally by the parents. This second large early contributor to unconscious worries about fear of aloneness with the feelings of lack of safety and security results also from the very early parenting and the carer's negative "definitions" of self and unreasonable ideals given to the child. Those that produce problems create self-esteem vulnerability. The details of this will be spelled out shortly. One may question why this is included here. Since understanding of the self and then ideals come from the early carers after separation-individuation begins, in certain ways the carer is not loving and accepting "enough" when labelling a little one "the ugly one", "the stupid one", being disappointed the newborn is not the right gender, or the newborn had too dark or too light coloured skin, or passing on belief that the ideal gender is boy or that one must be perfect. A certain demeaning and rejection comes from labels of self and ideals such as these and more. Without words these children not only feel rejected by the carer but again they fear aloneness due to their continuing helplessness at that age. But now they will have developed self-esteem problems that continue to make them feel others would not want to be with them or respect them. Shame is the affect experienced and is quickly defended in adults whereas it is easily noticed in children. These disorders are quickly hidden in the adults by defence activity resulting in new compromise formations. These adults continue to need reassurance throughout life to make them feel acceptable and worthy. They often get the reassurance through defence activity leading to strong efforts resulting in getting many to praise or think well of them. This may be done by having more and more titles and positions to feel good about the self. No gain is enough though and they must continue the behaviour as long as those definitions remain within, both conscious and unconscious. The motive was the wish for safety and security. Fear of aloneness was and is present. The self continues to use the object as a selfobject for reassurance of worth or to feel good enough about the self.

Various other situations like illness, war, famine, and other disasters often interfere with a successful journey on the early developmental road. When the early fear of aloneness continues into adulthood, use of the other as a selfobject continues in the adult. The dynamics and treatment in these cases will be reviewed shortly. Although fear of aloneness in the adult presents quite differently from that in the earlier periods of life, the basic need for connection(s), with its sense of safety and security, is always present. There are many things prompting the need for safety and security, but this fear of aloneness prompted the first need which was noted for safety and security in early life. This basic need is the underpinning of our partnerships, of close friendships, and of many sublimations that help provide that feeling of safety and security which is needed by every individual. The journey on the earliest developmental road will have lasting effects on that individual's reactions upon separation and upon his or her self-esteem equilibrium, with the accompanying beliefs that others will be there and appreciate the individual or not. In those with trauma of any type, the normal need for the object to be used as selfobject in childhood will continue into adulthood where narcissistic problems will prevail.

Throughout adult life, fears of aloneness may be experienced in many circumstances. They may occur upon leaving for college, upon graduating from training programmes and entering the working population, upon job changes, upon moving to a different culture, upon marriage, with divorce, upon taking the job of parenting, upon having successfully grown-up children leave, upon advancement and loss of position, upon accepting a position of large responsibility and/or leaving it, upon being turned down for a job or having one's creative endeavours rejected, upon reaching middle age, upon older aging, upon loss of one's partner or friend, upon illness, and when facing the end of life. It also surfaces during unsafe times as during violent behaviour in another and during war and natural disasters such as earthquakes and hurricanes.

Although fear of aloneness in the adult is never so frequent and usually not as severe as in the small child, it may recur intermittently at times of real or imagined change or danger until the end of life as just noted. Of greatest importance are the ways these fears were handled in early life. The ways the early fears of aloneness have been dealt with by the type of early "mothering" will become part of that individual's unconscious and conscious memory bank, casting their shadows over future times of fear of aloneness throughout life. These are responsible for our types or attachments and sublimations which serve as anchorages throughout life. With "good enough mothering", the fear of aloneness only surfaces in adults when real circumstances consciously or unconsciously call for more safety and security. Sometimes individuals are so traumatised in early life that there are signs and symptoms of the traumas on a daily basis. These may be frequent panic attacks. During the intermittent episodes of fear of aloneness, the responses may vary from some fear and sadness requiring one's calling upon his or her "connections" or anchorages and regrouping … to asking for counselling … to having severe panic attacks and sometimes thoughts that death would be better than this. The latter may require hospitalisation. Since separation-individuation is felt to go on for a life time, and since new stages in life often trigger a separation anxiety or fear of aloneness, the references to studies of adult stages of development will be noted.

Adult stages of development

Child development had been studied in England along with object relations in the early 1940s. It was not until later that the focus moved to adolescence and then adult periods of development. These were referred to by some as further stages of separation-individuation. In all the later developmental stages, all individuals will have experienced some planned and unplanned losses in the evolving stages of further separation-individuation. Is the individual experiencing loss, is there a resilient capacity or desire to restitution to remain in the mainstream? If not, what was the response? Recommended readings about the vicissitudes of separation-individuation during adult life are to be found in *Intimacy and Infidelity* (Akhtar & Kramer, 1996), and *The Seasons of Life: Separation-Individuation Perspectives* (Akhtar & Kramer (1997). These edited volumes contain many important essays, with the contributions of Ross (1996), Colarusso (1997), and Prall (1997) being the most outstanding. Besides the ordinary unfolding of the life span, another variable that affects individuation during adult life involves immigration (see Akhtar, 1995, for details).

Often with loss of family, culture, and country, to name just a few, these are far beyond losses normally found in further individuation. Under such circumstances, the fundamental developmental issues of childhood continue to be reworked though in somewhat altered form.

Dr Ross expressed the difference as follows: "Whatever its elasticity, it is not the core self representation that is being organized (in adulthood) but the more variegated and permeable layer of self closer to and more responsive to the social surround. The ego identity achieved in its felt actualization and affirmation is more dynamically affected and volatile in adult life than this primordial structure laid down in infancy and toddlerhood" (1996, p. 125). One last reference by Weinstein (1971) reported that Margaret Mahler (1965) addressed separation-individuation as a lifelong process because of the inherent threat of the object loss in every stage of independence.

Evaluation for basic anchorages in those with fear of aloneness in adulthood

When evaluating the individual who is having trouble adjusting to the changes in adult life, the evaluation should gradually include the type of early parenting, any early separation fears, and self-esteem problems from early life. These may elevate the symptoms from the new fears. The individual may be using the object as a selfobject now, but was that true earlier? Sometimes the results of defence activity are so successful, and one does not even realise the difficulty until this new fear of aloneness "upsets the apple cart". Examples of the problems being successfully hidden are found when a man or woman who has the inhibition of aggression is seen as a very kind individual for never saying no to others. With the woman or man with self-esteem vulnerability, the defences may have tilted towards reassuring oneself about worth through multiple successes. These are like temporary bandages over the wounds of not feeling good enough.

Safety and security will always be an important need. Since fear of aloneness is related to lack of this, we know that having good connections to people and sublimations of this are helpful to us on the journey through life. When "good enough" mothering promoted good enough connections in the child's world, that adult should be able to build basic anchorages or connections. To evaluate this, the following areas should be reviewed.

1. Does the individual have an intact home and family?
2. Is there a social anchorage (not familial)—school—play—work/career, etc.?

3. Economic security (e.g., the capacity to work and provide).
4. Is there a meaningful purpose to life (e.g., sublimations, religion, art, music, work)?
5. Does the individual have a healthy body? Often, long periods of excessive stress affect the immune system. Also, depression often leads to not eating and weight loss or may in same cases lead to weight gain.
6. Does the individual have a healthy body image? Problems with this are often found in those with self-esteem problems from early life such as the anorexics.

Two major situations which impede one's freedom to develop such anchors include the early development of (i) separation anxiety often along with inhibition of aggression, and (ii) self-esteem vulnerability. These two areas also should also be carefully reviewed.

Evaluation for inhibition of aggression

This is often found in cases where the early unconscious understanding of aggression is that it equals abandonment. Evaluate for attachment problems or separation anxieties ... Is there any history of separation problems in the earlier part of life, such as school phobia, or of later ones where the subject cannot go to camp as a teen or off to college. How did the mother deal with anger in the child? Does the individual use the object as a selfobject? Is the patient comfortable with anger from without and anger from within? Can the person set limits? Is there a history of panic attacks?

Evaluate for self-esteem vulnerability and defended shame

What does the individual feel about himself? How would he describe himself? What does he think others feel about him? How did he think the mother and father felt about him? How does he respond to insults? Does the individual use the object as a selfobject? Does the individual know the gender value and gender characteristics passed on in his or her family and culture? What ideals does he or she hold high for the self? Some are conscious and some not conscious.

Since self-esteem conflicts in adults rarely present as shame, does he or she have any of the usual presenting pictures or compromise formations? These include denigration of the other when frequently feeling insulted, having haughty behaviour, being very envious, externalising and inviting denigration, and shamelessness which is often seen in an adolescent with this, and other presentations (Hutson, Pulver, Kilbourne, Lansky, & Morrison, 2003; Morrison, 1989). In all the later developmental stages, all individuals will have experienced some planned and unplanned losses in the evolving stages of further separation-individuation. As noted before, is there a resilient capacity or desire to restitute to remain in the mainstream? If not, what was the response?

Clinical findings

Upon reviewing many of my adult cases treated with psychoanalysis and psychotherapy during the past two decades, I noted that those with problems involving fear of aloneness and lack of safety and security had required significant work with material pre-Oedipal in origin. Often, some of these individuals reported no early problems until the triggering losses in adulthood. At that point reactions to losses triggered a fear of aloneness and sense of lack of safety and security in adult life and symptoms developed. The most frequent problems found were problems involving inhibitions of aggression attached to early unconscious fears of abandonment or aloneness and self-esteem problems which required defensive activity to hide a sense of shame and expected lack of acceptance. Both fell under narcissistic disorders due to the pre-Oedipal origins. Over half of the cases were immigrants and the traumas from this had added to the early stresses. The early history of life was crucial along with understanding that in the transference, the analyst would be used as a selfobject at first. This is how those close to the patient would have been related to. With other adults there was diminished empathy. The only exception in some of the cases was their being able to have an empathic stance with children or helpless pets. Otherwise, the capacity for empathic connections was diminished in those with the narcissistic disorders.

In many cases, the analytic work revealed an early understanding that aggression leads to abandonment. In three cases in analysis, I found similar early fears of aloneness and lack of safety and security attached to sexual feelings. The important findings in these cases were those where the sexual drive in the very young children had been stimulated by an exhibitionistic parent or by a careless parent being too exposed. The parent demeaned the early child's normal responses as perverted or unacceptable. The demeaned and badly labelled young child had fears of aloneness and lacked safety and security. Without words, the understanding was that sexual excitement leads to abandonment. In one case, it was that sexual excitement leads to a type of castration. Again, this was from a time when children would have no words for sexual drive. In one case, this led to a vertical split of any type of libidinal feelings (from liking to sexual feelings) from age fifteen on when the patient was close to "loved" ones. In another case, sexual feelings in response to the exhibitionism came to be understood as unacceptable and the child would be damaged by the parent. This would be a "castration" of sorts. This threat has been found in both little boys and little girls. The individual with the vertical split suffered with this for over twenty-five years before being able to deal with it in therapy. Through steadfast work in therapy in midlife, he was gradually able to feel libidinal feelings as normal.

Many of the adult cases of fear of aloneness, which triggers the need for safety and security, include contributions from the early developmental problems to the occurrences of fear of aloneness in adulthood. Therefore this frequently requires working with the problems pre-Oedipal in origin. Because of this, helpful advances from various theoretical and technical paradigms and from early child research findings will be addressed. These concepts are useful when conducting psychoanalysis and psychotherapy in patients with fear of aloneness.

Studies of early development and mothering patterns

In the 1940s, object relations theories were advancing as well as early child development studies. Object relations referred to specific intrapsychic structures (Horner, 1984). These included intrapsychic self and intrapsychic object. Kernberg (1976) defined the objects relations theory as a psychoanalytic study of interpersonal relations and how intrapsychic structures grow from internalised past relationships with others. Child development research would spell out the timeline for the move into development of self representation separate from object representation in the mind. As the child development studies evolved, the first need/wish in life came clearly into view. This first need in life was for safety and security and would occur when the little one was aware, in some way, of aloneness through the separation. This early developmental period would be interwoven with libidinal and aggressive aspects as development evolved. How the adult would finally be able to handle fears of aloneness and thus periods of lack of safety and security in the future would especially depend on the mother's early handling of the child's assertive moves (aggression) and expressions of independence a little later on. The child research had shown that before there could be integration of the libidinal object representation with the aggressive object representation, these two are separate in the developing mind. If the mother can deal with the assertive moves and still be very loving, chances are the child will come to be comfortable when differing with a loved one.

Kernberg emphasised how intrapsychic structures grow from internalised past relationships with others. Good affective experiences are the basis for libidinal drives and bad affective experiences the basis for aggressive drives. He noted that in object relations, object related feelings of love and hate precede and build up the drives. These are the same findings as in the child research. The individual is innately responsive and relational rather than innately sexual or aggressive. In these studies, the focus is on pre-Oedipal development. Kernberg outlined five stages of development. The third stage roughly covered the same period as the separation and individuation stage described by Margaret Mahler (1965) and ran from six to eight months and from eighteen to thirty-six months.

With time, the road of integration of attachment theory findings and psychoanalysis evolved, as noted next. Bowlby (1940, 1969) had originated attachment theory, which is an empirically derived set of hypotheses pertaining to the infant's need for a secure bond with the mother at its core. This theory widened human motivation beyond the original focus on drives to stressing the early human motivation of attachment with the carer (mostly the mother) as a primary drive and the main factor in psychic structuralisation. The theory was based on observation and provided understanding of the gradual development of the self representation and object representation as separate in the developing mind. The development is addressed in the following reference on stress in the first year.

In her book titled *Scared Sick*, Karr-Morse (2012) reported on research which revealed that at birth, the thinking aspect of the brain is not fully developed. Anatomic and neuroendocrinology studies show that a child can respond to "danger" due to the inborn alarm system for survival purposes. The reaction is typically called "fight or flight". A neuro-chemical response occurs and leads to this. Thus, there may be a startle reaction. Only the amygdala is well developed at birth. Other parts of the brain will continue to grow in this early childhood period. Memo-ries recorded would be unconscious. The hippocampus, the mediator of conscious memories, does not come fully on line for three or four years. Noted before was the gradual development of the self and object repre-sentations. Among other things, this relates to biological development. The earliest memories are unconscious and stored in the amygdala. This is important to know and to work with in those traumatised very early. Research is continuing in this area and is leading to understanding of the connection of chronic stress to damage and disease. This can even happen very early if the infant is overstressed or if the pregnant mother is overstressed and lowered cortisol levels found in her are also found in the developing child.

This kind of information is helpful in the treatment of pre-Oedipal problems involving separation anxieties and the later self-esteem problems, problems causing early lack of safety and security. When memories cannot be recovered as compared to when they can, varied approaches can be used. In all, the lack of safety and security would have evolved due to too much fear of aloneness. Also in all these cases, the object will be used as selfobject and technically this is important to understand. Usually memories that became the first understanding of self and ideals developed after the development of self representa-tion and object representation in the mind of the child. Perhaps some of what was transferred into the self was through the process of transmut-ing internalisation (St Clair, 1996). Some memories of past trauma can be passed on by a parent this way, as in the case to be presented. In gen-eral, the memories constructed after development of self and object in the mind may remain unconscious but often can be recovered through an analytic approach. In cases of self-esteem problems, these results of psychoanalysis or dynamic therapy have allowed for changes or matu-ration in the sense of self and early ideals.

By the 1980s Emde, and McDevitt, worked at helping develop com-munication between attachment theory and psychoanalysis. Fonagy (2001; Fonagy, Gergely, Jursit, & Target, 2002) noted that attachment theory and psychoanalysis hold that personality development is best studied in relation to the child's social environment. Attachment theory takes the cognitive underpinnings of emotional development more into account, and psychoanalysts are definitely beginning to pay more attention to this part of development. Both theoretical models now emphasise and accept the crucial significance of the need for safety and security in childhood.

Kohut developed self psychology, which focused on personality development and functioning (1971, 1977). He developed the concept of narcissistic investment in objects as compared to libidinal invest-ment. Although Modell (1963) coined the term selfobject, Kohut used it to refer to any object that is (i) not felt as having intentionality and agency separate from oneself, and (ii) primarily useful in supporting the cohesion and vitality of the self (Akhtar, 2009b). Understanding the concept of the self using the object as a selfobject is crucial when working with those who have remaining trauma from lack of safety and security due to fear of aloneness from the pre-Oedipal early help-less origins. This will definitely come into the transference, which will be different than that when analysing Oedipal difficulties. Wolf (1994) categorised selfobjects into mirroring, idealisable, alter-ego and adver-sarial types. All of them help to sustain the vitality of the self through the differing means of affirmation, offering glory to bask in, offering twinship, and invigorating opposition. Whereas we see the use of the object as a selfobject as normal in childhood and not even called that, the continuing of the object as selfobject in adulthood represents dif-ficulties from early development. This would be true with our adult patients with separation anxiety and panic attacks as well as those with self-esteem instability.

Understanding of narcissistic disorders was advanced by the object relations theorists and provided a great deal of groundwork for those who have suffered fear of aloneness and lack of safety and security in the early part of life. But the kinds of problems which arise after the early separation anxiety issues and after the development of self rep-resentation and object representation in the self-esteem problems allow for the observation of the development of another strong contribution to fear of aloneness and thus lack of safety and security in the early years. This is the development of self-esteem problems. The definitions and understandings parents pass on verbally and non-verbally will become part of the sense of self. The ideals will be passed on the same way. Often it is done without the parents even realising what they are passing on, as in chauvinism. Various excellent analysts have written on self-esteem, but somehow it did not become an everyday part of psychoanalytic understandings. It was included under narcissism, but not elaborated upon. There were many differences over the terms such as self *vs.* ego, and over theoretical and technical approaches involving the elements of self. Ego ideals and definitions of the self are built into our first dictionary of life defined by parents in words and actions. The internalised automatic comparison of ego ideals to the self leads to one's self-esteem. Shame is the affect felt when self-esteem is unstable or lowered.

The American Psychoanalytic Association finally began a study group with Wurmser (1981), Morrison (1989), and Kilbourne (2002). All had contributed significantly to the studies of shame in the US. Because I had worked with patients with body image difficulties and limiting gender messages, I too became very interested in self-esteem difficulties. A large number of my patients were immigrants and many had had to leave their countries due to revolution or other threats of violence. All this had a strong effect on them and created fears of aloneness connected to the changes. The need for safety and security was increased a great deal in many.

In spite of the frequency of self-esteem disorders, these types of problems did not seem to have a consistent place in theory and did not seem to come into conferences perhaps as much as needed. Drs Morrison and Lansky and I were able to advance the first panel on shame, accepted and then presented at a national meeting of the American Psychoanalytic Association. This was in 2003 and it was titled "Shame and Intrapsychic Conflict". Papers presented were by Morrison, Hutson, Lansky, and Kilbourne, with Pulver being the moderator. Very briefly, we can see that self-esteem disorders are narcissistic disorders first developed during the early dyadic relationship with a parent after development of the self representation and object representation in the mind of the child. Self-esteem problems involved the internalied sense of self and ego ideals being automatically compared. If the labelling of the self is too demeaning, as in "You are stupid" or "Your skin is too black [or white]", the inference is the ideal is something else. If the ideals are specific ... such as, "Only As are acceptable grades for academic work", any grade less would create shame in the owner of the ideal for all As. When self and ideal do not match, the individual senses shame. Adults hide things they are ashamed of. But since shame is so painful, it triggers unconscious defence activity and responses or compromise formations. A number of responses can be seen. These include denigration of the other to feel good about the self, being driven to success (but no success is enough), the development of coveting, which in combination with the shame equals envy. There are many other compromise formations. As one can see, the understanding of defence activity and conflict is necessary when working with those with self-esteem disorders. The wish is not for drive discharge, but it is the same as with the separation fears. The wish is for safety and security stimulated by fear of aloneness.

Due to the very frequent findings of separation anxieties, often accompanied by fear of aggression and self-esteem problems in the individual with fears of aloneness in adulthood, these two areas will be further elaborated.

Early fear of aloneness in the child and fear of aggression

During early development when the young child is essentially helpless, fear of aloneness is a very frequent and intense feeling experienced in the infant's intermittent short separations from the carer. These are situations of total helplessness. Alarm follows the sense of separation in the helpless infant due to a built-in alarm system there from the beginning. At first, the infant cannot conceive of being separate from the caregiver (symbiotic state). But physical separations must occur intermittently and the infant does become aware of this foreign sensory state and of the wish or need for the safe soothing state. Mature "mothering" is crucial for healthy development. If the infant's show of distress not only brings the caregiver physically close to the child, but also creates comparable empathic distress in the caregiver, then the ideal situation is created for the infant to experience containment. The individuation can progress safely in this case. The early memory of the comfort and safety of not being alone is then in place in the child's memory bank.

With continued development of the young child, early stages of separation-individuation begin. The toddler gradually becomes able to be assertive and separate, by running into another room, for example. But the toddler also gradually becomes increasingly aware of his or her own helplessness when alone … and runs back to the mother. A mature accepting reaction by mother is crucial. The example of the lost toddler cited above depicts the child's helplessness to survive. Thus fear of aloneness and the need for safety and security is solved by being with the object, the carer.

In writing of the road from interaction to internalisation, Akhtar (2009b) clearly outlined and referenced the steps for this. Noted was that as the child makes rudimentary steps towards separation (assertiveness or aggressiveness), the other's availability (the mother who is still able to love and be relied upon) is a paradoxical requirement for the development of autonomy. This is crucial for the child's early understanding that aggressive or independent pushes for autonomy are not equal to abandonment by the object. However, when the carer's reaction is not accepting of the child's rudimentary steps for separation, then separation remains a most feared state. Usually these early understandings created by the parents' reactions remain unconscious and unchanged. When the parents or basic carers are intolerant of such independent pushes for autonomy, the memory bank of the child will hold the understanding that aggression or the independent push leads to abandonment. Often in the adult, these early memories remain unconscious and unchanged in the first "dictionary of life" for the child. This is frequently found in cases and referred to as inhibition of aggression. Here, fear of aloneness with its sense of lack of safety and security would require there to be no differing from or aggression against the important other.

When the early fear of aggression is unconscious, it remains with the same threat as in the earlier days. Thus, the individual cannot differ with an important other for fear of abandonment and lack of safety and security. This is true for aggression from without and from within. Each must be asked about separately. This is what I often find in adult cases with inhibition of aggression. Some have panic attacks of unknown origin while others have inhibition of aggression and present with results of defence activity. Examples will be depicted in the full case in this chapter, of Mrs Z.

Another patient with long-term panic attacks reported living with parents where the father was regularly violent with the mother, and at one point he killed a man in front of the children. The violence went on all through childhood. In adulthood, the woman could never differ with another. She could describe the good in some friends but not be aware of any bad, for aggression was inhibited in her. Aggression meant aloneness and lack of safety and security in her first dictionary of life.

She held a responsible job, but when it came to evaluating which people to allow as close friends, she could not see the immaturities. Even after marriage, she was unable to keep in mind the many negative concerns about the husband and thus experienced verbal abuse for years. Her freedom for critical thinking was inhibited and she became a victim. Her early trauma kept her in chronic stress and she was often physically ill when seen. She had panic attacks when her husband would be angry or when suffering any loss. So, here was trauma from the beginning of life with severe panic attacks. She could not defend herself and her immune system was impaired from the changes resulting from long-time stress. Medication was crucial as well as use of a combination of therapies, one being a psychodynamic approach.

Early fear of aloneness accompanied by self-esteem instability

Some may wonder why to include self-esteem problems as having anything to do with fear of aloneness. However, when a child has low self-esteem, the labels of self and ideals have come from the carers. If they are negative enough, the little ones feel diminished andunwanted. These feelings and definitions will become integrated into the self and also ideals. In the grown-up position, the adult may now think or say, "Who would want to be with me?" This is true in the case of Mrs Z, written below.

The carer who passes such negative definitions on to a little one is unable to do "good enough mothering", and fear of aloneness accompanies separation for the child. Safety and security are lacking. In addition to the labels given to the child, gender messages of value and characteristics are passed on verbally and non-verbally to boys and girls. One example of a gender message is that "the ideal gender is male". The self usually "knows" what gender it is. If the gender ideal passed on is to be male, and the girl knows the self is a girl, she will feel inferior and ashamed as a girl. This is usually well-defended and this is where analysis of defence in some way is helpful and gentle. This is often found in anorexic women. One gender characteristic passed on to the male may be that "boys don't cry". Thus, if he cries, even in war, he will experience shame.

Different cultures and countries may very well have different gender messages also. When shame develops, self-esteem vulnerability is present. Shame is such a painful affect, it is rapidly hidden through defence activity prompted by signal shame. This has often been called a shame conflict. In all people, the self is automatically compared to the ego ideal. Too large a difference leads to feeling unacceptable and experiencing shame. The unconscious defence activity may be to put others down, to act superior or conceited, to be driven to success, and other compromise formations. Another one of the results of defence activity may be coveting. Coveting does not occur without one feeling less about something to some degree. A drop in self-esteem results in shame, which is defended; coveting is one of the results of defence activity. The driving force for coveting is aggression and when this is conflictual, there will be new defence activity and a new result from this. Due to the presence of these two together, I have often referred to envy as the envy complex. One would expect to find both self-esteem problems and inhibitions of aggression in many of those with the early fears of aloneness. This patient presented here had both complexes. The concepts are summarised in *The Envy Complex*, (Hutson, 1996).

Conflicts involving shame are ubiquitous and have often been missed by the individual having the conflict and by those around. As mentioned earlier, in the child, one can recognise this by a child covering his or her face or running out of the room. In the adult, it is hidden rapidly through the results of defence activity. That is why it is often called "hidden shame". Shame is well described along with numerous results of defence activity in Dr Morrison's (1989) book, *Shame, the Underside of Narcissism*. Another reference to shame and defence is found in the book by Lansky and Morrison (1997). References to the wide number of defences are also found in Blackman (2003).

Some of the most driven people and some of the very successful people have self-esteem vulnerability and have unconsciously had their vulnerability covered with the success "bandages". Sometimes when someone loses a high position or other success, or the fortune which was a "bandage", fear of aloneness and severe depression quickly appears ... and sometimes suicide. Not only are successes being used to hold up the self-esteem, but the use of the object as a selfobject is for the same purpose.

The case being presented had very poor self-esteem. It is difficult for someone so shamed to be comfortable openly communicating about this. As for technique, I try to increase intrapsychic viewing first so it is like two adults (the more grown-up and observing part of the patient and the analyst) looking at the younger part of the patient (intrapsychic viewing). This facilitates analysis of defence which is so helpful in these cases. And as in all types of psychoanalysis, close process monitoring helps with this analysis of defence. Examples of this are included in the case material.

The case of Mrs Z

Mrs Z, a thirty-eight-year-old married mid-European born Jewish mother of four, was referred by her daughter's psychiatrist and a psychologist. A year before, she developed frequent disabling panic attacks following a small road accident she caused after leaving her children at school. She had been referred to a male psychologist who saw her for therapy and had a psychiatrist medicate her. While in therapy, she would bring gifts of information to him and he would be grateful and admire her. At that time, she and her husband decided to have another child. She felt the therapist was angry about this and she knew something was wrong. She sought a consultation, and this referral was made.

Mrs Z was a soft-spoken woman who was still upset by the therapist's anger. She was very active in raising her children and running the home. She was supportive of her husband who had a very solid business. Volunteer activities were within the Jewish community and the family was active in the synagogue. She had no idea why she had the panic attacks, but had had two previous episodes. One was at sixteen, when she went to Israel, and one at eighteen, when her boyfriend left her for college.

Her mother was a Holocaust survivor. Father was also from Europe. They met after the war and married. After living in Paris for two years, Mrs Z was born. Mother took in sewing to make a living but never took much credit for what she had done. When Mrs Z was two, the parents immigrated to the US. At three, her brother was born. She always felt he was the "cute one" and she the "ugly one". Although mother and father both worked, she felt mother doubted her worth. Father was the head of the family. Mother, a fearful woman who had been in concentration camps, always worried about what might go wrong. If a child cried, mother cried. Mrs Z said mother never talked about what had happened.

Father was often her main carer. When he finally got a job outside the house, she would smell his clothes for comfort when he was gone. She was frightened when he force-fed her in the basement when she was very small. (A few years later, I learned she had been told he had to do that for she was losing so much weight.) After WWII, cases of infants dying by not eating—after the mothers had died in the war—were reported in England. Some of the infants just stopped eating. In this case, mother was probably very depressed and disconnected from the child; father probably saved her life by force-feeding. Mrs Z recalls he would have frequent arguments with mother, and during adolescence, intermittently, he would sleep in her bed. She did not wonder about this or report anything different or strange in this. Mother would encourage her to accompany father to the synagogue for dinners, but later be jealous. Currently, Mrs Z is uncomfortable around father when in her exercise clothes, but she does not know why. She and her brother were not ever close, and to this day he is the one looked up to in the family.

Although she was an excellent student and wanted to go to Harvard, the family moved to Miami when she was in high school. Then her grades dropped. She did well in college and graduate school but could not sustain good feelings about herself. This was also true about her very helpful community activities. She was never close to girls, even to this day. All the events of puberty were "accurately anticipated" and she began to date. The parents would not answer any of her questions regarding sexual development. But mother would ask her about her sexual activity upon dating. This seemed normal. When she became sexually active, mother advised her to stop for she knew about it now.

She married a Jewish professional when they were in graduate school. She then worked as he finished up. She said she had no sexual problems, but in married life she never initiated sexual activity. He was in charge of that and she enjoyed it this way. It was the way she could respond.

In relationships with adults, she was uncomfortable with anger from within and without. A critical comment would erode her confidence and cause anxiety as it had with her first therapist. Good enough feelings about herself at the age of thirty-eight were still dependent on external events and comments. It had pleased her so much to have her gifts to the previous therapist appreciated and for him to think well of her. (As an adult, she still needed to use him as a selfobject.) Although she had many positive accomplishments, they did not "stay" with her in terms of stabilised self-esteem. During pregnancy, she would feel happy. As a mother, she left no stone unturned in this job, a job she did exceedingly well. But she would then turn to focus on what was not done yet. With her children she was very empathic, but this was not so with adults. In fact, she often thought they did not want to work with her on projects. Mrs Z loved her husband and believed he should make all the decisions. He, like father, was often enraged and she felt in a panic. She felt sure he would leave her. Yet the husband was very responsible to the family. The older daughters were self-conscious and in psychotherapy. On the other hand, the son seemed sure of himself and was doing well. She had a very young child when she started psychoanalysis.

Course of treatment

The panic attacks were severe and controlled with medication. Even though she left the last therapist due to his being angry, she needed to drive by or call his office to hear his voice. She hesitantly told me, saying that I would be angry about this. I asked her if she understood how it helped her. She described the calming effect it had on her. I then said that I certainly understood the value to her.

A few sessions later, she needed to feel I was responsible for her leaving the previous therapist. The intraspsychic viewing had to be developed before I would be able to deal with this. And so I began to use analysis of defence which uses the principle of psychic determinism. In my experience, this usually facilitates intrapsychic viewing. Thus we had a team, the more grown-up part of her mind looking at her associations and me with my training looking at the sequence of her spontaneous associations and those following my interventions. In addition, I carefully followed my own thoughts and feelings. Shame is probably the most painful affect and I had learned that this method was extremely helpful with those with self-esteem disorders. It was also helpful with separation anxiety.

An example will be cited—for it was the repetition of this which allowed her to gradually become free to be comfortable with her critical thinking.

PATIENT: I am so irritated with you. You think it doesn't have to do
            with you ... but it does ... Cocowalk [a shopping place down
            the street from my office] is pink ... it's silly to be irritated
            with you.

ANALYST: Did you notice in your thinking that you were free for a
            moment to be angry with me, but quickly your thoughts

were deflected elsewhere. Cocowalk … and then your mind reversed and belittled yourself for the anger … as if having an angry thought directed outward was worrisome somehow.

PATIENT: This morning I woke up scared … I was thinking about Dr X not being there for me.

ANALYST: By going to the memory of this disconnection from Dr X, perhaps you spell out the reason for the worry if you are angry with another … thinking that person would not be there anymore.

PATIENT: I think I was scared of loss all the time as a kid.

ANALYST: So that would all be recorded in your first dictionary of life … In your memory, even when not recalled consciously.

Turning critical thinking against herself or other defensive movements concerning anger was recurrent and analysed regularly. Eventually further understanding by her evolved about where that danger might have been true. She could not differ with the parents, especially the father, who would rage. Her anxiety seemed to be related to the disconnections in these early days, disconnections which meant abandonment and loss of safety and security.

Gradually she could differ in her conscious mind about her friends, husband, parents, and finally me. She could pause and decide what to do with the thoughts. One can check the dreams to see how much if any defence remains. She made a conscious decision not to express her different opinions with the husband, but she could think about these. He did not want any therapy to help with this. Later, when gender messages came into the analysis, this was understandable. "Men are the leaders and make the decisions." Both had similar gender messages when they married. The panic attacks were rare at this time.

Self-esteem problems related to gender messages

The second area of difficulty to come into the analysis had to do with gender messages of value and characteristics passed on by parents. The following is an example of how this came up and was analysed.

Mrs Z began to bring gifts of information to me like she did for Dr X: articles about politics, medicine, etc. Gradually, I was able to help her become curious about the bringing of these gifts. She said it was very helpful to her if she felt I would attend to and appreciate her due to the gift-bringing. I noted to her that her mind could have had other expectations more than my not attending to her. But she had automatically believed I would not attend without something special added, the "gifts" of information.

MRS Z: Who would want to talk to me?
            Analysis of the gift-bringing helped to further the uncovering of a view of herself of not being worthy of being listened to unless something special was added, the gifts of information in this case. Sometimes she concretised her not being "good enough" in a fantasy that her face was abnormal, as often expressed by anorexics. One day, when she had passed a man leaving, she indicated she knew I preferred to work with men. This was a projection of the template self and the early object and the person who felt that way: the mother.
ANALYST: You didn't interview me but perhaps that belief is from somewhere.
            Again my intervention prompted her curiosity about her choice of expectation in the other. She went on to say that men come to make their lives better and women come to be fixed. She added, "Girls are disgusting." So she walked in shame. She then recalled that before the panic attacks, she would be introverted around others and worried that she would not say the right thing and that people would not like her. She couldn't make friends. The question was always in her mind whether she was good enough. She identified with people with body defects and had worked with people with body defects. Self-worth fluctuated with what others thought of her and if she did something well. No success lasted though.

This is self-esteem vulnerability: for example, "Ideal gender is male … self is female." She walks in shame. Her defence is to be driven to be better in more and more studies, in more kindness to others, etc. Nothing sinks in due to the definitions from that first dictionary of life. As she continued, she began to verbalise her constant comparisons which led eventually to the covetous fantasies that are the second part of envy. An example of how it came into our sessions was as follows:

MRS Z: You are more organised than I am. So many things are wrong with me. This makes me feel awful. I had a dream of sewing a sleeve on a coat. Then I was finished. I guess that is what I want for me—to be finished.

ANALYST: The fantasy and then the shame of not being right is escaped by your completing something. But only by switching to two inanimate things could you spell out the idea of repair. Completing the coat by adding a sleeve. As if something about the repair fantasy after the comparison to me is too worrisome.

It is important to note that envy is made of two conflicts: (i) the shame conflict and (ii) the aggressive repair fantasy. There had been something remaining about aggression which was conflictual and needed further analysis. The rest of the analysis of this particular conflict was analysed through associations about her daughter. The displacement was necessary due to the fears attached to aggression. It was interesting that this helped her to be happy with her more accurate appreciation of herself. She began to be able to belong to groups. Later, we were to discover what further fear made her worry about abandonment or separation.

In the displaced form, she talked about an aggressive fix-it fantasy. One day after speaking about envying everything I have, she associated that Emmie (her two-and-a-half-year-old daughter) had told her that Darby, the dog, would eat her if she crossed the street (an oral incorporative fantasy). She next remembered Emmie had asked her that if she ate a pretzel, would she become one. I pointed about how, in a displaced way, this was about how to change a body. She then recalled when she borrowed the last therapist's umbrella, she felt better about herself as she carried it. As she gradually recovered these ideas of defect passed on to her, she began to use her adult thinking. She began to feel better about herself. This was maintained as we continued to work on it. When on the couch she finally spoke of good things, I noticed she would immediately raise the right forearm with the thumb between the index and third finger. Using psychic determinism—one of the guides Freud gave us and Paul Gray wrote extensively about, I noted to her the sequence. She laughed and said she hadn't even been aware of doing that with her hand. She did not know what it meant. That evening, she told her mother about it and mother said it is to keep bad things from happening (avoid the evil eye of envy).

She recalled then that right before the accident which precipitated her panic attacks, she had had thoughts about life finally going well. This was a thought she didn't often have. She began to pull out from the school and the "fender-bender" occurred. She then recalled her mother repeatedly warning her that if she were too happy she could lose all she had. In her daily life, this had taken quite a toll for she could only allow herself to buy one day's worth of food at a time. She completed many projects for the school and synagogue, but was not able to take credit for success in them. She recalled that often after making "too many good grades", she would automatically end up with lower ones. A few years later, I learned that mother cried a great deal throughout the patient's early life, and Mrs Z would have to do a lot of mother's duties. Seeing a friend's sad face once automatically made her forget everything else she was scheduled to do while she went to help that person. This occurred even though it was not a good thing for her to do; the person could easily have asked someone else for help. She felt the sad face made all else disappear in her mind. It reminded her of her mother's face.

The hand movement noted above is an example of a transgenerational warning passed on to her very early in life, at the time when children are so helpless. In reality, during World War II, the mother and her family had everything taken away. What Mrs Z came to believe was that "If you are happy, all you are happy about will be taken away." She acted out the solution by not being happy. When finally she became happy about something during the analysis, she automatically used a motion to avoid the envy of others. Therefore, in some way she did unconsciously know about losses and tragedy. This, along with the gender message that she was not the best gender, would contribute to her not ever feeling she is good enough.[1] As all of this was recovered, she became part of a group of women who had breakfast and lunch together fairly regularly. She was also able to enjoy her children's successes as well as enjoying her activities and new co-ed study group.

The last area of lack of maturation had to do with interruption of the line of development for the sexual drive. There were problems both on a dyadic and triadic level. Mrs Z always dressed in very plain dark clothes and without make-up. Her friends dressed up but she could not. She was able to help her children dress well, but not herself. She proudly said she never flirted. This would have left her shamed if she did. Such ideals would have had to come from her parents, for instance, "The ideal woman is not exhibitionistic." This is dyadic.

She did not speak about being overstimulated when dad slept in her bed, but as an adult in exercise clothes, she was uncomfortable around him. She did not know why. Three years or so into the analysis, sexual conflict came into the transference. She began to be able to talk about sexual attractions, but also had an intermittent return of severe anxiety and panic attacks. She worried about her control system and that of others around her. She would worry if I walked past her as she went to the couch. It was then that she was able to tell me she was very careful not to touch any man or woman for fear of being out of control. It would be her fault and that was not acceptable.

One morning she reported a feeling of shaking around her when she had awakened in the middle of the night. Her husband was sleeping so it was not him. Later, she had it elsewhere and then in my waiting room. Intermittent panic attacks continued. They had accompanied fears of abandonment before. She began to be worried about her control system and that of others around her. All sexual assertiveness by her had been inhibited in the marriage. She would just lay still. Only if her husband was the active initiator could she enjoy sex and be orgasmic. It was not her fault this way. She said her husband wanted it like this also: "An acceptable woman did not initiate sex." Otherwise, she would be shamed/abandoned. So here was an ideal that makes her unacceptable if she is active sexually. In the midst of this, she recalled coming into a room when her little boy was touching himself. She yelled at him if he did that again she would break his leg. She was shocked at herself and wondered where those words had come from. If a child shows excitement, these are words of severe rejection and damage to him/her. Therefore, sexuality leads to danger to the self and abandonment. She thought maybe this was her parents' response to her early excitement in life. This would be an early definition and heighten a feeling of lack of safety and security. Thus sexuality leads to abandonment.

She had never developed to the point of knowing that people could feel excited and then decide what—if anything—to do with it. Finally, she recalled playing with father's chest when he lay down with her and went to sleep. Later, she became conscious of having sexual excitement during the shaking spells. Shortly thereafter the shaking stopped, as did the panic attacks. As she continued, she gradually lost the fear that she and everyone could not control their sexual drives. She shared that she had never been comfortable around her girlfriends or any male friends, and certainly did not touch anyone. With further work, she lost her fears as the faulty ideals were analysed and as she realised she could feel excited and decide what if anything to do with those feelings.

She began to talk about Emmie getting into bed with her. She noted Emmie would be "all over her", and she realised it was the adult's responsibility to not overstimulate the child and to define it correctly if overstimulation occurred. Children hadn't developed a control system yet. But she—as the adult—had. She could feel excited now and decide. She felt her father would not have protected her in this way and then probably would have blamed her if she were excited. Somehow excitement would also mean abandonment. She found books for Emmie to help her understand the body and drives at a young level. She also made a point to help Emmie see that boys and girls are both "A-1" people.

When the analysis of the dyadic and triadic sexual conflicts was completed, she was able to be comfortable with herself as a woman, with her sexuality, and with aggression. Self-esteem was stabilised. It is important to note that a parent may label the sexual drive unacceptable in the dyadic relationship. This is just before the Oedipal period. Usually the sexual material is just focused on the Oedipal. So now, one can see how both sexuality and aggression may be defined on that dyadic level as leading to abandonment.

Concluding remarks

Fear of aloneness surfaces intermittently throughout life. In the earliest period of life when a child is essentially helpless, this fear is due to lack of safety and security. Safety and security is one of the first needs/wishes in all people and will remain one of the needs throughout life. The early solution is in the reconnection with the mother. The ways the first fears of aloneness have been dealt with by the type of early mothering will become part of the memory bank, casting their shadows over future times of fear of aloneness throughout life. Each individual who has experienced "good enough mothering" will, as an adult, be able to be alone, but also be able to couple and have good friends. They have usually developed other good anchorages which are helpful in weathering the various returns of fear of aloneness and lack of safety and security. Due to the "good enough" parenting, he or she will have freedom to differ (aggression) and therefore add clear critical thinking and mature use of it throughout life. Also, the parenting will have defined the self and ideals of the child accurately enough to enable the development of stable self-esteem and the freedoms this provides in facing life.

When the early mothering is not "good enough", many difficulties may remain due to the understandings in the memory bank of the child. Two frequent major difficulties which develop and usually walk with that individual throughout life involve (i) fear of aggression which had come to mean abandonment, and (ii) self-esteem instability which leaves the child fearing rejection in various ways. Both are pre-Oedipal in origin and thus based on a dyadic relationship. As the child develops, the need for safety and security will have triggered defence activity to rid the self of fears of aloneness. The individual automatically continues to use the object (and sublimations of such) as a selfobject to feel safe and secure *vs.* fearing being alone. As depicted in the material, these create limitations in life and often contribute to later fears of aloneness in adulthood. Many of the results of defence activity are unknown as such to the owner. Sometimes the early sexual feelings in the dyadic period are labelled as unacceptable by the carer. Early fear of aloneness evolves and the need for safety and security requires defence activity eventually. Later, this may present as an inhibition still required due to the early unconscious understandings.

Case material was presented which depicted panic attacks set off by a small accident. The patient felt she had been functioning fairly well in life before the accident. The analysis revealed excessive unconscious fears of aloneness due to transgenerational transmission of certain understandings about happiness causing loss of all and transmission of limiting gender messages. Also, the mother had been severely traumatised and this robbed her of being able to provide "good enough" parenting. The continuous fears of aloneness accompanied by a sense of lack of safety and security remained in the child's memory and unconsciously required new ways of being (compromise formations) to live with less anxiety about aloneness. The analysis allowed for the gradual unfolding of multiple contributions to these fears of aloneness. Both drives were involved and inhibited without the patient being aware of this. Self-esteem difficulties and fears of rejection and denigration were unconsciously defended. The passing on of gender messages which add to this was unfolded. The later fears of aloneness were added to by all these earlier unresolved fears. Various helpful methods aiding in this analysis were described. Of great importance is prevention! This would evolve through the passing on to the mothers of the future the importance of knowing about the different needs during development and ideas about providing "good enough mothering".

Note

1. As a side note, I have had quite a number of immigrant patients who have come from violent areas in the world, areas of great danger. People of that group have more of the ways of living, sayings, or amulets to avoid the evil eye of envy than those from more peaceful areas of the world.

CHAPTER FOUR

Fear of intimacy

Susan Kavaler-Adler

The fear of intimacy can relate to primal annihilation terrors or to higher level fears of object loss and loss of love. The terror of losing any differentiated subjective self and its autonomy, or any primitive sense of existing at all, or of killing off the part object mother-other with one's basic states of emotional need, are seen in character disorders. Higher level fears of retaliatory aggression, and of one's own aggression killing off the object, as well as fears of grief-laden loss, and fears of overwhelming longings for the love of a loving *other* who can also withhold love and thus create the pain of unrequited love—all can be seen in Oedipal level neurotic conditions (those already living a lot of the time in Melanie Klein's depressive position).

To break down some of the pre-Oedipal terrors (Winnicott's (1965) "unthinkable anxieties") as well as the higher level inhibitions that all together give us a picture of the "fear of intimacy", I will have two sections of this chapter. The first section will outline the concepts of major British and American object relations theorists who speak in their own particular ways of the developmental arrests due to primal trauma, and of the higher level intrapsychic dilemmas and conflicts that forestall intimacy in relationships. The second section will give clinical examples from my own psychoanalytic object relations private practice of almost forty years.

Theories

Harry Guntrip: schizoid phenomena, object relations, and the self

Harry Guntrip's (1969) "in and out program" (p. 36) is based on a primal and regressive splitting related to developmental arrest in character disorders. One is damned if one does and damned if one does not, in terms of basic human needs to be connected to the *other* (Fairbairn, 1952), to avoid abandonment and self-dissolution, and to simultaneously be free of the *other* enough to have one's own autonomy. One's autonomy feels threatened by terrors of entrapment, suffocation, and/or claustrophobia, when there is no psychic space (related to the internalisation of potential and transitional space between self and other) inside the internal world, due to the lack of internalisation of a separate other (e.g., mother of separation) during separation-individuation process. To be "in" is to crave connection, but in the developmentally arrested individual, who had not separated and self-integrated and who has not internalised the whole *other* (one who is, in Melanie Klein's terms, stuck in the paranoid schizoid position), there is no "connection" of a subjective self with another subjective self, that is, no interpersonal relationship. There is only concrete merger. Such concrete merger lacks the relief of relating to the *other* psychologically as someone represented by words, images, and symbolic meanings. Also, in concrete merger, one cannot differentiate if he/she is having thoughts and feelings about oneself or about the *other*; as well, there is no awareness about the subject of one's interpretations (see Ogden, 1986 on the "interpreting subject"). There is no dialogue, only a monologue in the mind related to reactive victimisation, when the "harmonious" fictive merger breaks down. Then, the *other* is always perceived as enacting hostile impingements, intrusions, and active attacks.

So there is no sustaining of contact within a connection through love and surviving through anger and hate. There is either merger that temporarily answers the primal human need for connection, which is the "in" part of the "in and out" solution, or there is the escape from the merger, through cutting off contact (abruptly if one is splitting and in the paranoid schizoid position), which is the "out" part of the "in and out program" (Guntrip, 1969, p. 36). The object and the dissociated self-parts that are attached to the "bad" and to the idealised part objects are split due to the lack of integration of love and hate. One loves the symbiotic object that one has inside the internal world; the object from prior to the early pre-Oedipal trauma resulted from the failings of mothering attunement during separation and autonomy. One hates the separate other who evokes the traumatising object of separation. The other is never an ambivalently loved and hated whole-object-other; and one cannot have anger within a sustained relationship with another, where the other can remain good enough to survive anger in one's mind, so that love could be renewed. As soon as anger is felt, it becomes hate, combined with a sense of betrayal and an accusation of abuse and victimisation. The other is no longer a "good enough" object to be accused and then loved again. The idealised object immediately becomes the hated "bad" object who must be totally spoiled, devalued, demonised, disowned, and left as soon as anger at the level of pre-Oedipal rage and hate takes over. In other words, pre-Oedipal separation-individuation stage trauma is relived and is experienced again. One feels disappointed, outraged, and betrayed! Later, the same cycle of traumatic disappointment occurs after one attempts to merge with one's symbolic pre-trauma mother, who is hoped to be the mother one never had. Now again, the new idealised object is devalued and becomes bad and demonised; and one relives being at the mercy of this "bad object" which failed to negotiate attunement during separation.

Guntrip's schizoid compromise is when intimacy must be avoided in a relationship because of polarised fears of either entrapment or abandonment—in relation to a split internal object, which becomes either idealised symbiotic mother or demonissed bad object mother of separation. Consequently one never offers one's full self to the other. One is never present in full intimacy, because parts of oneself must be dissociated and put out to others outside the relationship or displaced onto others, to avoid a full engagement, which feels like "putting all one's eggs in one basket". So one keeps contact to a minimum (e.g., therapy only once a week) or avoids marriage in life, as well as in psychoanalysis. The compromise is to have some connection, because of a profound human need to have some contact and connection, while also avoiding a need for the other or responsibility for the needs of the other. In this way, one attempts to avoid feeling trapped and engulfed in the other's needs, and avoids being abandoned by the lack of adequate availability of the other for one's own needs.

Ronald Fairbairn: psychoanalytic studies of the personality

Harry Guntrip derived his theories about the schizoid "in and out" solution and the "schizoid compromise" from Ronald Fairbairn's theories about the split self and object relationships that are incorporated within the psyche of anyone, but particularly of those who have primal failures in mothering in the first three years of life, when the self is forming. Fairbairn (1952) speaks of how the infant and child, who yearns for and desperately needs an attachment to another human being, attaches to the "bad" object, which is traumatically frustrating in terms of the human need for contact with the primal mother, because one must have a connection in order to psychologically survive as a human being. The "bad object" can derive from an abusive and/or abandoning mother (borderline), or a detached mother (schizoid), or from a false narcissistic mother, who demands that the child mould himself into the mother's narcissistic image and agenda for him/her. In all these cases, the child is deprived of the essential "good mother" contact and connection that could allow the child to move on and to relate to the father and to others in the world. Without an adequate "good mother" relationship in infancy and throughout the transitional stage (in Winnicott's language, later called separation-individuation by Mahler (1965)), the child gets helplessly attached to the actual external primal mother, who fails to provide the contact and connection needed, and thus fails to help the child's growth. Then, the child (as well as the adult with the child still undeveloped within) becomes addicted to the "bad" mother. This addiction results in aggressive fights with the mother who was overly aggressive and abusive. One can also become addicted to a mother who is overly detached and withdrawn. This results in the internal world's early sadomasochistic dramas with the detached (schizoid) mother, who also enslaves the child as an extension of herself. Also, this early primal object can be the mother's false grandiose self-reflection of the child, or an attachment to the mother's image of herself, in order to avoid the conscious experiencing of the internal mother's deprivation. Fairbairn writes of the child who is forced to relate through identifications rather than through the separate self-relatedness of emotional connection. This term of "relating through identifications" was picked up by Winnicott in his paper on "The use of an object and relating through identifications" (1969). The child who is unable to develop his or her own personality due to the lack of relatedness with a mother capable of being aware of the emotional needs and personality of the child, and who is then met with the failings of the father and others to relate, will be stuck in the position of relating only through being identified with the mother or with the image of the child created by her. Inside the internal world of the child, there will be an undeveloped primal self-craving to have contact and connection with the unavailable mother (see Fairbairn's concept of the "libidinal ego" attached internally to the tantalising and seductive, but unavailable mother object), and split-off and dissociated from that will be the part of the self ("the antilibidinal ego") that is attached to the rejecting part of the mother ("the rejecting object"). Both the libidinal ego and antilibidinal ego will be split-off in the internal world from any part of the primal innate self, called by Fairbairn the "central ego". This "central ego" will still be in touch with others in the external world through the intellect, as in the schizoid personality, but not through relatedness and emotional connection, as these have traumatically failed during infancy and toddlerhood (the transitional stage or separation-individuation). Then, the whole emotional life will be stuck in regressed attachments to the "bad objects" of the seductive and tantalising types, and the "bad objects" of the "rejecting objects". This will be a static drama in both the internal and the external world of the borderline character, as opposed to the totally sealed-off schizoids. This will be enacted in the external world as if every other person in the external world is the "tantalising" object (the mother one never had), but then, inevitable disappointments take place, and the "tantalising" object becomes the "rejecting object". Therefore the cycle of wishing for the object and being "in" is always inevitably followed by wanting to be "out". The internal world repetition is continually replayed outside through projections onto external objects (as in borderline personalities) or is enacted in a sealed-off and dissociated schizoid internal world. Each reliving of the traumatic primal disappointment initiates a new cycle of craving for an "exciting object", which then switches into the "rejecting object's" abandonment and/or attacking abuse, which is another form of emotional abandonment.

Donald Winnicott's concepts related to fear of intimacy

D. W. Winnicott's contributions to understanding the fear of intimacy are multiple. I will mention a few concepts of Winnicott that are important to an understanding of the fear of intimacy and the developmental theory that can be applied to clinical work. First of all, Winnicott (1960) spoke of the too "omnipotent mother" who impinges by substituting her gesture for the child's "spontaneous gesture" (Winnicott, 1963). This can be the mother who presumes to have knowledge of the child that interferes with the child discovering itself, or the too omnipotent psychoanalyst who interferes with the analysand (patient) discovering his own inner experiences as his/her own feelings and thoughts by showing too much "knowledge" of the patient with theoretical presumptions. This can be the mother who has her own narcissistic images of what she wants the child to be, and her own narcissistic agenda for the child's development along with this. Thus, the child becomes co-opted into acting as if he or she is the image of the parent; and any true impulses, feelings, and thoughts from the child's own individual being must be split-off, dissociated, and hidden or (in the higher level neurotic or Oedipal level individuals) it must be repressed. This narcissistic mother creates a false self in the child, which meets the mother's (and then usually the father's and siblings') images and agendas. There is also the schizoid mother who moulds the child into the caring false self that Winnicott explicitly speaks of, while the true spontaneous impulses, feelings, and thoughts of the child and the later adult are dissociated and stifled before they can be expressed. Also, there is the too "omnipotent" aggressive borderline mother who opposes the spontaneous gesture of the child with her own attacking gesture. This results in the child submitting and later identifying with an overly aggressive dominance, or an overly passive submissiveness, both of which obviate contact and connection with another that could grow into intimacy.

Intimacy requires that one person gets to know the authentic self of the other and vice versa, in a mutual progression of getting to know who the other is, and a mutual willingness to reveal to the other who one is. This cannot happen without true self development in childhood, because authentic relatedness is obviated by the "false self" (Winnicott, 1960) enacting its coercive narcissistic performance, its borderline fight-and-flight, or its schizoid coercive caring. Also, the contact and connection with one's true self has been so arrested by a sealing-off and splitting-off (or at a higher level—by a repression of authentic feelings and impulses), that one never reveals the self to the other. The other then never gets to know who one is, which is the essence of intimacy and interpersonal expression and responsiveness of back-and-forth intimate relations.

Other concepts of Winnicott (1965a, 1971) that are so pertinent to understanding the fear or failure of intimacy are the following: the "capacity to be alone", "capacity for concern", "object survival" (of the mother and of the object relations psychotherapist, in the face of the true self's most aggressive aspects), and the capacity for "play". Also, there is the theory of potential or transitional space, a third area for intimate relatedness to take place—between the self and other that provides "potential space" (originally transitional space during a transitional stage that is developmentally related to Margaret Mahler's (1965) separation-individuation stage). In addition, there is the contrast for the mother as the mirror of the child's true self *vs.* the mother as the narcissistic mirror. The narcissistic mirroring mother reflects back to the infant or child her own self, so the child cannot feel seen or known, which obviously obviates any hope that intimacy can take place with another.

Winnicott's (1958) "capacity to be alone" is a developmental understanding that one must be able to internalise a good enough maternal holding environment before one can be alone with oneself. This means that one must have a mother who can just be with oneself, as opposed to intruding her needs or demands on the child. If one does not have the internalised maternal environment to develop the capacity to be alone, one cannot have intimacy. This is true since one must be able to be a separate other who can be alone with oneself in order to connect with an "other" as *other*, and not as a projection of a part of one's own psyche. In fact, the greater one's capacity to be alone, the greater is one's capacity to be with another, because one does not cling, intrude, or attempt to merge with the other. One can tolerate the other only if he/she has a psychic space to be himself or herself. If one does not have the capacity to be alone, one will fear the needs of the other to be intimate, because this will feel like an intrusion on one's wish to merge or cling to the other for one's very survival (called the "co-dependent" in colloquial terms). The "capacity for concern" (Winnicott, 1963) develops as the mother (or therapist) allows the child (or patient) to experience tolerable guilt for his aggression along with an adequate dose of recognition for his "good" or loving aspects. This allows for guilt to turn into concern. Guilt can then be tolerated and not permitted to turn into hostile and retaliatory aggression or into the disowning of responsibility in life (because of intolerable aggression). Only through true concern for another can one be intimate. To not feel concern for who the other is, with all his/her individual desires and needs, results in using the other for one's own needs. This leads to exploitation of the other rather than in knowing the other and growing to know the other more, which is the essence of intimacy. When the mother has not offered the child the concern and empathy that results in developing concern and empathy in the child, the child will fear any prospect of intimacy (which would create vulnerability), since the other is feared as having a lack of concern. Then one will exploit in order to use the other for survival needs, and through projections, will fear exploitation when the other might be looking for intimacy.

Winnicott's (1971) understanding of "play" is the capacity to imagine the other as a subjective other, rather than only seeing the other as a concrete object that one might try to manipulate. Imagination of the other is necessary for intimacy to take place, and intimacy will be feared if one cannot enjoy imagining the other. If one can imagine the other, one can play with the other, which will evoke joy in getting to know more about the other in intimacy, and thus will enjoy imagining more and more about the other. If the other just is "it" (not a subjective self, but a concrete thing), there will be no imagination in the mind that creates play and its accompanying spontaneous gesture in relatedness. The mother who mirrors her own image or her own image of the child, will not reflect back to the child a recognition of who that child as a spontaneous being is. This will create a fear in the child of the other moulding him or her into the other's image, as opposed to being perceived and recognised as one attempts to reveal oneself in intimacy.

Margaret Mahler and fear of intimacy

Margaret Mahler's developmental theories from both her 1971 paper entitled "A study of the separation-individuation process—and its possible application to borderline phenomena in the psychoanalytic situation", and her 1975 book on *The Psychological Birth of the Human Infant: Symbiosis and Individuation* (co-authored with Fred Pine and Anni Bergman)—pertain to the fear of intimacy and the defensive dynamics around the prospect or threat of intimacy. Mahler's paradigm of separation-individuation, based on mother–toddler observation, helps us to understand Guntrip's schizoid "in and out" dynamics (which are based on traumatic pre-Oedipal mother–child bond disruption). Mahler's theory also helps us to understand the dynamics of Oedipal level conflicts over connection and separation in intimate relationships, since at this higher level, primal splitting does not predominate, and the conflict over desire for intimacy *vs.* the fear of intimacy within connection can be felt. Mahler offers a perspective for split enactments around self-and-other connection that express the conflict between yearning for closeness and fear of intimacy.

The original mother–infant symbiosis that Mahler describes at the initiation of the infant's life (while she discarded her "autistic stage" that was an adaptation to a Freudian view of "primary narcissism" that does not hold up) is a stage of life that is continually yearned for. In neurotics, who make it through separation-individuation to the Oedipal stage, the yearning may remain an unconscious fantasy with its accompanying wishes, that can be experienced consciously at the time of a normal experience of "falling in love", but the fantasy and wish can be relinquished in these neurotics once a true intimacy develops, in which two separate individuals with distinct identities come to truly know each other. However, for the person who was developmentally arrested during the separation-individuation phases (due to the failure of the mother to maintain sufficient attunement and emotional connection with the toddler of these stages), a perpetual addictive craving for the lost symbiotic mother will persist. The primal symbiotic mother (the Jungian "chthonic mother") will not just be yearned for, but will be continually recreated in fantasy (as in James Masterson's (1981) "reunion fantasy"). This will undermine all attempts to sustain a state of connection with another, since the wish for a symbiotic reunion will constantly be traumatically disappointing, resulting in the other being experienced as the "bad mother" who "failed" during separation-individuation. Such splitting at the point of disappointment will continually disrupt any relationship, as the perception of the other goes from being the idealised symbiotic mother to the "bad mother" of separation. So the relationship is constantly disrupted before any true intimacy can evolve, an intimacy that would require two separate individuals coming to know, accept, and love each other. In fact, not only can someone with a primal traumatic disruption in the separation-individuation stages not sustain connection, but as the other becomes the "bad object (mother)" the split-off self-part related to the bad mother will also be the aggressive hating part of the self. Consequently, one's very identity as someone who is capable of loving is lost.

In her 1971 paper, Mahler refers to the symbiotic era, which is developmentally prior to all the phases of separation-individuation, as the stage of "dual unity". This is a concept used by D. W. Winnicott and by other British object relations theorists, such as Margaret Little. Michael Balint (1968) uses the term "primary love" for this early dual unity stage, in order to distinguish an object relations axiom of the primal need for connection (also Fairbairn's axiom) from the Freudian idea of the "primary narcissism" before longings for relations with the mother and others took place. Balint opposed the idea of primary narcissism, a view that has been backed up by all infant research, including that of Mahler. Mahler relinquished her idea of a hypothetical primary "autistic" stage and revisited her view to make the "symbiotic stage" the most primal stage of human development. Emotional birth happens during the "hatching" of the separate self during separation-individuation, when the mother of separation is internalised, and a differentiated individual identity is formed. Mahler (1971) also speaks of the "coenesthetic" feeling of being one with the other, which is created physically during symbiosis, and which is yearned for to acquire comfort later on. This coenaesthetic feeling is more dramatically craved as a way of coming back to life in the toddler who is psychologically dropped by the unattuned and psychologically abandoning mother of the separation-individuation stages. The toddler who has tolerable levels of disruption of mothering presence and attunement during the separation-individuation stages will be capable of "imaging" the mother when she is temporarily unavailable. This child will be capable of tolerating the "low keyedness" or early child sadness related to feeling the loss of the mother, as long as the loss is temporary enough for the mother's image to be held onto and focused on by the toddler within his/her internal world. Managing this dilemma of temporarily losing the mother is a sign of a successful internalisation of mother's presence during separation-individuation (differentiation, practising, and rapprochement phases). Such a healthy toddler will not have his/her psyche disrupted by overwhelming tantrum rage that cannot be quieted, but will have enough of a solid ego-self to be able to tolerate the affect of sadness, a primal mourning experience that Mahler calls "low keyedness". Such a toddler will yearn for the mother, but will not feel like he or she is falling apart. A toddler with "unintegrated" mother image will instead be caught up in the frantic throws of "desperate crying" or perpetual tantrum rage. When this latter toddler grows up, he/she will try to hook into another to regain the blissful symbiotic phase of "dual unity" with the mother. However, when the symbiotic illusion fails because the other has separate and autonomous needs, there will be no internally sustained image of the other to have a sense of the other as "good". The other will become "bad" because there is no internal image of the mother of separation as a "good enough" mother (Winnicott's term), who is physically (but not psychologically) absent and living a separate existence. So, true intimacy will fail because of the desperate attempt to control the other and to keep the other as a part of the self or extension of one's own self, and it will undermine any relatedness through emotional contact and connecting communication. Instead of communication and interpenetrating mutual knowledge of each other as between two separate individuals who have a "good enough" mother internalised, there will be rage at the other, now seeming to be a "bad" object. The mother-other will then be experienced as having betrayed through not being the symbiotic other-half of one's self. The mother-other will be seen then as abandoning, abusing, or intruding and violating. So, fear of intimacy in Mahler's paradigm is always related to a fear that the other will abandon one (if closeness and dependence is achieved) or will entrap and engulf one because of the needs of the other, who is experienced as foreign, intrusive, controlling, and possessive, when not the symbiotic other half. The mother who tries to possess the child by attempting to keep the child in a state of symbiosis with her, will always create a powerful terror of intimacy. This is true because the adult with such a child inside his/her internal world will be afraid of being taken over by the other, and will talk of wanting to get away all the time in analytic treatment (the patient can come to learn about a continuous obsession about "escape", the escape fantasies). When the mother made a traumatic error on the other side—the side of abandonment—it can create constant fears of being left. The person with these abandonment fears may find a mate who is at first imagined to be the craved symbiotic other half, but who is actually someone with the "escape fantasies" that create an impasse with the "suffocation and entrapment" fantasies of the one who had the overly abandoning mother.

Theories of Melanie Klein and the Kleinians

Overlapping with Margaret Mahler's linear theory of separation and individuation in the developing self is the British theory of Melanie

Klein, which focuses on self-integration as a normal primal splitting is assumed and becomes integrated in the healthy individual; while pathological arrests in splitting result in increasing fragmentation of the personality throughout a lifetime, unless clinical treatment allows for the integration of the split-off self-states and split-off internal objects. Such treatment always involves a mourning process of primal mother object loss (which becomes combined with object loss related to the father and with later losses).

In Klein's theory, there are two basic psychic positions that each have a whole constellation of anxieties, self-states, and defences (see Kavaler-Adler, 1993c), where each has its individual fears of self and other relationship in the world, and thus each psychic position has its own fear of intimacy. These two psychic positions can alternate in one's unconscious and conscious states, so that there is more of a qualitative development from one position to the other without any absolute linear programme as Mahler proposes. Yet movement from the more primitive to the more advanced position does have a linear developmental progression, even though the more primitive state of perception is always returned to in states of anger, rage, trauma, and regression. One never totally leaves the earlier position. Modern Kleinians have more acknowledgement of the role of the actual mother, regardless of the actual position of the psyche achieved. The role of trauma has currently been more acknowledged than it was by Klein herself, and it is seen as the fixation or arrest in the more primitive position.

The more primitive psychic position is called the "paranoid-schizoid" position. In the paranoid-schizoid position state of mind, one is reactive and experiences oneself as an "it" rather than as an "I". One is always a victim, since one is just reacting to others, and not feeling autonomy or self-initiating agency. In this position, one is not a subjective self, and others are just intruding enacting monster others or idealised others, with whom one merges and who do not have their own subjectivities (their own feelings and thoughts and opinions and fantasies). One is either an idealised or devalued self, or a grandiose or bad self. There is no in-between and there is no ambivalence. Thinking is black and white, and one is not aware of making interpretations. The world is a mixture of concrete phenomena. One part-object person enacts the primal sadomasochistic scenarios on another. The other retaliates. All can retaliate back and forth endlessly, mirroring the internal world dramas. One either adores and attempts merger with the other (breast or penis part object figure), or one protects against being killed or destroyed by the malevolent bad object other. The internal world of split idealised and bad objects are projected outside, and are enacted against others to make them feel like the bad object enemies through projective identification, or to make them feel like the idealised perfect omnipotent part object others. The idealised object always turns into the bad persecutory other (persecutory breast from the oral stage or the persecutory anal object from the anal stage) as the inevitable disappointment takes place. One has to leave the idealised object that has turned bad to avoid being persecuted, and so one never loves and hates the same other. There is no such thing as a sustained relationship in this psychic position, because the idealised projection object always turns bad. Consequently, anger and aggression cannot be felt within a context of sustained love. The terrors of this psychic position are of self-annihilation and self-destruction through abandonment and persecution. So a relationship with an idealised other that has a primitive narcissistic state of infatuation—as opposed to an Oedipal level honeymoon—can never lead into true intimacy. To protect the self when the other turns bad, one must leave, escape and attack and kill the other to do so. Otherwise, one fears one's own extinction, and this extinction is annihilation, not just a death that would leave symbolic images and symbolic memories and symbolic effects of one's own existence behind with others in the world. This is a pre-symbolic position, so if one is persecuted and killed, one just disappears without a trace. One does not die and leave symbolic expressions of one's identify behind. To fear intimacy in this position is to fear being annihilated and "disappeared" by an alien other, because nothing lasts. Once one becomes angry at the idealised other with whom one craves merger, all is over. The hate in the anger wipes out the desirable image of the other, and there is no more love. There is no remembered history of the relationship. It becomes a phantom of a relationship that one was sucked into until one discovered the true "betrayal" and malevolence of the other. To leave or break up the merger relationship leaves no trace of a meaningful relationship. Without symbolic experience of one's own subjectivity and of the subjectivity of the other, there is no meaning. The past relationship that aroused a fantasy of love forever and a pseudo intimacy of merger becomes a lousy bum steer. Disillusionment within love cannot be tolerated. It is all over when the other turns bad, until the same other (person) is once more resurrected as the projected idealised other. This vicious cycle of idealisation and devaluation, corresponding also to the "in and out" solution of Guntrip, can only change when the rage and hate that transpires during devaluation can be tolerated by the other, with sustained loving attunement. This can only happen with the psychoanalyst who creates a "holding environment" (Winnicott), and contains affects and hated split-off parts of the patient's self that are projected on to the other (Wilfred Bion). Only in the relationship with the psychoanalyst can the rage and hate related to transference disappointment, with consequent devaluation, be tolerated. When such aggression is tolerated and affectively contained, a more intimate connection with the patient and analyst results that can serve as a transitional relationship (Winnicott) to intimate relationships with outside others in the patient's life. Without this transitional therapeutic relationship, the vicious cycle of splitting the object into idealised and then demonised and devalued bad objects continues. So the pathological "in and out" solution of trying to merge with the object when it is idealised, and trying to escape contact with the object when it is devalued and demonised, perpetually continues.

In the more sophisticated psychological position, the "depressive position", one experiences the subjectivity of the self, as one becomes aware one has thoughts and feelings and needs. One is no longer just reacting to others. Most important, in terms of capacities for true object relationships and thus for intimacy, in the depressive position, one can sustain relationships because one can tolerate ambivalence, that is, loving and hating the same object, and having love survive the hate in anger, because one is also symbolic, and communicate about the meaning of one's anger so that it does not last forever, but can be relinquished while love renews and survives. One can have conflicts over loving and hating an other person as one enters the depressive position. Hate never totally destroys love, because the other is experienced as a subjective person, not as an "it". The other can have a separate point of view and have feelings and thoughts of her/his own. So, intimacy through communication becomes possible. Even in states of anger, the communication of one's reasons for one's anger, or one's reasons for one's hurt feelings, can result in feeling understood and understanding the other, if one can talk with the other/lover about why one is angry. So even at times of anger, relatedness is maintained. Consequently, intimacy can evolve as one gets to know oneself, and the other one is with, as anger is communicated.

The fears in this psychic position are of losing the other for whom one yearns, rather than attempting to possess the other. Yearnings for the other can be tolerated, but one fears losing the other one loves and yearns for and desires, as subjectivity within sexual instincts turns into differentiated desires of the self towards the other. Instead of fearing self-extinction, one fears object loss, or loss of the other whom one loves, and one fears guilt for regretting one has hurt the one that one loves. One also fears loss of love from the other, and fears disappointing the other, as well as fearing the actual literal loss of the other. Separation and break-ups of relationships can be tolerated since the meaning of the relationship and its history is maintained, allowing one to wish to recreate it with another if one loses one love.

Masud Khan's contributions

In his 1972 article on "Dread of surrender to resourceless dependence in the analytic situation", Masud Khan speaks of the terror of intimacy in people who have been overly possessed by mothers during the "dual unity" stage, which he calls the "omnipotent symbiosis", in which one has been so extremely catered to that a regressive symbiosis is maintained far beyond its time, resulting in the failure of a normal expression of childhood aggression that would allow for the autonomous development of a separate self with its own agency. Khan likens the consequent demands to return to such an "omnipotent symbiosis" in the analytic situation to Michael Balint's (1959) discussion of "malignant regression" *vs.* a benign one, while in analytic treatment. The patients of Balint's "malignant regression" demand that the analyst give them the relationship that they had in the regressive symbiosis, and even what they never had, as in the fantasy of a totally omnipotent symbiosis. The demands for the analyst to deliver this defend against feeling the horrors of regressing into dependence on another who is not fully controlled as an extension of the self. In the "benign regression", the patient can feel the loss and grief of the wished for omnipotent other, who would fully cater to the self, and who would not demand any autonomous functioning or self agency. However, in malignant regression, the demands for the analyst to be the omnipotent symbiotic other persist. Masud Khan points out, in relation to D. W. Winnicott's theory of true self development and the analyst's "object survival" of the most primitive rage in the patient, how critical it is for the analyst to allow the patient to risk the terrors of "resourceless dependence" in order to develop true self agency—through aggressive demands and criticisms, and through rage towards the analyst for not providing what they never had. The analyst allows and meets the patient's accusations of the analyst's failure to be the fantasy mother-other, the fantasy mother who would never cease to be omnipotent and perfectly attuned. When the patient is allowed to express all the rage, which naturally and spontaneously emerges from within, true self development can begin again, even after its arrest after the "dual unity" or symbiotic stage. Khan (1972) writes:

> Hence the crucial task of the clinical situation and analytic relationship was for the analyst to present himself in his person vis-à-vis her with that authenticity of mutual rapport where she could register how he failed her and get angry about it, and how she failed him and be reparative in a genuine way. (p. 6)

Fear of intimacy at this level relates to a terror of being trapped in a profound dependency where one's aggression is cut off and/or stifled. It is a fear of being unable to have a voice as one's primal level of rage and aggression (which is at the core of developing an independent voice) and an independent self (with self-initiating agency) is obviated by the opposition to one's aggression. The analytic situation is the only place where the primal aggression can be allowed without hostile retaliation or abandonment (Winnicott's "object survival"). This is the Winnicottian holding environment, which also requires the containing and processing abilities of the analyst. Eventually the patient learns to appreciate, understand, and thus process and contain his own aggression. The analyst's ability to tolerate and understand, at a symbolic level, the primal aggressive affect and complaints of the "malignant regression" allows the patient to develop the capacity to process his aggression, and to thus communicate it symbolically in relationship (from sarcasm to direct expression of anger). This also allows the patient to developmentally proceed to a level of grief, that is, proceed to the mourning of the loss of the primal object as an external mother. Through grief, affects become more subtle and self-parts become integrated. Hate and love become symbolic anger and sustained communication. This radically lessens the fear of intimacy, since intimacy can be tolerated when dependence does not leave one feeling resourceless, but rather allows one to communicate all that is felt. Anger, hate, and aggression do not have to be split-off or run away from by running from the relationship. Meeting the aggression of the patient also means setting limits and making the expression of aggression tolerable—by keeping it within an analytic frame as much as possible. Both Michael Balint and Masud Khan propose limit setting in clinical examples, in order to transform the malignant regression into the benign regression.

Otto Kernberg: love relations

In his book on *Love Relations*, Otto Kernberg (1995) speaks of a gender divide in relation to the nature of conflicts (fears) of intimacy. Kernberg speaks of men having difficulty surrendering to commitment in marriage, while women have difficulty surrendering to sexual intimacy within marriage. He states that

> Men's discontinuity between erotic and tender attitudes toward women is reflected in the "madonna-prostitute" dissociation, their most typical defense against the unconsciously never-abandoned, forbidden, and desired oedipal sexual relationship with mother. But beyond that dissociation, profound preoedipal conflicts with mother tend to reemerge in undiluted ways in men's relationships with women, interfering with their capacity to commit themselves in depth to a woman. For women, having already shifted their commitment from mother to father in early childhood, their problem is not the incapacity to commit themselves to a dependent relationship with a man. It is, rather, their incapacity to tolerate and accept their own sexual freedom in that relationship. In contrast to men's assertion of their phallic genitality from early childhood on in the context of the unconscious erotization of the mother–infant relationship, women have to rediscover their original vaginal sexuality, unconsciously inhibited in the mother-daughter relationship. One might say that men and women have to learn throughout time what the other comes prepared with in establishing a love relationship: for men, to achieve a commitment in depth, and for women, sexual freedom. Obviously, there are significant exceptions to this development, such as narcissistic pathology in women and severe types of castration anxiety of any origin in men. (pp. 84–85)

In the section on clinical cases, the marriage between Judith and Allan illustrates such dynamics. Kernberg (ibid.) also speaks of the fear of receiving love or feeling love, which can be seen in the case of Paula (to follow), where such a fear interacts with a Fairbairnian concept of addiction to a "bad" internal object, and also with a terror of resource-less dependence, as described by Masud Khan.

Salman Akhtar: love and its discontents

In referring to various psychopathological syndromes of love life (e.g., inability to fall in love, inability to remain in love, falling in love with the wrong kinds of people, inability to fall out of unrequited love, and inability to feel loved), Salman Akhtar (1996) describes the varying developmental levels that interact in the inhibited and pathological modes of loving. Akhtar writes:

> ... the fact is that each of them [each syndrome] contains deficits and conflicts from various developmental levels. The inability to fall in love, for instance, might represent the lack of activation of early psychophysical eroticism through a satisfying symbiotic experience, and a defense against unconscious envy of the love object, and, at times, even a pronounced inhibition resulting from intense castration anxiety. Similarly, the inability to remain in love might emanate from a futile search for a transformational object, anxieties regarding fusion with the love object, and/or conflicts related to narcissism, aggression, and the Oedipus complex. (p. 173)

In his critique of Person's (1988) views, Akhtar (1999, p. 78) writes that she emphasised that brevity is an essential feature of passionate love. However, the capacity of the two partners for mature object relations helps them convert the flame of intense emotions into the steady glow of affectionate companionship.

My own viewpoint

Fear of intimacy can be understood from the viewpoint of a failure to mourn the primal parental objects and to internalise them symboli-cally, and to thus psychologically benefit from the resources of related-ness that they provide, while simultaneously separating from them as external objects, so that one can relate to others as true differentiated others in the present. My theory of "developmental mourning" (Kavaler-Adler, 1985, 1988, 1989, 1993a, 1993b, 1996, 2003a, 2003b, 2005a, 2005b, 2006–2007, 2010, 2013a) deals with mourning as a primary developmental process, following the contributions of Melanie Klein (1940) in her article on "Mourning and its relation to manic depressive states" and following Klein's view of guilt and loss being an essential part of self-integration in the "depressive position". Klein was the first to see mourning as a primary and fundamental clinical and developmental process.

My theory of "developmental mourning" follows from Klein, but it also integrates aspects of Margaret Mahler on low keyedness, James Masterson on the abandonment depression, and D. W. Winnicott on "object survival". Developmental mourning can proceed as long as one has attained whole-object relationships both within the external world and within the internal world. When developmental arrest due to failed pre-Oedipal mothering traumatically occurs, mourning of the other as a separate and symbolised whole-object other cannot proceed. Then splitting of the object becomes pathological and perpetual, resulting in the sealing-off of the internal affective self, or in the compulsive externalising projection of the affective internal world, with its part-self and -other constellations. As long as such splitting is perpetuated, no true intimacy can occur, because the other is looked to as an idealised symbiotic other half or is feared as a malevolent, persecutory, intrusive object, or is feared as an inadequate or dead object that would drain one of one's very life.

When developmental mourning of primal objects occurs from the early pre-Oedipal time of separation-individuation and throughout life, aggressive affect states are being contained by a predominantly loving and attached self and other relationship in a symbolised form (see Kavaler-Adler, 1992, 2013b). Then, there is more love than hate in mourning of the losses of both primal figures and others throughout life, with whom one must separate. Anger and aggression yield to the affects and memories of grief. Sadness modifies hate into tolerable experiences of anger within loving relationships, and the pain of grief yields to love within loss and loss within love. Increasingly then, disappointments and disillusionments within relationships can be tolerated, so that relationships can be sustained to the point that true intimacy can take place, where one person gets to know the other and vice versa.

Mutuality occurs as one's own subjective experience can be conveyed to the other. The subjective experience of the other can be perceived, listened to, understood, and internalised. Internalisation of affective relationships at the level of intimacy is part of a "developmental mourning" relationship that takes place throughout life. With benign internalisations, the fear of intimacy lessens, since one does not fear that the other will destroy one's self, and one no longer fears one will damage or harm the other by just being one's full self. One's own unconscious aggression becomes more conscious and understandable, and thus increasingly less frightening. As one's own aggression becomes less frightening so too does the aggression of the other, which is always partially perceived through the projections of one's own aggression, and through the projections of one's internal objects' aggression. One's internal objects' aggression gets modified as love trumps hate with the tolerance of anger and loss within the developmental mourning process.

My delineation of the "demon-lover complex" relates to the perpetuation of primal splitting that cause the idealised god-muse object to continuously turn into a bad object due to the repetition of primal separation-individuation trauma. However, in addition to the instant vicious cycle of the idealised object turning bad, there is the eroticisation of the "bad object", which results in the projected image and internal world experience of a "demon-lover". Also, the Jungian concept of a "demon-lover" archetype can interact with the bad maternal-paternal object in early pre-Oedipal childhood. This is related to a complex that results from failed mothering before the whole and subjective self is formed through whole object internalisations. When the psyche is split and eroticised in this way, intimacy is terrifying because it threatens to be an experience of another destroying one, or co-opting one's self and identity, or of seducing and abandoning on the level of oral and anal sadism that has terrifying and nightmarish internal world images related to it. One loses one's validity, self agency, and self-identity in merging with the idealised god-muse figure, which is sought for a merger. This merger with the muse is experienced as transforming the muse into the diabolical demon-lover; it brings possession rather than transcendence. The longed-for muse, from whom one seeks inspiration and transcendence, turns into the dominating demon-lover, an eroticised primal bad-trauma-object. The demon-lover then turns into the image of death, as its dominating and raping, and eventually abandoning or murderous character emerges (Kavaler-Adler, 1993b, 1995–1996, 2003a, 2003b).

Clinical illustrations

The case of Leonard

Leonard demonstrates the pre-Oedipal level of fear of intimacy. In his own words, he intensely craved intimacy while also being intensely terrified of intimacy. However, through a "developmental mourning process" which reaches back to his mother's death when young, and back further to infant and toddler trauma, Leonard finds a marriage that gratifies his sexual and emotional desires. He begins to face his terrors to sustain the relationship. Prior to this evolving marital relationship, Leonard had been profoundly isolated. He self-medicated by having part object sexual relations with massage therapists, and dream and fantasy relations with his female analyst in a role of a "sex slave", but he had been too frightened of rejection (related to unmourned loss) to risk a relationship with a whole-object woman. However, Leonard continues to fantasise about escapes from commitment. Sustained intimacy is terrifying, both because of the shame that makes him fear being seen and known and because of the terror of being back in the high chair (where he is helplessly controlled and abandoned). It stirs up annihilation anxiety and a numbed out sense of being invisible. Leonard, as an infant in a high chair, had to split-off from himself and had to look back at himself from across the room. His mother had left for an intolerable amount of time, traumatising him, and (psychologically) almost wiping him out of existence. Resourceless dependence has to do with this level of terror. As with Masud Khan's patient, Leonard needed to express aggression all the time to feel any sense of power, when he felt so helpless inside. He had to say "No" to everything in his mind, and often in reality, to the point of devastating loss and self-sabotage. Through the psychoanalytic process, Leonard made increasing progress towards true emotional intimacy, no longer just continuing to fill up the void with a hyper-sexuality and an overly sexualised romantic and then marital relationship. Yet, during the first few years of his object relations psychoanalysis, he would fend off any mutual rapport with the analyst. He would polarise himself and the analyst by distorting the analyst's statements, to maintain a stance of opposition in order to pathologically guard his fragile sense of autonomy. At times, he might allow a few moments of actual rapport, where he would surrender this oppositional mode of obstructing relatedness. However, he was sure to unconsciously time this so that it only occurred at the end of the session. Then he would immediately run out of the room (the "in and out" solution of Guntrip). This anal stage opposition, which reflected developmental arrest trauma during separation-individuation, came after an earlier period of symbiotic harmony in his relationship with the analyst. This is symptomatic of Mahler's separation-individuation stage child who cannot "image" the mother enough to sustained a positive internalisation of her because the mother is too absent during the separation period, when she was more present in an earlier symbiosis. Leonard's maternal abandonment was associated with the time he was left in a high chair for so long that he had to split-off from himself and see himself from across the room. In analysis, the couch became the high chair he feared being trapped in and imprisoned by, in a state of "resourceless dependence", and he would always have escape fantasies along with his polarised oppositional enactments. When Leonard would surrender to encounter, he could be sure he could escape the couch and the room at the end of the session.

The case of Judith

Judith's fear of intimacy involved an over-reactivity to statements by her husband that re-evoked insults and contemptuous attitudes and critical comments from her brother and parents in childhood. She feared her own anger and would avoid responding to her husband. Then she would turn her anger inwards and develop all kinds of visceral and somatic body tensions, knots in her stomach, back and leg pain, and also cramping in her feet. She would also attack herself with her anger turned inward, saying to herself that she was not as good as others in her academic community and inhibiting herself from speaking up and having a voice. This held her back at work, just as her reticence in her marriage, or her long delayed articulation of anger inhibited intimacy.

In Kleinian terms, Judith demonstrates a depressive position conflict over anger, rather than paranoid-schizoid terror of outward retaliation, but they both interacted. In terms of fears of resourceless dependence, Judith feared humiliation that could extend to terrors of self annihilation. The childhood memories that re-emerged through psychoanalysis illustrate why. One memory was of being on a table in the kitchen of her childhood home, at four years old, while a doctor was attending to her wounds after her brother "accidentally" hit her with a baseball bat. In a state of extreme physical and emotional vulnerability she was tortured by the doctor, the same doctor who was hired by her mother to save her and heal her. When she cried from the terrible pain as the doctor stitched up her wounds, the doctor screamed at her for crying. The doctor angrily told her to shut up, while he flirted with her mother, and while both the doctor and her mother ignored her pain. No wonder Judith became terrified of anger, and of her potential internal rage, forcing her to continually repress her aggression so that she had to use distancing from intimacy in marriage to protect herself.

Also interfering with marital intimacy was Judith's fear of being defined by the other or moulded into the image of the other, rather than having her own autonomy of self-definition. She feared having her subjective experience being visible to any other, and particularly with the partner of potential intimacy in marriage, her husband. Her parents had always defined her rather than hearing her. Judith was often called the "sensitive" one, as her mother fantasised of being Judith's confidante, while exploiting Judith constantly. She was also defined by her parents as "the fat one", or "the too sensitive one", with all her vulnerability being seen as an imposition. If she walked down the street with her intrusive and sexualising mother as a teenager, and her mother said to her that some older man was leering at her as a sex object, her own experience of feeling disgusted by her mother's comments was totally ignored. Judith's subjective state was denied. By denying her subjective state, Judith could be further defined by her mother—a mother who also felt free to barge into her bedroom at any moment and demand that Judith listen to her, regardless of what was going on with Judith. When Judith's husband started to define her or mould her into his image by proclaiming her political beliefs, she would feel enraged, but the rage had been unconscious before her psychoanalytic psychotherapy. Now, the repressed rage appeared in dreams and in sleepy feelings felt by the therapist. These rageful dreams would always disappear as soon as Judith could express her anger and understand it. Often, her rage would strike her the next day, and meanwhile she was unaware of why she was distancing during sex, splitting off, and watching herself in the sexual act, rather than being able to emotionally surrender, even if her body had orgasms. Bringing Judith's awareness about her anger, while on the couch, helped in communicating her anger to her husband and to relinquish control during sex, and surrender without being inhibited by an unconscious fear of submission.

Judith had many dreams in therapy. However, one stands out as a transformation of self through modification of repression. The dream is as follows:

> There was a tsunami, tidal waves of water heading towards me. But then suddenly the tidal waves of waters stopped and just stayed suspended in an archway around me, so that I wasn't in danger of being hurt or drowned. Also there were walls that had been holding the water in place that gradually fell away. Yet the waters remained static above and around me and I felt safe.
>
> The patient's associations to the dream: "I was wondering why the walls could fall away and yet I could be safe and not be drowned by the raging waters. It felt like something could be let go of that was like a defensive wall that I needed before to survive. Now the walls could move away and I still survived and even felt safe. I think the raging waters are the multiple levels of my rage, my anger, and my sexual and erotic feelings too, all mixed together, but now no longer threatening to overwhelm me, despite the immense force of the waters. Somehow the waters are containing themselves now. I don't need rigid walls around me anymore, like the repressive wall barriers in my mind, or the wall of muscular obstruction that I experienced before in physical and emotional constipation.
>
> "When I was about six years old, I remember being terrified when I would be in the family car with my family, and we would drive through tunnels. I always feared the walls would come tumbling down on the side of the tunnel, and that we would be destroyed by the waters coming in and drowning us. My parents did comfort and reassure me when I had had this fear, unlike the times when they laughed at me for having nightmares, or ignored my pain at four when I was on the table being operated on by the doctor. Maybe I've revived their comfort as I let go of the rigid repressive walls that kept my anger at them silenced. I had also kept my love for my mother silent, since I feared my mother would manipulate me into some obligation to her if I expressed love to her. Here was another side of them when they were being parents. Also, my mother had been very tender and loving with my children when they were infants. Maybe that maternal love had been there for me very early on before the problems began."

This was the analyst's interpretation:

> Yes, your dream seems to articulate a vision of the rigid defensive walls falling away since they are no longer needed. You seem to be unconsciously declaring that you can surrender now to your internal emotional life, without fearing that either your anger or your sexuality will be too much for you. As you allow your anger into consciousness, and we sort out all the different reasons for your anger, you have been freer to speak up distinctly and assertively to your husband, when you feel he doesn't hear you, or is trying to mold you into his image, or co-op you for his agenda and miss your subjective experience. Also you can speak up quicker with your anger ("in the moment"), as the tidal waves of rage become moments of understandable anger that you can find words for, allowing you to surrender your rigid walls of opposition to your internal life. You have been able to speak up to me in your anger now too, with less fear of alienating me or of provoking alienation.

The case of Carol

Carol holds on to her internal bad object family by expressing their disapproving judgments against herself when she feels judged by her husband. Her turning against herself with a regressive attachment to the hostile attitudes of her bad objects, just when she needs understanding, is a manifestation of her fear of intimacy. Instead of speaking up to her husband at these times so that he can understand her, her fear of losing him (depressive position fear) causes her to attack herself with the very accusations that her childhood family used against her: calling herself selfish for having her needs and wishes, calling herself a whiner and complainer, calling herself "too angry" and aggressive.

The case of Richard

Richard speaks of "time out of time", or "time out", and times of compulsive work. "Where is the third way of being?" he asks. Only in this third state of being, which he begins to find in the analytic situation, can intimacy, as well as the true self spontaneity and mutuality needed for intimacy, become possible. This evolution towards allowing being, not just doing, is related to D. W. Winnicott's theories. Going to sleep to escape and not being able to get up in the morning, as well as his taking leaves of absence from work, and earlier from graduate school, are all part of the way Richard tries to create a "time out of time", or "time out" experience for himself, since he cannot possibly tolerate the tension and anxiety of his defensive work mode, in which "doing" has dominated over all states of "being". As a developmental mourning process begins in treatment, Richard starts to see the alternative state of spontaneous or quiescent being that he can allow himself, within the "transitional" and "holding" therapeutic environment and with the "containing" analyst. These moments of freedom (of being rather than doing) come gradually, and mostly, at the end of Richard's double sessions, as he is able to surrender to being in his body and feelings. First his anger comes. Then his grief and loss. Then the pain of longing for intimacy and commitment with his partner. As Richard yields to this pain in treatment, he realises that he carries anger that his mate cannot rescue him. He confronts a helpless feeling about life turning against him after his transfer to junior high school. With this awareness, Richard's compulsion to work non-stop when back at his job begins to yield to more freedom engaging emotionally, and also to suspend work and let go. Consequently, he escapes into sleeping day and night or into perpetual vacations. He is able to express the huge "no" that he had been compulsively working against all his life. This "no" may have gone back to a two year old needing autonomy. However, the "no" became a huge "no" towards life in general. Behind the "no" is the anger that he could no longer get his way through just being in his own narcissistic and instinctual self as he was in elementary school. When in junior high school, his first girlfriend rejected him, and competition arose. Richard unconsciously gave up on relationships, fearing that they all would result in rejection. Then in his thirties, Richard finally takes a risk in having a relationship. He is pursued by a homosexual younger man, and he succumbs to a strong emotional need for this man, only slowly opening to sexual relations and often feeling resistant. This new relationship is threatened until he can find his repressed feelings, dreams, and memories in treatment. Lying on the couch and discovering his repressed feelings and the fantasies, memories, dreams, and thoughts related to these feelings, which engender a developmental mourning process, Richard is gradually able to move past the emotional "in and out" schizoid solution, or Guntrip's schizoid compromise. He begins to stay in the relationship as he becomes capable of being more inside himself. Instead of just being there for his boyfriend as a mentor, and instead of unconsciously wishing for his boyfriend to be his mother, or for his psychoanalyst to be a mother who could rescue him from life, Richard begins to see that he could be his own mentor. However, this requires him to sustain a connection with himself that allows for empathy and compassion towards himself, instead of a severe judgmental view of himself, which perpetuated its own compulsive mode of negative thinking. Surrendering control in analytic sessions has been critical. He cries and sobs on the couch, thus discovering the two-year-old child self within that wants to kick, scream, and cling to his mother. He learned that his saying "No" to life was a defensive demand for an oppositional autonomy, when the challenge of risking true and authentic autonomy through saying "Yes" was too frightening. As he sobbed out his pain of longing for his lost mother, when trying to reunite with his boyfriend after a separation, he realised that he was very angry. He then realised that he feared that consciousness of his anger would leave him all alone without anyone. He came to realise that the opposite was true. Richard's consciousness of his anger became part of moving towards more intimacy with his boyfriend, and with others. He began to sense that he was less alone. He gradually came to express his love. He also began to express his sexual desires, which had been greatly inhibited, causing a large rift between him and his boyfriend.

The case of Phillip

The case of Phillip serves as another example of resourceless dependence in the fantasy of a patient who was in a transference regression, while having achieved the depressive position and Oedipal stage level of development. His dream-fantasy symbolises his fear, but also resolves it through an internal world that already housed a "good enough mother".

In the third year of his three times a week psychoanalytic treatment, Phillip has a rich and vivid fantasy of being a small infant, just placed on a bed by me, his transferential mother. In the fantasy, I leave him on the bed and go into another room. In his fantasy, Phillip feels such intense rage that he thinks his rage has pursued his mother and killed her. This expresses Phillip's abandonment terror within a "depressive position" psychic state. In this mature psychic state, as described by

Melanie Klein, Phillip's core anxiety is not related to losing his self, nor is it the fear of another's angry retaliation, nor is it even a terror of the abandonment by the mother herself. Rather it is the higher level terror of one's own rage when one is killing off the one one loves. Also, since he views himself as an infant, the one he loves as his internal mother in the outside world, his psychoanalyst, who is his transferential mother, is also the one he feels totally dependent on when on the couch in a therapeutic regression. Nevertheless, instead of resourceless dependence, Phillip feels the power to kill off another with his rage. He also experiences the power of his sexuality. As Phillip evolves in his own fantasy, he says that when his mother comes back into the room and picks his infant self up off the bed, he is not only relieved, but he is also suddenly gripped by seeing me, his transferential mother, as a demon-lover mother, because he feels his desire for me, making me sexual and thus evil. He finds the power of his sexual desires in this fantasy along with the power of his aggression, and his capacity to symbolise these passions in psychic fantasy allows him to no longer fear so much either the destruction of his aggression or his sexuality. This allows him to commit to his wife much more fully, and to save his full erotic self for her as he was unable to do before.

In Phillip's words, the fantasy story has its fear of resourceless dependence plot and its own resolution. Phillip narrates his vivid fantasy to me, his psychoanalyst, with awareness of his maternal transference (see Kavaler-Adler, 2003a, pp. 182–183):

> I see myself in a room as an infant. I see you in the room also. You're my mother. You're standing there in a black bra and black slip, holding me. You put me down on the double bed, where I can't roll off. Then you leave the room to go into the next room to get whatever dress you're going to put on. I'm lying on the bed and I don't know if you are going to come back or not. I can't tell if you're going to walk back into the room twenty seconds later or whether you'll walk out and I'll never see you again. Maybe you'll be dead. I am lying on the bed staring at the ceiling, and my neck doesn't even lift my head to see what's happening. My legs are these useless pieces of toy flesh. I can't move about on them. I want to speak and all that comes out is this inarticulate wail. I've got no power at all to take care of myself [he's crying]—no power to feed myself— no power to say what I want and need—no power to move myself.

I'm just like utterly and completely dependent on you; I don't want to feel all this stuff. You know I don't want to feel this vulnerable, needy, and powerless experience. I don't want to feel so dependent on someone who clearly doesn't have the judgment or love for me to not walk out of the room all the time. I can't take care of myself. I can't even walk. I don't speak. I can't even lift my head. I just feel this amazement seeing that all that is true—seeing that I'm completely powerless and dependent in that way. And you would walk out of his room, knowing what the implications are, and it fills me with this rage towards you—this feeling I could just crush you or strangle you—for failing me so acutely and so insensitively, as I see this force coming out of my little infant self, a force of rage leaving my heart and body, like in a third dimension—going off to accomplish its intent. I see it leaving me and going out and this phantom that's left my body is gone. It's accomplished its mission and dissolved. What's left in its place is my knowledge that I've created the very thing I most feared. I truly am alone. There's nobody coming back for me.

All of a sudden I'm aware of birds singing, the breeze blowing, the curtains, and the sunlight coming back into the room. I realise I'm utterly alone. All of a sudden I wake up to the present moment. To the beauty of what's around them. It's wild! I was expecting that this phantom would go out and destroy you and I would be alone. This is what I had feared. Instead, all of a sudden I'm gurgling happily with birds singing. I'm alive to the moment—having released my rage and my fear. What do you know? OK, so now I'm on the bed, alive to the moment—a happy baby gurgling on the bed. You walk back into the room with a dress on a hanger. You say something affectionate. Everything's OK again. Then we start a new cycle. You put the dress on and then leave the room again, and once more I think, wait! Hold on! My legs don't work, and you're leaving me alone!

The case of Paula

Paula represents a case of pre-Oedipal trauma compounded throughout childhood and causing a wall against intimacy. Paula reveals a "resourceless dependence" (Khan, 1972) dream related to developmental arrest due to trauma in the pre-Oedipal infant-toddler period—in contrast to Phillip's symbolised phantasy of maternal transference abandonment, which exposes a transference regression to fear of a primal object loss. This contrast highlights the paranoid schizoid self-annihilation terrors in Paula with the depressive position object loss fears in Phillip (who was regressing from the Oedipal stage through his intrapsychic fantasy). This is Paula's dream:

> Paula is on the top of staircases in a large house. The house is like her childhood home. She feels entrapped and imprisoned, in a state of aloneness and isolation. She finds herself trying to hold on to the wooden banisters, but she falls down all the flights of stairs. The wooden banisters all break and fall apart as she tries to grab them. She finds herself toppling downward and there is nothing to grab onto that would stop the fall. She is about to smash into a cold white marble floor that lies at the bottom of the crumbling wooden banister staircases. I, as the psychoanalyst, then interpret to Paula that she is in a nightmare version of her childhood home that seems to reflect her annihilation terror in the face of a detached and unavailable father who was never there to protect or support her, i.e., the wooden banisters. But even worse is her fate of falling onto a cold ice-cold marble breast mother. She falls onto this mother who can kill her rather than hold her, just when she seeks support to stay above this cold marble mother from her father. Her parents are both paranoid-schizoid position part objects in this dream. The father is represented by wooden banisters that crumble in the face of her dependent need, and which fail to support her. Her part object primal object (at the base) mother is a cold marble inert floor object. Due to Paula's dependent need for mother, the nightmare dream threatens murderous annihilation, as she seems headed to smash into the cold floor, which is like the immured wall of a cold breast mother who cannot hold or contain or nurture her. The dream is a nightmare, because there is no resolution of primal self annihilation terrors. There is only the murderous and destructive ending of her core true self internal child being in the face of dependence on two part object and bad object parents.

Paula's dependence is thus the resourceless dependence that Masud Khan referred to. So naturally she has to fight any emotional dependence on the psychoanalyst or on her husband, as this dependence would threaten to awaken the pre-Oedipally arrested child within her. She has many memories of her mother threatening to murder her, or ignoring her presence and abandoning her. A memory comes back to Paula that once again highlights the endangered state of her childhood. Paula's nightmares of the archetypical terrors are interpreted in relation to her distancing and devaluing of the analytic process. Paula's own interpretations as she becomes "an interpreting subject" show her growing ability to tolerate her rage so that she can symbolise her "damned if you do and damned if you don't" dilemma (need/fear dilemma) and to understand her unconscious "pact with the devil" (representing Fairbairn's addiction to the bad object).

The memory is of Paula running into a bathroom in her home of her teenage years (around thirteen)—to escape her raging mother, who was screaming that Paula deserved to die and that she (her mother) would kill her. Paula remembers running into the bathroom to escape her mother, and then she remembers standing behind the bathroom door, crying out "I hate you!" to her mother, while she shivers and shakes behind the door. Shivering from terror, Paula prayed that the lock of the bathroom door would hold. This was not the first time she was threatened with death by her mother. When only four years old, her mother tried to trap her in her mother's lap. Her mother seduced her by offering to play with her mother's ear or to suck her thumb. The mother wanted to hold Paula for her own comfort. Paula felt imprisoned by this gesture just as she would at times feel while lying on the couch during analysis. At only four years old, Paula escapes her mother's grasp, and runs out in the back yard where there are chickens that she likes to play with. Her mother's retaliatory response is to go after the chickens. Frantic with rage, Paula's mother grabs the live chickens and puts them into a bag. She then marches to the butcher to have the chickens beheaded and cooked. Paula is enlisted to march with her mother to the butcher. Her mother grabs her by the hand and drags her with her. When Paula cries and objects, her mother threatens: "I'll kill you too if you tell anyone about this!" That night Paula's mother calls her down to dinner in a voice that sickens Paula. There, on the dining room table, are the pet chickens, cut up and cooked. Paula doesn't want to eat, but her father acts as if all is well, and her brother is in his usual dissociated and out of touch state. She has no choice but to eat the murdered pet chickens, and she feels the nausea until this day. Her own rage makes her nauseous but so does the unconscious reliving of being force-fed the murdered pet chickens.

Paula's problems with intimacy become obvious when one gets in touch with her internal world. Within this internal world, Paula is "addicted" (through primal attachment), to her malevolent, hated, and murderous mother. Lying on the couch, Paula becomes aware for herself that she could never allow herself to receive the sustained loving interest of a man. Recently Paula realised that she was sabotaging the interest of a man, whom she dated and had sex with in the past, and who is trying to reconnect with her. She becomes aware that, like in other cases, she had interpreted his interest as purely sexual. She becomes aware that she never could believe that anyone was genuinely interested in her for herself, beyond sex. In line with Otto Kernberg's (1995) discussion of those who cannot receive love, Paula forgot about an invitation to a special party, where she was supposed to meet her male friend's mother. In her internal world, she maintained a "pact with the devil", in which she could escape the murder of her primal maternal object if she stayed wedded to this voracious and rageful mother forever, by continuing to believe that she, Paula, was the "rotten kid" her mother accused her of being. Paula was addicted to her internal bad object and to her bad object's view of her character (Fairbairn, 1952), so how could she ever think that someone would want her? She could understand a man's sexual hunger for her, which only made her interpret her position with the man as an exploited sex object position. This position was comfortably familiar to her in her mind, since she was an exploited child. However, to believe that she was wanted for herself was unthinkable, since she never had that experience with her primal relationships. Therefore, she was stuck in a state of alienation from any intimacy, walled off against the intimate emotional state. In fact she got out of bed and lay on the floor after sex with one man because she feared imprisonment in the merger with the other (the merger her mother demanded of her when she was not threatening to murder Paula or was not actively abandoning her). Paula had to wall off from emotional contact to avoid reliving the resourceless dependence she has suffered with her mother (being force-fed the murdered pet chickens). So she lived "in her head" and only intellectually communicated with others. Or, she lived in her body in sex or yoga. But she could not experience emotional connection that would allow for heartfelt intimate relations. So how could she believe she was wanted for herself? She forgot the men who might truly want her, just as she "forgot" therapy sessions she had had, in which she reached her more vulnerable feelings of need and longing for connection. All could become vague, abstract, or totally forgotten in her mind, despite briefly opening herself to her sadness and tears. I would need to interpret her fear of remembering any authentic emotional connection in her treatment sessions, understanding how dangerous it was for her to remember our sessions, which would make her aware of her emotional needs. To sustain connection with the analyst would mean that she would feel the need for the analyst, who would put her in a position of possession, or would shame her for being, in her words, "needy". By staying wed instead to the internal murderous mother (her pact with the devil), she walled off against the threat that she would be murdered by the external relationship with the analyst. She would need to become more aware of her fear of abandonment if she would sustain connection with the analyst. Gradually, Paula became aware of the other side of her "damned if you do and damned if you don't" position, the side of fearing being abandoned by the mother so that she would be in a totally isolated and thus unsustainable state. Forgetting the analyst and her analytic sessions, just like forgetting men who were seriously interested in her, was her unconscious way of controlling the abandonment. She would become the abandoning one, the one who was more in (false self) control, rather than feeling the need for the other that would abandon her. In Wilfred Bion's (1989) terms, she would attack the links of relatedness in her mind, to protect herself from the vulnerable position of emotional need that threatened to bring Khan's (1974) "resourceless dependence". In Klein's (1940, 1946, 1957) terms, she used a manic defence to defend against the vulnerabilities of the depressive position. By forgetting, Paula defensively opposed the developmental progression described by Mahler (1971) in her discussion of the child "imaging" the mother who was externally absent. Such "imaging" during the separation-individuation phases of development could keep a good mother alive and present psychologically, so as to build inside in the internal world the sustained imago of a present mother, allowing her to "go on being", in Winnicott's (1971) terms. By forgetting, Paula regressed to the paranoid-schizoid level of Klein (1957), where she continued to fear her own rage and the retaliatory rage of her mother, rather than to enter the more vulnerable state of the depressive position, where she would pine for the mother, and would thus feel loss in her absence. The forgetting forestalled the whole developmental progression of mourning the primal mother, in order to separate and self-integrate, described in Kavaler-Adler's theory of "developmental mourning".

Paula would relive her rage repeatedly, but would resist the sadness and grief of feeling need for the other. However, Paula became aware of this in treatment, and gradually she would more often acknowledge the sadness and tears she kept inside her. Nevertheless, Paula still returned to her addiction to a demon mother whom she eroticised when merged with the distant and absent father who lived as an internal object within her. This was her personal demon lover theme and complex. Only gradually could Paula relinquish the primal and profound ties to the internal bad object parents, and risk any need for the external object, the female psychoanalyst. Only as she became increasingly aware of how alone and isolated she felt inside (when not intellectually living in her head), could she tolerate feeling lonely, and tolerate sharing this loneliness with the analyst. Only as the loneliness came up in dreams— where she was on the outside as the excluded one, or was misplacing or losing herself through losing major possessions such as her car or her house keys—could Paula admit that her attempts to escape relationship left her stuck in a fearful state of aloneness, without any emotionally needed intimacy.

Back to the case of Phillip

By contrast, Phillip's internal mother is a whole object mother who leaves him for a few minutes, but who returns to nurture him, be affectionate, and to contain him. She makes sure he is safely placed on the bed before she leaves the room. He fears the loss of her, which, he fears, would leave him alone in a resourceless dependence, but instead his rage shows he has a sense of self agency and intention and empowerment even in the totally dependent infant state. He fears object loss but not self-annihilation. In fact Phillip symbolises the whole experience of a feared object loss all at a conscious fantasy level, and thus works out the fear as his mother returns. He sees that his rage can be survived by both him and his mother, and by both him and myself in his state of maternal transference in his analysis, as well as in his marriage. This allows Phillip to have erotic thoughts, without self-consciousness in his psychoanalysis, and in parallel to have erotic intimacy within his marriage. Phillip relinquishes all his avenues of escape from monogamy once he sees that his relationships can survive his anger and aggression, and even his more unconscious pre-Oedipal infant rage. Even in fantasy of infant dependence, he has the power of his rage and is not resourceless.

Phillip's fears of intimacy in marriage emerge in his transferential fantasies in treatment. He fears that the female analyst will either be a traumatised mother who could be devastated by any honest reaction to her, or would be a contemptuous father, who can humiliate and ridicule him. He fears the analyst is secretly making contemptuous judgments of him that she does not say overtly. He fears she would be devastated if he were critical of her, rather than just generally devaluing the treatment for many years. When he evolves to a place where he experiences the analyst as truly understanding him and as providing, in his words, "a sustained holding presence" for him, it has to do with his being able to see that she is not the mother he dreamed of as a mother who drops her infant, or shows him off to boost her narcissism in her inner insecure state. He also gets there by realising she is empathic to him over many years in a way that he finally is convinced distinguishes her from the bad object contemptuous father he had carried in his internal world. Now he is more capable of intimacy than ever. However, in becoming so he has to again confront his wife's fears of intimacy, which his wife still expresses by her projections onto him of a rejecting and irresponsible and excluding father. He has to face that his wife still continues to set up with him the very abandonment that she fears by hostile rages, although she now apologises. He persists in communicating to his wife that she can still speak to him in a scapegoating, demeaning, and dissociated manner. Phillip is continually faced with the difficulty of seeing how he can remain open to relationship when his capacities for intimacy are closed off by his wife's attacks. Through his analysis and his object relations work of internalising a more secure and containing relationship, he has learned to assert himself and stay emotionally open, rather than dissociating and closing off as he once did.

Return to Paula's case

The case of Paula relates to Margaret Mahler's theory, in terms of the fear of possession by a borderline mother who wants to pull her into a regressive symbiosis, or attack her and abandon her. Paula is most conscious of her fears of entrapment with the female analyst, who quickly becomes the feared mother in the transference. She is less conscious of her terrors of abandonment. She is less conscious of yearning for the mother she never had than of wishing her mother would drop dead. In fact, Paula imagines her psychoanalyst as dropping dead when on vacation. She fantasises that if I drop dead, she would be freed from any difficult choice about committing to or leaving therapy. She is less conscious of the need for me. This need was so traumatically frustrated in childhood that Paula has dissociated from her whole internal child core self, and a whole life lived in an intellectual false self to avoid being aware of the primal and profound need in her for a mother.

Unlike Margaret Mahler's two year olds that can "image" the mother, and who consequently begin to keep the mother symbolically within the self, when the mother is temporarily absent during separation-individuation, Paula could not "image" a mother that was emotionally absent even when physically present. She was left empty with a void inside, where the primal connection with the mother should be. She had been numb, when originally in psychoanalytic treatment. Then she became consciously enraged. Now she gets to a feeling of sadness and tears in a "developmental mourning process" that continues through her analysis, as anger and rage now alternate with a feeling of need and longing. However, Paula also regresses to cutting off, but much less than before. Her memories tell of a mother who threatened to kill her at the age of four, and who later raged and attacked her until she picked up a knife at fifteen and threatened to kill her mother. Then her mother continued to emotionally attack Paula, only giving up the physical attacks. Her father was mostly absent. To be made aware of the need for her female analyst, every time she repeatedly thinks of escaping prematurely from treatment, becomes part of the process of the treatment.

Mahler (1965, 1971) speaks of the double-headed monster of a traumatic separation-individuation period, where the borderline individual always ends up feeling damned if they do or damned if they don't. Paula had always kept more conscious the side of this terror related to fear of engulfment and entrapment. She tried to be totally independent, through using her very fine intellect in a schizoid mode of false self-defensive self-sufficiency. She dissociated from her inner self where the vulnerable child and toddler self remained sealed off, walling off against feeling the agony of needing a mother who was never emotionally attuned or in touch with her. The analyst was able to interpret this side of things once the effects of the "abandonment depression" mourning process (James Masterson) and the "developmental mourning process" had been felt. This involved feeling void states, rage states, and ultimately deep grief and loss states. As dreams spoke of Paula symbolically losing herself by losing her car, or of being lost without any guidance or connection, Paula began to see that she was feeling as terrified of being alone as she was of being entrapped in the treatment and in her marriage. She began to feel the true internal needing self that was her only avenue to connection and certainly to intimacy with another.

Paula could finally begin to feel the therapist feeling her. At first she could not remember this when it happened. But gradually she started to remember that there was someone there. After every session that would begin with how Paula resented the time and money for treatment, and with travel plans that were in part a plot to get away from psychoanalytic treatment, a transition began to occur. As the analyst pointed out Paula's unacknowledged need for the analyst and for the analytic process, which was evident in her dreams, Paula began to see it, too. She also began to surrender to her inner pain in sessions, despite her fears of depending on anyone as she now needed to depend on the analyst.

Conclusion

In all these vignettes, we see how there is a need-fear dilemma related to the human need for intimacy. We also see the many levels of fears related to surrendering to needing the *other*. The theories described initially are highlighted within the case examples. In this way abstract concepts, such as "resourceless dependency", the "in and out" solution, "developmental mourning", the "demon-lover complex", "imaging" the other to restore a coenaesthetic experience in order to soothe the self, the "depressive position" *vs.* the "paranoid-schizoid position", addictive attachments to "bad objects", etc.—can all come alive.

CHAPTER FIVE

Fear of injury

Jerome S. Blackman

T he disciple, in search of meaning, approaches the Zen master. The Zen master tests him: "What is reality?" The disciple responds, "Reality is an internal construction. Reality is the manifestation of mental aggregations. Reality is your mind's personal creation." The Zen master then takes a stick[1] and smacks the disciple on the head.[2]

Not to labour the point, when we speak of fear of physical injury, we are dealing both with reality and fantasy. Sometimes it is difficult to distinguish between the two. Yet, in our everyday lives, we see the operation of the reality principle (Freud, 1920g; Schur, 1966). We could not drive on the highway if we did not trust that other people did not want to be physically injured. We rely on the idea that the vast majority of human beings possess a self-preservation function that leads them to try to avoid road accidents. We drive "defensively". On the other hand, there are people who are afraid to drive a car, or even get into one, citing the average of about 40,000 deaths per year in road accidents in the US.[3] How realistic are they?

To begin, let us start with some considerations about how fear of physical injury develops throughout childhood and adolescence, in both boys and girls. Although a vast topic, I will try to touch on some of the nodal points in development that contribute both to reality testing of physical danger and to inhibition and symptom formation (Freud, 1926g). Then, after examining some clinical examples, I will take a look at how diagnosis and treatment selection[4] are affected. Finally, I make some brief comments upon cultural, national, and international implications of this ubiquitous fear.

Developmental considerations

The beginning of the fear of physical injury is similar in girls and boys, in that, during the second year of life, when they begin walking, they realise that when they fall, they get hurt. If there is a sibling or playmate who pushes them, they will, early on, recognise that physical injury can be caused by the action of another person as well as themselves. Also, in both boys and girls, the destructive-aggression mobilised towards their mothers and fathers in the service of separation (Mahler, Pine, & Bergman, 1975) can also be projected. Thus, the child experiences the capacity to make other people angry and begins to fear what that other person could do to them if the other person is too angry.

Roiphe and Galenson (1972) discovered, in their studies of toddlers, that the first genital phase begins just before the age of two and Knight (2005) found that this phase lasts until about six and a half in boys and until about seven and a half in girls. Much research on girls (e.g., Blum, 1977; Lerner, 1976) has found that during the first genital phase, girls find their vulva and entroitus, finger them, and discover and conceptualise the inner canal (the vagina), whether the mother names these anatomical parts or not. When girls learn that babies come through the vaginal canal, their integrative function and reality testing lead them to realise that something could also go in that opening, and perhaps hurt them. The sensitivity of the external genitalia clue them in that those could also be harmed—"feminine genital anxiety" (Dorsey, 1996). However, many girls during the first genital phase deny their vulnerability to being penetrated or hurt, and sometimes this denial persists.

Boys' fear of being physically injured begins with reality experiences and is reinforced by projections of hostility during separation-individuation (at the ages of one to four years). Overlapping the anal/separation phase, they also begin to finger their genitals for pleasure just before the age of two. By the age of three, their competitive feelings towards either parent will likely be projected, so that either parent is feared, even if the parents are gentle. For boys, the witnessing of the female genitalia (mother undressing, or girls being diapered during play groups) creates a thought of being without their pendulous penis. This thought adds to what is dramatically referred to as "castration anxiety" (Freud, 1905d).

The reality of social experiences with other boys during latency will confirm for any boy that there is danger of physical injury from other boys. During these school-age years, the physical differences between boys and girls are minimal, although there is the beginning of some differentiation in terms of strength. Nevertheless, I have treated a number of girls who were such wonderful athletes that the school-age boys insisted on having those girls, for example, on their baseball team. This prowess, however, almost always dissipates as girls move into adolescence, since the post-pubertal muscular development of boys is so dramatic, and the girls' relative weakness compared to the boys also becomes dramatic. During this phase, girls may use any number of defensive operations, including painful shyness, avoidance, or devaluation of boys. During adolescence, we see the boy-crazy type develop, using counterphobic seductiveness (seduction of the aggressor) to manage their anxiety, which is based partly, again, on their reality perception of the differences between the genders. Finally, healthy adolescent boys and girls must begin to recognise the paranoid psychotics and vicious psychopaths who begin to show their feathers during the teen years. In one of my favourite movies, *Back to the Future* (1985), Marty, a teenage boy, goes back in time to help his father face up to a psychopathic bully. When Marty returns to the present, the entire world has changed because of this action. Healthy aggression in men is often referred to, even by women, as "having balls". A refined, Southern-reared woman physician, married to a physician friend of mine, once complained about a particular group of male physicians she disrespected as "a bunch of pussies".

As are all things in life, all things in developmental theory, and all understanding about the genders, no generalisations are true 100 per cent of the time. There are women who are much stronger than most men, and there are men who are much weaker than most women. Men also experience fears of rape in certain situations and women also, at times, use counterphobic mechanisms (Raphling, 1989).

Fear of physical injury in men

Some people immediately mention fear of physical injury as a chief complaint. Much more commonly, however, we see people in our offices who have other problems, where fear of physical injury may be kept out of consciousness by defence mechanisms (like suppression—as Anna Leonowens used when approaching the King of Siam)[5]. Below is an example of a man whose major problems included, as one unconscious motivation for his personality problems, a fear of physical injury of which, at the beginning of treatment, he was completely unaware.

A case from my practice

Lance, a thirty-seven-year-old divorced man with no children, consulted me originally because of severe procrastination, some difficulties with delayed ejaculation, and occasional abuse of alcohol. He was currently dating a woman seriously, and they were discussing the possibility of getting married. After two years of psychoanalytic treatment (four times a week, using the couch), Lance told me that he had "done something stupid". At the beach with his girlfriend and another couple, he decided to go for a swim in the ocean. He decided this although there were signs posted, clearly visible, that the surf was high and dangerous, and swimming was prohibited. His girlfriend and the other couple did not seem to notice when he slipped away and dived into the water.

Within a few minutes, he was a couple of hundred feet off shore, when the rip tide caught him. He could not swim back to shore, but being a good swimmer, he rode the rip tide. His girlfriend and the other couple then noticed that he was not able to come back in, and followed him, running and screaming, for over a mile down the beach as the rip tide carried him. He eventually was able to pull himself back to the beach, but commented to me, "I don't know why I did that. I could have gotten killed." His girlfriend was frightened but furious at him for "being stupid", and the other couple was nonplussed.

Lance and I discussed this matter for many sessions until we could understand what had been motivating him to make such a terrible mistake. First, he did not like to think he was vulnerable to being hurt. We could see that he partly used denial of reality—by means of a deed (A. Freud, 1936) and a counterphobic mechanism (Blackman, 2003), that is, doing something he was terrified of in order to prove to himself that he was not scared. In other words, his dangerous behaviour was a defence against anxiety. But what was he frightened of? He confirmed that he did not like to think that he could get hurt or get killed. This feeling had been around, not just since adolescence (when it is extremely common in boys), but had started during his grade (elementary) school years. When he misbehaved and did not listen, his father would take him "to the woodshed". Literally, Lance's father would drag him to a shed in the back yard and beat Lance with a belt. The first time, Lance cried and screamed—lost control of his emotions.[6] After that, Lance said, when his father beat him, Lance "learned to take it". He would not show any sign of emotion. His stoicism was reinforced by his father's admonition that if he would "keep crying, I'll give you something to cry about!"

I then engaged in a technique Kanzer (1953) called "reconstruction of the present", in that I explored the immediate situation on the beach that preceded Lance's misbehaviour. Lance recalled that he had actually been feeling bored and frustrated by the lively conversation his girlfriend was having with the other couple. Strangely, although they attempted to draw him in, he resisted because he did not want to feel "controlled". The emotional closeness also bothered him, to a certain degree. Much like a teenager (or a toddler), in order to feel separate, he ran away. He did something dangerous that disturbed the people who loved him (much as the toddler makes his mother angry during the separation-individuation process) and simultaneously got them all to pay attention to him. Lastly, he brought likely punishment on himself to relieve his guilt over wishing to retaliate against his father for his father's physical abuse.

Lance's periodic binge drinking was connected to his father, as well. Lance had not had a drink until he was twenty-one, at which time his father, who was a weekend alcoholic, took him out to celebrate: they got drunk together. We could see that Lance's identification with his father relieved him of his guilt over his anger towards his father and relieved his "father hunger" (Herzog, 2001). Additionally, Lance proved that he was macho: he could live through the danger of being harmed by over-imbibing a toxic substance.[7]

He connected "feeling controlled" by his girlfriend's attempts to draw him into conversation with the other couple with the way his mother had forced him to go to cotillion dances during his school-age years. He hated this activity; he thought cotillion was for "sissies" who "who kept their skirts clean". When Lance behaved himself, as he usually had professionally and most of the time socially, he was "keeping my skirts clean". When he misbehaved or did something dangerous, he felt like a man. As we discussed these connections, Lance recalled a dream: "There's a group of elders, and they're finding me guilty of something. I run away, and then I'm in a back room somewhere. In the next scene, I'm sucking my own penis, and it is about three feet long so I don't have to bend over. Maybe I'm on the roof of a skyscraper." This dream had many meanings, which we elucidated over a period of time. One glaring connection between Lance's misbehaviour and this dream was his wish to have a three-foot penis. The three-foot penis made him feel masculine, which guarded him against infantile wishes to depend on his mother. The penis also represented, among other things, a breast which he could suck himself, not having to rely on anyone else. By sexualising his oral dependency wishes, Lance felt "masculine" and not vulnerable to control and castration (feminization).[8]

Lance showed anxiety based on conflicts deriving from different stages of development. He experienced some anxiety about closeness and distance—selfobject fusion and separation anxiety (Mahler, Pine, & Bergman, 1975). He showed castration anxiety from the first genital phase, which was aggravated because of the beatings he received from his father then and during latency. He associated being "good" with being a girl, which meant, to him, someone without a three-foot penis. When he proved that he could do dangerous things or even live through dangerous behaviour that he instigated himself, he felt manly and punished simultaneously. The anxiety about punishment seemed to derive from his latency phase of development.

Remnants from his late adolescence (in his case, this began around the age of twenty-one, when he also first engaged in volitional masturbation) included a sense of revelry associated with drinking and misbehaving, as well as his persistent defensive pseudo-independence (Blackman, 2003) and wish to see himself as invulnerable.

Lance got better, eventually behaved himself without feeling feminine, and eventually married his girlfriend. He was successful in his work. He stopped doing dangerous things, and he stopped abusing alcohol. His reactions to me, in fantasy, paralleled many of his reactions to his father, and sometimes his mother: "transference". In a dream towards the end of his treatment, he reported: "I am lying on my back, and you are sort of floating above me. We have our clothes on, but I am like kissing toward your face. I don't actually kiss you, but it's like I am kissing in that direction." When I asked him what direction that was, down or up, Lance answered, "Up." Interpreting upwards (Loewenstein, 1957), I told Lance that it sounded like he was "kissing up" to me.[9] He responded, "I always kiss up to you! You're my father!" He laughed, and so did I.

It is tempting to continue telling you more about Lance, his dynamics, and his treatment. But I would like to shift gears here, and focus on the related, but somewhat different issue of women's fear of physical injury.

Fear of physical injury in women

Women's fear of physical injury also has a developmental story, a little bit different in each woman throughout her childhood and adolescence. Again, to illustrate the features that contribute to this fear, let us look at some clinical material. This time, instead of a case of mine, I offer a recent experience taken from my teaching activity.

Coincidentally, one group of third and fourth year psychiatry residents [graduate trainees] I taught at Eastern Virginia Medical School (one hour per week for the year) was made up entirely of women. In total, including the residents and the psychology interns [house doctors] who rotated through, at any given time there were about nine women in the room. In teaching them psychoanalytic theory, I had offered them the opportunity, at any time, to "trump" any assignment I had given them by inviting one of their own outpatients to come to class for me to treat during the hour. Their patient had to agree to it, and understand that I would stop periodically during the "session" to explain their dynamics; I would also explain the intervention that I was going to make before I made it. If a patient was amenable to this agreement, I would go ahead and demonstrate to the residents some dynamic techniques, much as a chief surgeon might teach a surgery resident during an operation.[10]

A supervised case

Jack, a thirty-five-year-old divorced businessman was in treatment with a female resident. She was worried about him because he had started having fantasies of having sexual intercourse with her. His wife had divorced him when, after several months of no sex, she caught him looking at pornography on the internet; and he was unable to stop this activity. He was aware that this was a problem, but was not aware why he felt compelled to do this.

I did a brief mental status assessment, which revealed no deficits in his integration, abstraction, reality testing, or self-preservation functions. As I discussed his problems with him, he could "mentalise" (Bouchard et al., 2008): he described his difficulty maintaining close relationships, particularly with women. Jack, himself, thought that some of his problems had to do with the way his mother raised him. His father had left the home when he was five, after which he slept in his mother's bed for several years. During those years, she would hold him for minutes while she pinched his cheeks and repetitively kissed him on the lips. In addition, one of his mother's boyfriends began watching pornography with Jack when he was about six, and although he was curious about this, he felt peculiar and uneasy watching it.

During the brief "session" with the residents sitting in the room, I indicated how I gently confronted Jack's defensiveness when he stopped talking (Gray, 2005). This led to him revealing some shame that caused him to become inhibited in speaking. In fact, this shame, in front of the group, pertained to revealing sexual material in front of all the women (although they were physicians). During this discussion, I was able to help Jack think about his relationship with his mother. As he reflected on their relationship, he thought he actually never felt emotionally close to his mother or his father. He agreed that he could feel some closeness with a woman sexually, but also used pornography to defensively distance himself from his wife. In using pornography, he would turn away from fears of closeness with actual women but simultaneously gratify wishes for closeness, symbolically, by imagining himself involved in a sexual fantasy where he was having sexual intercourse with the woman in the porn video.

We could link his fantasies about having sexual intercourse with his female psychiatric resident to these dynamics: fantasies of sexual intercourse were a way of establishing closeness without admitting the oral (dependency) elements or wishes for object relatedness. Simultaneously, he avoided emotional closeness by simply imagining sexual intercourse, as he did with his porn fantasies. He also imagined having sexual intercourse with her to avoid his embarrassment over exposing his wishes for love and closeness from her.

At the end of that interview, Jack asked me what I thought of him. I responded that I was impressed with his ability to think about his problems and because of that, I felt some optimism about his treatability. In other words, although he had painful problems, I saw that he showed good ability to observe himself, to understand symbolism, and thoughtfulness. Therefore, I thought further understanding of these conflicts could be useful to him in feeling better. He felt quite relieved, reporting to his therapist (she told me) in a following session that he was happy to have heard from me that he was treatable, and that he found the session with me "enlightening".

The following week, in class, I asked the residents what they thought of the interview. Almost all of them, one by one, said they felt "creeped out" by this man. All of them expressed some surprise that I had been able to establish a working relationship with him, help him develop insight, and that I did not seem "creeped out" by his symptom. My first response to these comments was that I was familiar with psychopathology in men that involved masturbation. Almost every man (and many women) I have treated has revealed masturbatory fantasies during treatment; these masturbation fantasies (Marcus & Francis, 1975), like dreams (Freud, 1900a) and daydreams (Raphling, 1996), can be the "royal road" to understanding their unconscious conflicts. I gave the residents an analogy to medical students and surgery residents, who get used to handling rather grotesque, bloody situations, which might "creep out" the average person. Similarly, in psychoanalytic psychiatry, we get into people's inner thoughts, which often involve fantasies that are embarrassing or disturbing, and involve both sexuality and hostility, at times. Sometimes even more graphic sadomasochistic fantasies emerge and must be understood and deconstructed.

I asked them if they understood the sexualisation mechanism (Coen, 1981), which Jack used as a defence against his shame and selfobject fusion anxiety, but also expressed his wishes for closeness. They all said they saw that, but still, the group laughed as they discussed how "creepy" this particular man was. With their permission, I suggested that we possibly explore what they all meant by "creeped out". Several of the women translated this idiom as meaning anxiety, but were not quite clear about the type (i.e., thought-content) of the anxiety this man caused them (Brenner, 1982). One thought she noticed Jack "smirking" as he revealed that he liked to watch porn movies of men having sexual intercourse with women. Another woman commented that the impersonal nature of his masturbation fantasies, without any love, made her feel "creeped out".

After these clarifications, Dr Jessica Campbell, the chief resident, a particularly astute student of psychoanalytic theory, volunteered, "All men can creep you out." I asked her if this was a generalisation. She said, "No. It's one thing women have to face: the average man is much stronger than the average woman, and therefore, there is always some danger, particularly if you don't know a man, that he could overpower you, hurt you, or even kill you." This declamation brought a silence to the group. After several seconds, I mentioned that this seemed a bit uncomfortable, and I wondered if the other residents agreed with Dr Campbell. As I went around the room, various women said things like this: "Well, it is true, you do have to be careful, although I don't know if it's quite as dangerous as Jessica said. But when I think about it, that's probably right." Another woman said, "Yes, that's true, especially if you're a young child. I'm not so sure about adult women, but I think in general that she is right." Dr Campbell responded, "Let's face it: men are bigger and stronger, and they can hurt you. You have to know if they've been socialized and care about you. If you don't know the man, he could be armed, or even have a knife in his pocket!" At this point, I commented to Dr Campbell, "That's interesting symbolism, isn't it?" She and I immediately agreed that "the knife in the pocket", symbolically, represented the fear of a dangerous penis, or in common terms, a fear of being raped. The other women in the room agreed that this was a constant, although generally somewhat minimised risk that all women face.

Their fear of physical injury from a rather timid, shy, inhibited, and sexually disturbed man occurred because of his supposed "smirking" while he was talking about impersonal sex. This had triggered in all the women in the room, almost simultaneously, a fear that this male did not associate sexual activity with love and concern, which of course made him more dangerous. His smirking suggested sadistic gratification, which I explained to the group. Jack expressed anger and defended against it, much as Arlow (1980) described as the "revenge motive in the primal scene". In other words, Jack made the group listen to his sexual fantasies rather than him being the victim of overstimulation by his mother and others. This defensive reversal could be eventually interpreted to him, although I thought the first order of business was to understand the content and the defences that caused him to have difficulty establishing closeness with women. I explained that if you first pointed out to him that he was overstimulating the therapist by talking about such things, this would probably cause him to feel that he should not talk about porn, and thus interfere with the treatment: a type of countertransference (Marcus, 1980).

The fear of physical injury in all nine women partly involved their reality testing as adults: that, being of the female gender, most of them would be somewhat unequal to a physical battle with a man who might want to hurt them. We did not address the issues of projection and displacement (which I have found in so many female analysands), where the woman's reality fear of a man is augmented by seeing in him her own hostile-aggressive feelings towards some other man in her life (where she wanted to physically hurt a man). Often, anger and fear, either from childhood or adolescence, has been displaced onto another man who was showing surliness. Then, because of shame and guilt over her own hostile impulses, the woman projected the hostile wishes onto the man—and therefore imagined he was more dangerous than he actually was. In the case of Jack, I thought that was also occurring in the group.

Nevertheless, the reverse can also be true. I have observed that many mature women seriously minimise the potential danger of physical harm by men—and of course, parents of teenage daughters worry about their daughters' frequently cavalier attitude towards the danger of physical harm. Moreover, adult women who are dating and looking for a partner may not know how to assess any man's object related empathy, his conscience functioning, impulse control, and whether his ideas about sex are connected to love or to sadistic physical harming of the woman (Blackman, 2012). I noticed some mild defensive inhibition of judgment about danger (Blackman, 2003; Freud, 1926d) in a few of the female psychiatry residents—who minimised Dr Campbell's maternal warnings. Nonetheless, they were "creeped out"—a sort of euphemism—by a man with object relations deficits and obsessions about porn. Facing the horrors of dastardly, ruthless men in the world, such as Uday Hussein,[11] can be overwhelming. The history of sexual atrocities against women in many totalitarian regimes run by men is legendary;[12] such acts of viciousness occurred under the Nazis and in the Soviet gulags, for example.

Diagnostic issues

How dangerous is anyone? And how much fear should anyone have of physical injury? What constitutes normal cautiousness? When does fear arise from neurotic displacements and fantasies? And when is fear produced by psychotic projections of hostility?

Fear of physical injury by psychotics and psychopaths

As I have pointed out elsewhere (Blackman, 2010), the major elements in assessing a person's dangerousness include that person's ego functions, ego strengths, object relations, and superego functioning. These terms are a shorthand way of describing sixty parameters, at least, that contribute to any person's dangerousness. These functions, if damaged in a frightened person (by heredity or overwhelming affect), can create a situation where the person's fear of physical injury is delusional.

In the clinical setting, if questionably dangerous people's abstraction, integration, reality testing, and self-preservation (AIRS) are damaged, intact they turn out to be more dangerous physically. If you add a deficit in superego functioning (no guilt or shame),[13] the person becomes even more dangerous than a garden variety paranoid psychotic. A colleague of mine once referred to people with deficits characteristic of psychosis, who also possess deficits in impulse control (of violent impulses) and show deficits in superego functioning, as "schizopaths".[14] Others have more formally referred to such people as pseudo-psychopathic schizophrenics (Rosen, 1971). Presumably, the multiaxial system suggested by the DSM-IV-TR allowed the diagnosis of schizophrenia on Axis I and the diagnosis of antisocial personality disorder on Axis II—although that manual did not require the use of the Axis system, and apparently it is being eliminated in DSM-V.

In assessing dangerousness, it is also critical to examine the person's capacities for empathy, trust, and closeness (ETC).[15] When there is damage to these three elements of mental functioning, the person will have no empathy (or "feelings") about others, and therefore does not feel guilty or ashamed about violent impulses (no conflict leading to defensive control). A person who does not trust others can easily project any hostility onto others and see them as dangerous. Be careful: if you are dealing with a so-called "borderline" person, who has intact AIRS but defective ETC, you can stimulate them to feel violent aggression towards you if you offer them too much emotional closeness. If they have a superego and feel guilty about this, they may then turn the aggression on the self; after a friendly "meeting of the minds", they may attempt suicide (to relieve selfobject fusion anxiety) (Harley & Sabot, 1980). If their superego contains lacunae (Johnson & Szurek, 1952), however, such people may well turn their hostile-destructive wishes on you. In general, in people with object relations damage, the risk of them causing physical injury to somebody is higher than in normal or neurotic people.

Additionally, we must consider people's ego strengths, or their capacity for impulse control, for affect tolerance, and for keeping primary process material in abeyance. The capacity for affect regulation and control of violent, hostile impulses is conditioned on: 1) a sufficiently securely organised attachment to parental figures during early childhood (Bretherton, 1992), and 2) the ability of such children to establish a separate sense of self, internally (Akhtar, 1994; Kramer & Akhtar, 1988). The development of a concept of a separate self-image involves the use of hostile-destructive aggressive tactics on the part of the child (Parens, 1980), and is sort of the obverse of attachment. When there either has been insufficient attachment (Bowlby, 1944a, 1944b) or insufficient separation-individuation during the toddler years (Mahler, Pine, & Bergman, 1975) and/or adolescence (Blos, 1966), a person is liable to become more physically violent. Finally, reality experiences with siblings often confirm people's fears of physical violence, which can persist into adulthood unconsciously and augment reality-based fears.

Fear of physical injury in neurosis

When a person's ego functions, ego strengths, object relations, and superego functioning are all within normal limits, fear of that person physically is generally not realistic. When people voice fear of violence by someone in the face of that someone having the intact functions I just described (as in the case of the man I had evaluated in front of the female residents), their fears of physical violence are usually due to other elements in their own thinking. The usual causes of their fear are projection, fantasies, and transference, where fear of physical harm is primarily the manifest content (symbolic) of anxiety that has many other meanings.

The typical "normal" or "average expectable" phobias of the first genital stage are sometimes characterised as the five Ds: that is, fears of doctors, deep water, dentists, dark, and dogs. The fears of physical injury engendered by each of these objects is due to symbolism and projection of hostile-aggression onto them. Here is an example:

Another case from my practice

Melinda, a thirty-nine-year-old married woman with two children, consulted me because she had developed an acute fear of being injured while riding a horse. This was troubling her because she was an equestrienne, and loved riding horses. I found out, as I explored the timing of this acute fear, that it seemed to have come into being just after her husband fell off a horse (while they were riding together) and broke his leg. The "real" danger to her was minimal because she was an experienced rider. Her fear of injury, we felt, must have symbolic meanings. In the course of her psychoanalytic treatment, we discovered that, at the time of her husband's accident, she had been making excuses for her husband in an attempt not to be angry at him. She engaged in such rationalisations because she felt guilty—that maybe he did not deserve her being angry at him, even though his frequent business trips interfered with their life: he had not even been present at the births of their children. As she defensively avoided riding, she punished herself for this anger.

Not coincidentally, her father had died, when she was twelve, in an accident involving horses. He had been on a sulky (buckboard) with Melinda, alone, in the country, when a wheel hit a rock. The sulky fell over, and her father suffered a severe closed head injury. A few days later, he succumbed to it. Ironically, this happened when she felt close to her father, so it was difficult to know where her guilt arose. She later recalled that at around the age of six, she had a nightmare and wanted to sleep in her parents' bed. She found the door locked. Instead of knocking, she got angry and wished her father would die—so that no other woman could have him; she hopped into bed with her brother instead.

She could see that when her father actually died, she felt guilty because several years earlier, she had had a fantasy of wanting him dead—and she felt like her hostile-destructive wish towards him then had come true—as though she were the culprit. Her overreactions to her husband's physical injury, it turned out, had included a thought that she would be physically injured if she rode a horse again—as a punishment for her wish to have hurt him, augmented by displacement onto him of all the conflicts she had about her father.

Once Melinda understood all this, she was able to reintegrate, and was no longer afraid of being injured while riding a horse. She also expressed some of her frustrations to her husband, instead of passively hiding her feelings due to guilt over "destroying" their relationship. Because of her capacities for abstraction, integration, reality testing, verbal ability, object relatedness, and conscience functioning, her understandings about herself were curative.

As I noted earlier, the picture changes as the variables concerning ego and superego functioning, and object relations capacities, change. When a person's abstraction ability, integrative functioning, and certain pockets of reality testing are damaged; when object relations capacities for empathy and trust are virtually non-existent; and when guilt and shame are also apparently non-existent, the danger of that particular person doing harm is greatly increased. People with damage to these basic mental functions tend to fall into some psychotic diagnostic category, and if they become violent, they may kill people with impunity.

Interestingly, deficits in these important functions may not be associated, in any given person, with their social skill. Therefore, a sexual abuser and murderer, like Ted Bundy, can be attractive and socially appropriate.[16] Even Saddam Hussein, who murdered hundreds of thousands of people, showed highly developed social abilities and refined ways of interacting with diplomats from other countries.

Therapeutic considerations

In our consulting room, a person's appearance, self-care function, hygiene, gestures, and language usage can easily obfuscate severe danger of which the therapist should be afraid. I found this dichotomy, between highly developed social ability and severe, dangerous psychopathology, often to be the case in heinous child abusers I evaluated. These men had raped or otherwise seduced small children into grotesque sexual activity. Although I have never evaluated a producer of child pornography, my educated guess is that they would fall into the same category.

Treating people who are afraid of physical injury involves helping them to understand the realities of life and to acknowledge their reality perceptions of danger. Also, we help them assess, differentially, which situations pose real danger of physical injury versus those where they are "over-reacting". In the latter situations, the danger of physical injury is either minimal or absent, but the person is inhibited, counterphobic, or using other unnecessary defences against fears of physical injury which may have arisen in childhood or adolescence. When people's fears of real physical injury are not being faced, we show them their denial, counterphobic mechanisms, minimisation, intellectualisation, and rationalisation—so that they do not get themselves injured, for real.

For "over-reactors", the main thrust of therapy is to find the developmental conflicts that have persisted, causing them to fear physical injury even when such risk does not exist. In those people who possess enough abstraction, integration, reality testing and self-preservation, who can form a relatively trusting relationship with the therapist, who have enough superego functioning to attend appointments, and who possess enough affect tolerance to withstand facing some unpleasant emotions, an insight-directed (psychoanalytic) approach to their fears of physical injury can be very effective in relieving their symptoms. In this approach, we try to find the developmental phases during their childhoods where conflict occurred that left them with a fear of physical injury. The conflicts from the separation-individuation phase of early childhood (ages about one to four), the first genital phase (ages about two to seven), latency (ages about seven to ten), pre-adolescence, and adolescence may all be implicated, or any mixture of those conflicts (Brenner, 1982, 2006). I have referred to conceptualising problems from the various childhood phases (Freud, 1905d) or "planes" of conflict (Blackman, 2012). Usually, I have found it best to stay within one conflict plane when attempting to explain the elements of the conflict to people in treatment.

During the treatment of people who have been physically injured, they often have some fantasy that the therapist will hurt them. When this occurs, showing them how they have been guarding against this fear, and tying it to the developmental phase of their lives when this fear seemed to have become aggravated, can help them de-repress the actual incidents that happened to them (Good, 2005). As they recognise the childhood nature of the conflicts that produce their intense fears of physical injury, their intact reality testing and integrative capacities as adults will help them differentiate those from the actual situations in their current lives, and should relieve their neurotic defensiveness, inhibitions, or counterphobic mechanisms.

In contrast, for those people who show damage to their reality testing, abstraction, and integrative capacities (in other words, those who have psychotic features), we usually try to suppress their anxiety by giving them powerful, neuroleptic medicines. These medications, as of this writing in 2013, all have extremely serious side effects and are only effective, depending on the study (Sadock, Sadock, & Ruiz, 2009) in forty to seventy per cent of cases. Cure is not usually obtainable. Nevertheless, maintenance on these medications may protect their lives as well as the lives of others.

Cultural factors

Greenspan (1994, 1996; Greenspan & Lewis, 1999), in his series of books on latency, clarifies that "playground politics" among boys and girls is considerably different. This seems to be true not only in the US. I have personally also heard about these differences between the genders from people I have taught and treated from India and China. My students from Europe (including Germany and Romania) and from South America (in particular, Argentina) have also confirmed that the different latency experiences of children in those countries are quite parallel to the dissimilar experiences of latency boys and girls in the US.

The role of play

Most boys engage in "rough and tumble play" (Lamb & Oppenheim, 1989), and much like bear cubs, hit and push each other in a somewhat playful way. Nevertheless, most boys learn the "real" danger of the bully, and the need for self-defence of a physical nature at some point during their grade (primary) school years.[17] Card's (1994) award-winning novel, *Ender's Game*, dramatises this difficulty in the development of boys. During Ender's development, which is described from about the age of three to twelve or thirteen, he kills two bullies, inadvertently, while defending himself from attack by them—first on the playground, and later in a washroom.

The need for this type of protective-destructive physical aggression is very often not experienced by girls, especially during the grade school and middle school years. For girls, the fear of physical injury usually comes from their contact with boys. (One tall woman recalled her feeling of absolute paralysis when held down by a somewhat "smaller" boy during middle school. It then dawned on her that she needed to be very careful about the boys to whom she became close.) Most girls' fears centre on the verbal and social viciousness of some other girls who exclude them, as "cliques" are born and change.[18]

Environmental triggers

Interactions between environmental realities and the development of anxiety regarding physical injury may also differ from population to population. For example, I once ran a therapy group for inner city, ghetto-reared, African-American boys with behaviour problems; they were all between the ages of nine and eleven, and I treated them at their school. In one initial meeting, a ten-year-old boy warned me, "You come in the ghetto, and I'll have blood on my knife and shit on my dick!" This expostulation (which caused the other boys to laugh) was frightening enough to me—although he was ten years old and just over four feet tall. Had he been sixteen years old and six feet tall, my fear of physical injury would have been much greater. With him, and with some other boys in the group, I was eventually able to clarify many reasons why they frightened me this way. One was to indicate the degree of fear that they experienced growing up in situations where the terror of rape and murder was an everyday reality.[19] Another factor was their identification with the aggressors who said and actually did such things in the ghetto.

In the United States, the unusual violent massacres by psychotic people in recent years (e.g., Columbine, CO; Newtown, CT; Virginia Tech, Blacksburg, VA) have been viewed by some as a current cultural phenomenon. I disagree. Massacres committed by psychotic individuals have been known throughout history, in other countries and earlier in the US.[20] Tatiana Tarasoff's death at the hands of Prosenjit Poddar at the University of California, Berkeley in 1968 highlighted the real fear of physical violence that we mental health practitioners must anticipate, unfortunately, in dealing with paranoid psychotic people. Under the "Tarasoff Rule", mental health practitioners have, for decades, been required to notify any potential victim that a person in treatment threatens to harm physically. How to deal with such situations legally, morally, and professionally is a topic of constant debate in both mental health and legal circles (Walcott, Cerundolo, & Beck, 2001). The realities of the social environment in any country also may change in any given era. For example, G. William Whitehurst, PhD, a former congressman and professor at Old Dominion University, recently told this story[21]—in turn, told to him by a fellow soldier in the Pacific theatre during World War II. His friend had a friend named Hans, a German who had grown up in Nazi Germany as a child. When Hans was about six or seven years old, he had belonged to the Hitlerjugend and believed in Nazism. Hans felt crushed when the Nazis lost World War II. It was only after that loss, while discussing Nazism with his father, that his father openly opined that Nazism was a horrible business and that he had only allowed his son to be drawn into it to protect everyone's life. Specifically, Hans's father had been an attorney. At a point in 1934, when Hitler, upon gaining power (after Hindenburg's death), immediately banned all Jewish lawyers and judges from entering courts, a Jewish man had approached Hans's father to represent him when the Nazi government demanded he sell property at a tiny fraction of its value. The attorney (who was not Jewish) offered to help. However, a week before the hearing, three SS thugs appeared at his house and insisted he sign a paper indicating that his client agreed to sell the property. At first, the attorney resisted, saying this would not be honest. The SS then told him that if he did not sign it, he would be placed in the black car sitting outside, and his family would never see him again. Under this threat to him and his family, Hans's father signed the paper, but now that the war was over, he admitted to his son he was ashamed of it.

The point is that the fear of real physical injury can be used by any despotic tyrant to force passivity and even some identification with the aggressor (the so-called Stockholm Syndrome) in the victims living in that country. This was quite true not only in Nazi Germany, but in the Soviet Union and its occupied countries during the Cold War.

After World War II, Lifton (1986) interviewed doctors who had cooperated with the Nazis; he felt they had disavowed their primary identity (as healers) as a defence against fear of their own physical injury and death. Anatoly (Natan) Scharansky, an amazing man who risked his life to make the persecution of Jewish people in the Soviet Union known to the world, later theorised that people living under a tyrannical government develop a dual manner of thought (Scharansky & Dermer, 2004). One aspect identifies with the persecutory rulers and obeys their totalitarian, inhumane rules. Once the totalitarian regime falls, and people regain personal freedom, most drop that identification and become conscious of a completely different set of values predicated on autonomy of the individual—which had previously been shut out of consciousness.

A few words on national defence

It is perhaps a sad reality of life that fear of physical injury must be considered, at times, in the service of one's own self-preservation and self-protection. It is for this reason that peaceful countries, like the United States, must maintain a robust military. Throughout history, it is only the fear of physical injury that seems to stop some nations and their leaders from attempting to attack, control, and invade other countries. The recognition that such leaders in other countries exist is not a pleasant one, but since Chamberlain's disastrous experience in Munich in 1938 (Dimbleby, 1938), the danger cannot be denied. Even then, Churchill psychoanalysed Chamberlain's denial (by means of words—A. Freud (1936)), saying, "You were given the choice between war and dishonour. You chose dishonour and you will have war." Since then, of course, if any persons doubt the need to maintain a military to protect ourselves from physical harm, we can remind them about September 11, 2001, when Saudi al-Qaeda terrorists killed almost 3,000 people in New York City.

From a psychoanalytic standpoint, the major problem that I see throughout history seems to be the use of projection, denial, and minimisation on the part of object-related people who possess a solid superego. It is hard for such people to imagine the horrifying destructiveness, sadism, and grandiosity in people like Adolf Hitler, Josef Stalin, Saddam Hussein, and more recently, Mohamed Morsi (Kirkpatrick, 2013), the ayatollahs of Iran (Ledeen, 2007, 2009) and Kim Jong Un (Sanger &

Sang-Hun, 2013). Most normal people, who get angry once in a while, project the image of themselves onto these leaders, and think they are angry because something has happened to them—and thereby do not really face the extreme danger of physical injury such leaders pose.

Summary and conclusion

It turns out that fear of physical injury is a complicated matter. The Zen student and the Zen master were actually both correct. Fear of physical injury includes matters that are perceived by human beings that depend on reality testing, abstraction ability, and capacity for self-preservation. In addition, however, perceptions are affected strongly by inner conflict, some current and conscious, and others somewhat unconscious, but persisting from earlier stages of development.

From a clinical perspective, treatment of psychotic people who are fearful of physical injury due to projections of their own violence (causing delusions of violent conspiracy) involves monitoring, frequent hospitalisation, and the use of powerful medications. In cases where the reality of the danger is miniscule or non-existent but reality testing is adequate and abstraction ability good, insight-directed work can help people understand the contributions to their fears of physical injury from various stages of development where they experienced difficulty. This type of treatment is usually at least ameliorative if not curative. When people are confronted with real physical dangers which they may be denying or minimising, an approach to the defences that are blinding them to the realities of their current situation is usually best.

Notes

1. A *kyosaku*. Kapleau, Tisdale, and Deshimaru (1998).
2. Thanks to Albert P. Koy, MD for first acquainting me with this ritual.
3. US Census Bureau, Statistical Abstract of the United States (2012).
4. Another vast topic. A separate paper (or book), for example, could be written about people who have already experienced physical injury. They may suffer with different types of depressive affect over the loss of function, and those who may have developed post-traumatic stress disorder may be frightened of being re-injured. These situations require differential diagnosis—including but not limited to: simple grief, depression with psychotic features, schizo-affective depressions, *bona*

fide PTSD, conversions symptoms, established pathological mourning (Volkan, 1982), and malingering. For more on this topic, see Blackman (2010).

5. According to Rodgers and Hammerstein (1951), in *The King and I*, Anna supposedly advised her students, the children of the king, to "Whistle a Happy Tune" when afraid. Her actual documentary writings about her experiences in Siam in the early 1860s suggest she was more reality-oriented, circumspect, and became the king's trusted advisor. She also was witness to the brutal torture the king's bureaucrats used to keep the populace "loyal" to him and, from her descriptions, was able to affect these rituals only slightly, and periodically (Leonowens, 1870). Contrary to the musical, she was not present when the king died, but her son later partnered with one of the king's sons to establish the extremely lucrative Louis T. Owens Company.

6. In my opinion, beatings (physical injury) that cause the child's pain and rage to break down his affect regulation, cause a transient psychotic state in the child—an abusive "trauma" (Lansky, 2000) that results in an intensification of shame over the disorganisation so caused. The mind then institutes any number of defensive operations to manage both the shame and the disorganisation.

7. The "macho" cowboy image who can "hold his liquor".

8. The so-called "mother–breast–penis equation" described by Marcus (1971).

9. For readers who are not native US English speakers, this is an idiom that means being passive and sycophantic towards an authority figure. We were able to understand that his kissing up to me was related to the various conflicts that we had understood regarding his mother and father. In other words, when he misbehaved, he was not "kissing up" to anybody, with all the meanings that that had to him.

10. This technique was originally suggested to me by Robert Braswell, MD, when he was a resident, and led to a project and a paper about this teaching technique (Blackman, 1997).

11. Uday Hussein, the son of Saddam Hussein, had maintained a series of "rape rooms" where Uday's military officers would bring unwitting women who had been kidnapped off the streets of Baghdad to be tied down and raped by him (Harrison, 2003).

12. For example, *The Rape of the Sabine Women*. Taken from Plutarch's *Life of Romulus*, the painting by Poussin illustrates the moment when the Romans seized the Sabine women in order to take them for their wives (Guillaume, 2013).

13. Superego functions include: fairness, integrity, reliability, ethics, lawfulness, deals, guilt, honesty, trustworthiness, and shame

(mnemonic: FIRE LIGHTS). These features are somewhat difficult to assess during evaluation, and sometimes requires external data about a person's actual activities (Blackman, 2010).

14. Thanks to Philip Sullivan, MD for this clever neologism.

15. *Warm-ETHICS* is a longer acronym I made up to remind trainees of the clinical manifestations of healthy object relations functions: warmth, empathy, trust, holding environment, identity, closeness, and stability (Blackman, 2003).

16. "… Ted Bundy confessed to killing thirty women in seven states before he was executed by electric chair on January 24, 1989 … He was known as a charming man, who earned the trust of his victims before luring them to a secluded place to murder them. He would also enter the rooms of sleeping college students and bludgeon them to death …" (Epstein, 2012).

17. In spite of elementary school teachers' best efforts, the sneaky bullies will forever attempt to terrorise other boys in their classes—when the teacher is not looking. Although I applaud schools' attempts to limit bullying, over and over I have noticed that most boys still must fend for themselves (physically) at some point during grade school—when the teacher is not looking—to end the bullying. Although I know of no actual deaths due to fights in elementary schools, Card's book deftly characterises the murderous fantasies produced by bullies even in boys of the most pacific nature (like Ender).

18. As so beautifully (and fairly accurately) depicted in the movie, *Mean Girls* (Wiseman & Fey, 2004).

19. For more on this topic, see Meers (1970, 1973–1974).

20. Examples might include Jack the Ripper in London in the late 1880s (Metropolitan Police), and the Unabomber in the US 1978–96 (FBI 100, 2008).

21. Professor Whitehurst presented this material at a public forum entitled: "Lawyers without Rights: Jewish Lawyers in Germany under the Third Reich", a programme created by the German Federal Bar Association. The programme, moderated by Susan R. Blackman, was co-sponsored by the Hampton Roads Chapter of the (US) Federal Bar Association and the Institute of Jewish Studies and Interfaith Understanding at Old Dominion University in Norfolk, VA, where the programme was held on April 17, 2013.

CHAPTER SIX

Fear of success

Andrew Klafter

Psychological conflicts which interfere with confidence and motivation to pursue success in various aspects of life are among the most common emotional difficulties observed in patients who seek psychoanalytic and intensive psychotherapy. The Merriam-Webster and Oxford English dictionaries both define success in two ways: (1) a desired or favourable outcome, and (2) the attainment of wealth, status, fame, and honour, thus reflecting the subjective and personal dimensions of success, as well as the most common external signifiers of success in Western culture.

The subject of this inquiry is to explore the dynamics of "success neurosis", a term coined by Lorand (1950). This term originally referred to a phenomenon, already described by Freud (1916d), of people who respond to their successes with feelings of guilt and intense self-condemnation, and in some cases inflict punishment upon themselves. The term "fear of success" is often credited to M. Horner (1968), an experimental psychologist who pioneered a projective test to study the anxieties of college men and college women provoked by academic success (Griffore, 1977; Miller, 1994). Colman (2009), in his *A Dictionary of Psychology*, reserves the term "fear of success" for individuals who are inhibited from exerting efforts at achievement, and "success neurosis" for individuals who punish themselves in response to actual successes. However, this distinction is idiosyncratic. Other authors use the term "success neurosis" to refer to both phenomena. It is reasonable to assume that any conflict that induces self-punishment upon achieving one's goals may well inhibit the same person from trying to reach them, and indeed some authors note patients suffering from both phenomena (Levy, Seelig, & Inderbitzin, 1995). Therefore, for the purpose of this chapter, "success neurosis" and "fear of success" are interchangeable terms and can refer to any psychological conflict or emotional problem which prevents people from pursuing their goals and ambitions, or enjoying their success in attaining them.

A central question in this chapter is whether psychological conflicts are actually centred around *success* and *achievement*. In other words, is it actually *success* which stirs up unpleasant emotional experiences, and which triggers the defensive responses which pre-empt or spoil one's achievement? Or, do such patients have no unconscious discomfort with success, per se, and experience difficulties only due to the increased responsibilities and pressures which accompany greater academic and professional achievement. A related question is whether "self-sabotage" is a helpful formulation for how we listen psychoanalytically for evidence of unconscious motivations in our self-defeating patients. Do some patients truly possess an underlying wish to damage or spoil the possibility of attaining their life goals? Or, does the psychoanalytic exploration of unconscious fantasies reveal that self-sabotage can be better understood as a way of shielding oneself from failure, humiliation, or some other fantasised, highly unpleasant experience?

To address these questions, this chapter will review Freud's classic paper on success neurosis, as well as subsequent developments in the literature. Then, three clinical cases of patients who pre-empt or sabotage their academic, professional, or social achievements will be presented. Discussion of each patient will focus on the psychoanalytic exploration of unconscious fantasies associated with self-sabotaging behaviours and the use of transference.

Freud's views

Generally speaking, Freud's views on the so-called "success neurosis" are equated with those he enunciated in his 1916 paper subtitled "Those Wrecked by Success". The fact, however, is that Freud returned to this topic a few years later and proposed an additional aetiology of difficulties in tolerating success. In the following passages, I will summarise the two perspectives Freud held on this phenomenon.

Those wrecked by success

In his 1916 paper, Freud describes and formulates three distinct personality disorders: (i) the "exceptions", (ii) those who were "criminal from a sense of guilt", and (iii) "those wrecked by success". Freud portrays this last variety of individuals as suddenly and inexplicably sabotaging their achievements after attaining a goal for which they had strived for many years. This can perhaps be seen as a forerunner to what would later be classified as the "self-defeating personality disorder". Freud offers a very specific psychoanalytic formulation for this symptom: when the goals of certain neurotic patients are unattainable over an extended period of time, these ambitions become associated with unconscious, Oedipal fantasies. Therefore, for these patients, the successful realisation of these goals after a long struggle is experienced as the gratification of forbidden, incestuous, libidinal wishes. The primitive ego (not yet referred to by Freud as "superego") unleashes merciless punishment on the perpetrator in order to prevent the individual from enjoying his or her success. Therefore, individuals who ruin their accomplishments are suffering from unconscious, Oedipal guilt.

Freud's paper, nearly 100 years old, was (to my knowledge) the first attempt in the history of our field to offer psychodynamic formulations for discrete personality disorders. His paper has also become the starting point for all subsequent discussions of fear of success and success neurosis. In light of the magnitude of the paper's influence, it is worthwhile to consider the basis for some of its remarkable claims. From a contemporary vantage point, there are a number of methodological problems with the evidence Freud adduces to support his understanding of the phenomenon of individuals who sabotage their achievements. In addition, the paper's conclusions rest on a number of metapsychological assumptions which Freud himself would later substantially modify with the innovation of his structural theory and the tripartite mental apparatus.

In "Those Wrecked by Success", Freud presents four examples of individuals who have sabotaged their achievements. Two are clinical case illustrations of patients, each consisting of a brief, one paragraph summary, with no presentation of process material or description of the treatment offered. In fact, based on the content of the essay, it is unclear to me whether or not Freud himself treated these two patients, or whether they were described to him by colleagues. The first case is a woman who rebelled against and ran away from her family as a young adult. She moved in with a man who, after a number of years, obtained approval from his family for their relationship, which prompted them to marry. Following their marriage, she "… imagined herself persecuted by his relatives, who in reality wanted to embrace her into their family." She felt "senseless jealousy" and attempted to isolate her husband socially. She later "succumbed to an incurable mental illness". No additional details about this "incurable mental illness" are mentioned. We are all familiar with patients whose disturbed object relations cause them to feel severe distress when anyone else is present in the lives of their lovers and spouses. Based on the information presented in this paper, it is unclear why her story suggests a conflict over success, as opposed to borderline psychopathology and distress over triangulation with her husband and his family of origin. The second case is a male "academic teacher" who, upon his mentor's retirement, was chosen as his successor. Once he learned of this promotion, he "depreciated his merits …" and "… fell into a melancholia which unfitted him for all activity for some years." Freud does not explain whether he eventually recovered from this, or, if so, how he recovered. It is true that the rough outline of this story fits the pattern Freud is seeking to describe. However, we are given no information of the patient's fantasies, his feelings about his mentor, or even the details of his job and what it was he anticipated he would be unable to do successfully in this new role.

The third and fourth cases are literary characters: Shakespeare's (1606) Lady Macbeth, and Ibsen's (1886) Rebecca (from his masterpiece, *Rosmersholm*). I believe it is important to state the obvious: examples from literature may provide helpful illustrations of a clinical theory, but they cannot serve as actual evidence to support it. In fact, Freud admits the following about *Macbeth*:

> What, however, these motives can have been which in so short a space of time could turn the hesitating, ambitious man into an unbridled tyrant, and his steely-hearted instigator into a sick woman gnawed by remorse, it is, in my view, impossible to guess. (1916d, p. 323)

Although a detailed, microscopic critique of Freud's literary analyses of *Macbeth* and *Rosmersholm* is beyond the scope of this chapter, I will explain briefly why I do not find his study of these works to be persuasive in terms of demonstrating an unconscious wish to punish oneself after achieving success. Lady Macbeth's guilt is not pathological, unconscious guilt derived from Oedipal fantasy; it is conscious guilt over the actual murder of the man whom she sought to eliminate in order to clear the way for her husband's ascension to the throne. Lady Macbeth's motives are greed and power, not illicit carnal pleasure. Ibsen's Rebecca is incapable of enjoying her relationship with Rosmer due to her guilt over having manipulated his wife into killing herself. She also has a history of a sexual relationship with her foster father and teacher, who may have actually been her biological father. However, Rebecca's end does not involve self-sabotage of financial, professional, or academic success. Furthermore, her guilt is driven by real (not fantasised) deeds.

Regarding the metapsychological details of Freud's theory of self-sabotage, it is important to remind ourselves of the stage Freud was at in the development of his thinking when he authored this paper. This was still 1916, seven years before Freud would articulate his tripartite model, in which anxiety would serve as a warning signal against dangerous impulses and forbidden wishes. Freud states in the opening paragraph of "Those Wrecked by Success":

> A pathogenic conflict of this kind takes place only when the libido … is deprived of the possibility of an ideal ego-syntonic satisfaction. Hence, privation, frustration of a real satisfaction, is the first condition for the generation of a neurosis, although, indeed, it is far from being the only one. (p. 316)

In other words, neurotic symptoms (at this stage in the evolution of Freud's ideas) are caused by sexual frustration, by the absence of libidinal gratification. In congruence with his early drive theory, Freud then makes it clear that this pattern of self-inflicted punishment occurs only *after* a success has been achieved:

> People occasionally fall ill precisely when a deeply-rooted and long cherished wish has come to fulfilment. … There can be no question that that there is a causal connection between their success and their falling ill. (p. 316)

What is critical for our purposes is that Freud here claims to explain only the type of self-sabotage which is due to guilt triggered *after* success is achieved. He is clear about this. However, patients whose conflicts cause them to avoid the pursuit of success, which all of us see in our practices, and which are probably more typically referred to by the term "fear of success", are not addressed by Freud in this paper. Therefore, the theory of success neurosis articulated in "Those Wrecked by Success" cannot explain their difficulties.

Freud's letter to Ernest Jones, June 4, 1922

Six years after the publication of "Those Wrecked by Success", Freud wrote to Ernest Jones about a challenging psychoanalytic patient that Jones had referred to him. In this letter, Freud presents another case of a patient who suffers from symptoms when she experiences success or praise. In contrast to the case examples in his 1916 paper, Freud here provides a descriptive synopsis of his analytic work with this patient:

> Let us turn to Mrs Riviere. If she were a sheer *intriguante* she would have insisted on her sweetness with me until she had got out of me all she needed. Now she did not. She soon became harsh, unpleasant, critical even with me, tried to provoke me as she had done with you. I made it a rule never to get angry at her. Now I cannot give you the result of our analysis, it is not yet definite nor complete. But one important point soon emerged. She cannot tolerate praise, triumph or success, not any better than failure, blame and repudiation. She gets unhappy in both cases, in the second directly, in the first by reaction. So she has arranged for herself what we call *"eine Zwickmühle"* [a dilemma], ask your wife for the explanation of the term. Whenever she has got a recognition, a favour or a present, she is sure to become unpleasant and aggressive and to lose respect for the analyst. You know what that means, it is an infallible sign of a deep sense of guilt, of a conflict between Ego and Ideal. So the interest in her case is turned to the narcissistic problem, it is a case of a character-analysis superadded to that of the neurosis. To be sure this conflict, which is the cause of her continuous dissatisfaction, is not known to her consciousness; whenever it is revived she projects her self criticism to other people, turns her pangs of conscience into sadistic behavior, tries to render other people unhappy because she

feels so herself. Our theory has not yet mastered the mechanism of these cases. It seems likely that the formation of a high and severe ideal took place with her at a very early age, but this ideal became superseded, "repressed" with the onset of sexual maturity and ever since worked in the dark. Her sexual freedom may be an appearance, the keeping up of which required those conspicuous compensatory attitudes as haughtiness, majestic behavior, etc.

Now I don't know if I will succeed with her better or how far success may go, but for the time being we are getting on quite satisfactorily and analysis is full of interest. I confess to a kind feeling towards her, partly based on her intellectual capacity and practical efficiency. I would not give her a bit of chance if she was not possessed of these highly valuable qualities. But so she is and "active therapeutics" could make use of this fact to initiate the reconciliation of her Ideal to her Ego. A due recognition of her ability, while the treatment conquers her incapacity for her enjoying success, is to her advantage as well as to ours. (Freud, 1922, cited in Paskauskas, 1995, pp. 484–485)

This precious letter reveals several points of great importance to our understanding of Freud's ideas about success neurosis. Unlike the literary or clinical examples in "Those Wrecked by Success", Freud here describes in detail his actual psychoanalytic work with the patient, and it is clear that his understanding of her problems is informed by his direct experience of her conflicts through the transference. It is noteworthy that Freud does not formulate the patient's discomfort with success as Oedipal guilt. Rather, Freud observed the derivatives of unconscious, grandiose fantasies. One manifest derivative of such fantasies was that the patient had set unrealistic and unattainable goals for herself. This made it impossible for her to enjoy any positive accomplishments because they would never fulfil her unreachable ambitions. Freud phrase, "a conflict between Ego and Ideal", refers to a discrepancy between her self-representations and her ego-ideal. In lay terms, this describes the patient's sense (conscious and unconscious, cognitive and affective) that she has failed to become the person she should be, and has failed to achieve what she believes she is capable of accomplishing. Freud here anticipates the definition of "self-esteem" which Edith Jacobson (1964) would later develop. Freud therefore formulates her success neurosis as a symptom of narcissistic character pathology, and not as structural conflict. Freud's suggestion of how to intervene is also significant. The cryptic phrase, "active therapeutics" refers to non-analytic interventions, such as advice, suggestions, and practical guidance. "Active therapeutics" is intended to distinguish such interventions from the abstinence and neutrality which Freud believed should typically characterise psychoanalytic work. In another paper, Freud had already elaborated at length his ambivalent attitude towards "active therapy", which is undoubtedly a thinly veiled reference to the supportive and non-interpretive aspects of Ferenczi's analytic technique (Freud, 1919h). In the case he is discussing in his letter to Jones, Freud asserts that it would be helpful to provide the patient with assistance and guidance in choosing a career or cultivating other activities which would allow her to make use of her considerable talents and intellectual abilities, thus reducing her sense of failure. We therefore see from Freud's letter to Jones that the sweeping generalisations in "Those Wrecked by Success" were not his final thoughts on the subject. In his actual clinical work, he did not apply a standard formulation to all patients suffering from success neurosis. He also felt free to deviate from his standard technique when he believed it was in the patient's best interests. Therefore, in light of this clinical anecdote, it is clear that even Freud himself took the bold claims of "Those Wrecked by Success" with a proverbial grain of salt.

Subsequent psychoanalytic contributions

Ovesey (1963) expanded on the conceptualisation offered by Freud in "Those Wrecked by Success". Ovesey asserts that fear of success is caused by the stifling of a child's assertiveness through pathogenic intimidation of the child by parents or other caregivers. While it is true that such intimidation may occur through Oedipal castration anxiety, Ovesey would suggest that it could just as easily be caused by a frightening or aggressive parenting style. Szekely (1960) emphasised the role of the negative Oedipus complex. He describes in depth a case where a young man's conflicted, unconscious longing for his father and for his father's love have played a substantial role in the development of problems later in life with success and achievement. Along the same lines, though they did not address success neurosis as a specific topic, both Blos and Herzog have greatly expanded our understanding of the key importance of an early, close, loving relationship between son and father for the development of ambition and confidence during adolescence and adulthood.

Kohut's self psychology offered a new paradigm for our understanding of ambition and success in the context of narcissistic personality disorders as well as in healthy patients. In Kohut's model, the development of normal and healthy self-esteem starts with the young child's grandiose needs for love, praise, and adoration, and the parents' or caregivers' capacity to empathically and adequately provide for them. Kohut emphasised that this grandiosity is normal in childhood. Later, the child requires the presence of role models that he or she can admire, and who inspire the development of goals, ambitions, and values. Occasional failures by parents to meet their children's narcissistic needs are inevitable; as long as these deficits are within the child's capacity for coping, such failures actually promote maturation and emotional autonomy. But pervasive and severe neglect of these needs will result in significant narcissistic disorders, which may either inhibit such individuals from seeking to fulfil their ambitions or expressing normal assertiveness, or may lead them to pursue their narcissistic needs frantically and resort to exaggerated grandiosity and exhibitionism. Because professional and academic success has such profound narcissistic meaning, conflicts over academic and professional achievement are hallmarks of patients with narcissistic personality problems.

Levy, Seelig, and Inderbitzin (1995) present the case of a man who engineered serial catastrophes immediately following each milestone in his life, including acceptance to a prestigious graduate programme, new jobs or promotions, and an engagement to be married. In the course of their case presentation, they state that in their judgment, the division of patients into discrete groups of success-avoidance *vs.* success-wrecking is artificial, as patients may suffer from both of these problems along a continuum. They also report their observation that patients who suffer from success neurosis often possess special talents or giftedness. They emphasise the important roles of envy, grandiosity, and exhibitionism for the psychoanalytic treatment of patients with these problems. They observe differences between men and women suffering from fear of success in terms of their family constellations. Gender differences have been described by other authors as well. Ruderman (2006) describes the analytic treatment of two women suffering from fear of success, and suggests that identification by women with the mother's role as a caregiver may impede their assertiveness and ambition. Miller (1994) discusses, from a psychoanalytic perspective, the significance of empirical studies showing differences in fear of success among men and women, and suggests the need for research which can explore specific theoretical, psychoanalytic paradigms.

Kavaler-Adler (2006) describes vividly, in-depth, and from a contemporary object relations perspective, the lengthy analysis of a woman with profound inhibitions in her pursuit of professional success. Important points from Kavaler-Adler's work include the inadequacy of Oedipal guilt as an explanation of her patient's inhibitions, the importance of recognising that the paranoid-schizoid position involves a distinct set of unconscious fantasies, introjections (in this case of the patient's mother) of an internal saboteur, and the necessity of the analyst's ability to recognise and tolerate idealising and merger fantasies in the transference.

Finally, a unique perspective is offered by Holmes (2006), who observes that previous literature on success neurosis has failed to acknowledge the profound role of race and socio-economic class in most societies on the development of self-esteem, confidence, and ambition. In addition to being at a relative disadvantage in terms of education, political power, and social connections, ethnic minorities and the economically and politically disenfranchised are bombarded with constant messages of being undeserving of, unfit for, or incapable of professional and academic success. These messages created an additional form of success neurosis for minorities and the underprivileged. Holmes argues that analysts are insufficiently trained in the identification of racism and classism as powerful factors in personality formation, and further suggests that until our professional analytic associations and institutes embrace diversity as an explicit, concrete goal, our lapses as analysts over issues of race and class will continue.

Non-analytic approaches

It is worth noting that "fear of success" has been studied by non-analysts as well. A perusal of titles in the self-help section of any major bookstore will reveal that "fear of success" is a significant industry. Pop-psychology terms for patients with such problems include "Peter Pan syndrome", "the imposter syndrome", "self-sabotage", and "compulsive procrastination". Experimental psychologists have developed numerous valid and reliable psychometric tests to measure fear of success (Griffore, 1977). Non-analysts who have written from a theoretical and clinical perspective on fear of success include some of the most innovative and influential writers in academic and cognitive psychology. K. Lewin, in 1935, proposed his theory of "approach–avoidance conflict". According to this paradigm, he suggests that all goals in life have both positive and negative experiences associated with them, and human beings are therefore inherently ambivalent about all goal-directed behaviours. As individuals approach their goals, negative experiences can begin to outweigh the positive experiences, leading them to display avoidant behaviours towards the very goals they wish to pursue.

Maslow, in 1971, employed the phrase, "the Jonah complex", to describe individuals who are unable to pursue their ambitions. Just as the biblical Jonah attempted in vain to flee his destiny as God's prophet, patients suffering from this syndrome attempt to evade their own potential for achievement and success. Maslow's description includes "fear of one's own greatness", "running away from one's own best talents", and "evasion of one's destiny". Maslow characterises his perspective as "non-Freudian", and asserts that there is an inherent fear of self-actualisation: "... We fear our best as well as our worst, even though in different ways" (p. 35). As evidence for this formulation, he cites the discomfort that people feel when consciously acknowledging their grandiose fantasies. I would suggest that Maslow's observations are good evidence for conflicts involving shame and narcissistic vulnerability, and that they are better explained by the insights of Kohut's self-psychology than by what Maslow believes is an actual fear of self-actualisation inherent in the human being. The cognitive therapist, Burns (1980), in his highly influential book, Feeling Good, lists "fear of success" among what he believes are the thirteen causes of "pathological procrastination". He does not propose any explanation of underlying dynamics, but he recommends that when treating individuals who suffer from procrastination, clinicians consider that one potential aetiology may be an avoidance of anxiety-provoking or otherwise unpleasant aspects of success.

I will mention a final example from the Jungian literature: Steinberg (1987) has written on fear of success from the perspective of Jung's depth psychology. He proposes the Jungian concept of an independent drive for regression (which is reminiscent and perhaps derivative of Freud's death instinct). This drive manifests itself as a wish to avoid any psychological progress or personal success. Interestingly, Steinberg outlines a therapeutic approach which includes the necessity for the therapist to process the countertransference feelings aroused by patients who regress during treatment due to a fear of psychotherapeutic progress.

Clinical illustrations

Having reviewed the psychoanalytic and non-psychoanalytic perspectives on emotional difficulties caused by success in some people, I am now prepared to offer three detailed clinical vignettes. While similar in some ways, each of these cases highlights a slightly different dynamic constellation and, therefore, a slightly different technical approach.

The case of Charlie

Charlie has been in psychoanalytic treatment for eight years. He first came for treatment because his life was at a standstill. He had already developed a pattern of "dropping the ball" at critical moments in his life, just prior to accomplishing important goals. For example, shortly before starting his analytic treatment, he had completed all the coursework required to attain a master's in English. He completed a draft of his dissertation, but never proofread it or submitted it for graduation. In the meantime, his thesis advisor has retired and moved out of state, and Charlie assumes that he will never be able to attain this degree. After a period of about three years of unemployment and inactivity in pursuing any goals, he enrolled in another graduate programme for a master's in education. I saw this as a sign of progress in his psychoanalytic work. He thrived academically, and felt like he had finally discovered his calling. He completed his thesis and succeeded in obtaining his degree, but then he procrastinated completing the paperwork required to obtain a teaching licence for over two years. He has done similar things with jobs. He was recently offered a good job in a local school district, but failed to complete a required background check and therefore lost the position because he could not start on time. When asked to describe his subjective sense of what happens when he fails to complete these tasks, he says, "I just can't imagine that anyone would want to hire me. I mean, I wouldn't recommend hiring me!" In situations where he is already hired, he imagines that they will discover how ineffective and unreliable he is, and that they will regret having hired him in the first place.

Charlie is the son of two highly accomplished academics. When Charlie was three years old, his mother completed her doctoral dissertation and took an academic position. The plan was that until his father completed his PhD, he would stay at the university during the week and join Charlie and his mother at weekends. He remembers his mother converting a room in their new house into an office for his father, with built-in bookshelves and an oak desk. But Charlie's father hardly ever came to see them, even at weekends. Charlie resented the fact that his mother persisted in trying to make the relationship work. "I was fine with not having a dad, but she wouldn't accept that he wanted nothing to do with us. It was like she kept dangling him in front of me."

His parents finally divorced with he was seven years old. Charlie and his father had infrequent visits for the next few years. He was a chubby boy, and his father implored him to eat differently and to exercise more. In addition to sensing his father's disappointment in his body and lack of athletic prowess, Charlie also felt that his father dreaded spending time with him. As he reached the age of ten, his father planned an extravagant, month-long sailing trip in the Pacific Ocean. Charlie was led to believe that he would be responsible as a member of the crew to steer the ship. He was terrified of being away from home for so long, and imagined making a catastrophic mistake which would jeopardise the safety of everyone aboard the ship. On the other hand, he feared that if he did not go on the trip his father would think he was a coward. At the airport, just before his flight, he had "a total mental breakdown", and his mother had to bring him back home. Charlie's father never invited him for another visit. "I felt like I had let him down so badly that he was just disgusted with me." To avoid the pain of this rejection, Charlie adopted the position, "I don't care about my dad, he's a jerk anyway." Over the next several years, he rejected all paternal figures in his life. He remembers when he was on a little league baseball team, his coach noted that there was no father in his life who could play catch with him, and offered to spend extra time helping Charlie outside scheduled practice. Charlie was deeply insulted by this suggestion. "I didn't want a charity dad." In fact "charity dad" has become an emblematic phrase in his analysis, which refers to his feelings of being patronised and belittled by any male role model who shows interest in him. He rebelled in middle school, was bullied and ostracised, and got into numerous fights. He was caught shoplifting, and started smoking marijuana on a daily basis. At the age of sixten, Charlie embarked on an intense exercise regimen and an extreme diet. It is not clear what might have triggered this. After losing forty pounds, he called his father and told him that he had got into shape. "During that phone call, I felt so lame and pathetic, trying to get the attention of a dad who wanted nothing to do with me." Charlie became so uncomfortable that he abruptly ended the phone call, and they have not spoken since.

Charlie's relationship with his mother is also complex. His mother never dated after the divorce. "She confided in me like I was an adult. She actually asked me for advice with what to do about problems at work, or about issues with my grandmother." He and his mother slept in the same bed until he was twelve years old, at which time he was humiliated by his mother's awareness that he was sexually aroused. Charlie then moved into the basement, which was set up like an independent apartment. He characterises his mother as very indulgent, catering to all his needs and whims, and never making any demands on him. He is grateful for her devotion, but feels infantilised by her. "I wonder if my mom had been more of a hard-ass and put some pressure on me whether I would be more accomplished."

Charlie fears that I am losing patience with him, and that he will be "fired" as an analysand if he does not make some progress. He correctly senses that I do, indeed, feel frustrated when he stops just short of a success and retreats to inactivity. "It's gotta be hard for you to just sit there, watching me shoot myself in the foot, over and over again." Charlie has recently become aware of how desperately he wants me to respect him, and feels that there is something horribly wrong with him for having such feelings towards me.

"There is nothing more pathetic to me than the idea of me wanting you to be proud of me. My worst fear is that I'm getting my teaching license just to make you happy, and not because I care about getting a job. I think that this is why I have been procrastinating doing it. I don't want to be doing this for *you*."

This closely parallels his feelings about his father. He had successfully convinced himself that he wanted absolutely nothing to do with his father. But, through discussing his transference feelings, he has also become aware of the following fantasy about his father:

"I get a job, lose weight, get married, start a family, and then I take
a road trip with my wife and kids to meet my dad. He says, 'Man,
I'm truly sorry that I let my personal, psychological problems interfere with our ability to have a father-son relationship, but I'd sure
love to get to know you now.' And then I guess I have some sort of
normal relationship with him."

Charlie is deeply ashamed of this fantasy, which he now realises has
been on his mind every day since he was an adolescent. Striving for
success and achievement, to Charlie, feels like losing weight in order
to make his father proud of him. Conversely, "When I don't care about
working or about anything, it's like I'm going on strike. I'm refusing to
try to impress him." From a self-psychological perspective, we see that
Charlie's conflicts over his longing for his father have contributed to the
stifling of the development of his idealised parent imago (i.e., his ability
to imagine himself as a powerful, mature, productive, admirable man).
While it is true that Charlie's relationship with his mother involves
many feelings which provoke Oedipal conflicts, our work thus far has
not revealed that these issues are a significant factor in his avoidance
of success and achievement. Rather, the psychoanalytic exploration of
the fantasies associated with Charlie's fear of success centre around his
father. Specifically, disavowal of his wishes for his father's pride and
encouragement lead him to sabotage efforts to accomplish academic
achievement and professional success.

The case of Melanie

Melanie, now fifty, began her psychoanalytic treatment five years ago.
She presented with depression and insomnia, conflicts in her marriage,
and a fear that her daughter-in-law hates her. Her son had married
into a prominent family and Melanie found her in-laws intimidating,
snobby, and condescending. Her daughter-in-law had recently over-
heard Melanie make disparaging remarks about them, and subsequently began acting distantly towards her. Like Melanie, her husband
grew up in humble circumstances. But he became a highly successful
real estate developer, and they are now wealthy. They socialise with
many affluent and powerful people. While Melanie's husband enjoyed
their new wealth and their new friends, she felt increasingly uncomfortable in her own skin. She said, "Since my husband starting doing

so well, I'm actually miserable. I don't like hanging out with people who are *above my level*." When asked what "above my level" means, she responded, "Oh, you know, rich and famous people who think they are better than me, or think I have no taste or no class, or something like that." She worried about whether her clothing was stylish enough. She obsessed over whether her jewelry was "classy enough" or whether she looked like she was "trying too hard" or "showing off". She felt jealous about attention during conversations, and even measured the amount of laughter she received in response to her jokes in comparison with others present. She said, "It's like I'm back in high school, at a party with all of the super-popular kids, and none of them want me there." She dreaded dinner parties, and avoided having neighbours over as guests in their home. Her husband felt increasingly awkward about her conspicuous absences from social events, and the fact they never reciprocated invitations.

Melanie was the oldest of five children. She describes her mother as "... easygoing and affectionate, but simple and had no idea how to be a mother or how to run a house." Her father was a hard-working man who was profoundly ashamed of their poverty. "It was weird. He hated rich people for looking down on him, but I think he actually believed he was low class and less of a person." He had a volatile temper, and demanded total obedience from his wife and children. She recalled being invited to the home of a girl she met at school. Her father screamed at her mother for allowing Melanie to befriend the daughter of a wealthy doctor. "My mother did whatever he told her to. It felt like my dad was trying to protect me from something dangerous that my mother had overlooked because she didn't understand how things worked."

As Melanie grew older, her relationship with her father grew darker. She came to realise that he was racist and sexist. He became increasingly controlling. He called Melanie "fat" as she developed breasts and an adult figure, and accused her of being a slut when, in fact, she had never been on a date or kissed a boy. When Melanie was a junior in high school, she signed up to take the SAT examination. Her father told her she was not permitted to attend college and that if she did so, she'd be disowned from the family for this highly selfish act. This was one of their last conversations, as he died of a sudden heart attack when she was sixteen years old. Melanie became responsible for the care of her four younger siblings. She immediately realised that her mother was incapable of balancing a chequebook, paying bills, organising a schedule, or even cooking and cleaning in a reliable way. (She has since come to the conclusion that her mother probably suffered from a form of mild mental retardation.) Melanie was given a full-time job in the store that her father managed before he passed away, and she fulfilled her work hours at weekends and after school. Her income, along with some financial support from her father, sustained the family.

When she began her analysis, she was unable to say a critical word about her father. She felt horribly guilty narrating stories about her father's bizarre obsessions with her weight and odd behaviours, some of which were truly abusive. Because her siblings were significantly younger when their father died, they never developed a realistic, adult appraisal of his personality. The idealisation of her father by her entire family contributed to Melanie's inability to acknowledge her anger and hatred. She revealed that she had always felt like her disdain for him somehow caused his death. She has felt particularly culpable for the thought that her life is better because he died, and that only because of his death was she was able to obtain a college education and have her own career as a paralegal. Countless analytic sessions have involved Melanie's recovery of repressed memories of his bizarre obsessions and her adult reflections on how damaging he was to her. Examples include weighing her before each meal, interrogating her on who she spoke with at school, forcing her to recount her whereabouts after school, etc.

Another major aspect of our work has been to explore her fantasies about rich, powerful, upper class socialites who laugh at her clothing, mock her unrefined speech, and consider her to be "an insignificant hill-billy". She notes that this is how her father made her feel about herself. He scrutinised her body, her posture, her motives, and her feelings. "It seems like he really wanted to make sure I was never proud of myself, and I think to a large extent he succeeded." Working through all of this in her analysis, Melanie has developed the following theory: "He took everything he was ashamed of about himself, imagined that rich people felt that way about him, and made me feel that way about myself."

A significant moment was when Melanie noticed that I added a teaching award from the university to the wall where I display my licence, medical degree, and training certificate. She expressed her amazement that I could openly display awards. "This tells me that you are proud of these awards and that you need things like this to feel better about yourself." This was a startling revelation for her. She had previously imagined me as a "... someone naturally happy with who you are, who doesn't need any external validation, and who doesn't need to show off in front of others." This revealed to her a cocky, exhibitionist, prideful streak in me. "Dr Klafter, you are the kind of person my father would have never let me be friends with. He would have hated you, and he would have been afraid of you." Melanie has largely resolved most of the difficulties she was suffering from prior to her analytic treatment. She has become much more attuned to other people's feelings and experiences. She sees that human beings, including the wealthy and powerful, are also struggling with challenges and are also full of insecurities.

The case of Katherine

Katherine is a forty-six-year-old woman who presented for treatment, stating, "My life is a mess, it's all my fault, and I have no idea what to do now." The precipitating event is that she impulsively quit her job just a few weeks after being hired, and immediately afterwards horribly regretted it. After years of underemployment, in positions which pay far below what would be commensurate with her graduate nursing degree, she was offered a full-time job as a director of nursing at a small community hospital. "This was the first time in my life that I had ever had a reliable paycheck. I could finally afford a new car, house repairs, and braces for my daughter." But she became suspicious about the motives of the hospital administration. "Why would they hire *me* as an administrator when I had only been working as a part-time nurse?" She suspected some ulterior motive. She imagined they must be paying her below the typical salary for this position. Or perhaps they were keeping her in this job only as a placeholder, and that they would soon fire her after hiring someone with a more impressive résumé. She had panic attacks at work, and felt uncomfortable around others in the hospital. She skipped meetings. "I became convinced they were going pull the rug out from under me." One Friday evening, she packed up all her things, cleared out her office, and simply did not return. She did not respond to their phone calls, or even open the certified letters she received from the hospital. She resumed working for the agency which placed her in temporary positions. It provides less reliable income and involves an irregular schedule which is a hardship for her teenage children. It is also a logistical problem which makes it difficult for us to deepen her therapy and convert to analysis, which I believe is the treatment of choice for her problems.

Katherine's life history is essential in understanding this episode of professional self-sabotage. She grew up in a chaotic home with a psychotic mother and a series of men invited by the mother into their home, one of whom physically and sexually assaulted her. Among other horrors, her little sister suffered a nearly lethal head injury as an infant by the hand of the same man, and is moderately mentally retarded as a result. At the age of six or seven, Katherine was removed by Child Protective Services and sent to her grandparents' home where she enjoyed a several month reprieve from her torment, until her mother persuaded the court to restore custody. "As soon as I let myself imagine that I was safe with my grandparents, it all went to hell." This pattern repeated itself several times over the course of her childhood and adolescence. Her mother's chaotic behaviour would attract the attention of the police, she would be placed in a loving and stable foster home of relatives or neighbours, but her mother would eventually persuade the court system to allow her to return.

Katherine's stellar academic performance earned her a scholarship to a private Catholic school. She impersonated her mother by telephone and forged her enrolment documentation. She worked as a waitress every evening to avoid going home and also to pay the small portion of school tuition for which she was responsible. A teacher at school caught on to her situation, and personally hired an attorney on Katherine's behalf. The court permanently severed all custodial rights and granted Katherine status as an emancipated minor. She was given a room in the dormitory where the nuns affiliated with the school's religious order resided. Katherine reacted to all this by transforming from a dutiful, model student into a disruptive rebel. She started smoking on school property, defied the dress code, brought boys into her room, and became a class clown. After a year or so of this behaviour, she was expelled from the school. (She was allowed by the nuns to stay in the same dormitory, and graduated from a public high school. She is still included in the school's alumni reunions and has maintained relationships with some of the teachers and nuns.)

She shared a fantasy, which she has always felt was a living reality:

> "There are people spying on me, waiting for me to think that I'm in the clear and that things are good, and then they will kidnap me, rape me, and murder my sister or my children. I say to myself: 'These people are going to take everything away from me anyway. Don't get too comfortable. Don't give them the satisfaction.'"

She can see these people, and they are a ghoulish cartoon of her mother and stepfather. In the transference, Katherine is frightened by her long-ing for reliable nurturing. She experiences my empathic communica-tions as "the food I have been starving for all my life", but quickly becomes angry at me and feels like I am manipulating her for financial or perhaps sexual exploitation. We are able to talk about this, and she sees that the way she feels towards me is very reminiscent of what she has done in friendships, romantic relationships, her career, and all other positive developments in her life. When she is treated kindly or respect-fully, it feels like she is reliving her time with her grandparents, "which they took away from me and sent me back to hell". She has come to see her sabotaging behaviours as a pre-emptive protection against what she feels is an inevitable crash. While it is true that Katherine's self-sabotage resembles the pattern described by Freud in "Those Wrecked by Success", the themes emerging in Katherine's analytic therapy do not reveal a wish to punish herself for an Oedipal victory. Rather, they reveal that she continues to long for a mother and father who will pro-tect her. This triggers a need to protect herself from the violence and deprivation which, in her unconscious fantasies, invariably follow any attempt to receive nurture and support.

Concluding remarks

Freud's observation that some individuals, upon the achievement of a desirable goal, destroy their success rather than enjoy it has stood the test of time. Later authors noted that another manifestation of the same problem is that some individuals sabotage themselves in a pre-emptive manner so that their goals are never realised in the first place. At the time Freud first wrote about this phenomenon, his model of the human psyche was at an early stage of incubation, as he still subscribed to the theory of the drive which posited that neurosis was caused by a lack of sexual gratification. Therefore, in composing "Those Wrecked by Success", Freud had a limited theoretical toolbox to for-mulate an understanding of this phenomenon. By 1922, as his letter to Jones attests, Freud was free to formulate the same superficial symptom presentation according a totally different model of psychopathology, as well as to deviate from his standard psychoanalytic technique accord-ing to his clinical intuition and judgment. As psychoanalytic thought has expanded over the decades, clinicians have a broader and deeper array of theoretical perspectives and clinical tools at their disposal to understand challenging clinical phenomena. Therefore, subsequent treatments of fear of success in the psychoanalytic literature reflect the developments of self-psychology, contemporary object relations, and sensitivity to the impact of race and class.

The clinical cases presented in this chapter reflect various dimensions of success neurosis. Charlie avoids efforts at success, or sabotages his progress at the last minute. Melanie feels uncomfortable with the new people in her life since she and her husband have become wealthy. Katherine ruins things once they start going well for her. What all these patients have in common is that they avoid progress or sabotage success when it stirs up unpleasant affects which can be traced to the derivatives of unconscious fantasies. Charlie feels alone, abandoned, and rejected in response to fantasies about earning the love and respect of his father. Szekely's emphasis on disavowal of negative Oedipal longings as well Kohut's conception of the ambitions and the idealised parent imago are extremely helpful in conceptualising Charlie's difficulties. Melanie feels guilty for betraying her father, and devalued by her father's abusive criticism when she embraces a life of wealth and status. Her problems are reminiscent of Kavaler-Adler's patient, whose problems she explained on the basis of dyadic object relations and introjections of a parental saboteur. Class and gender are certainly central to Melanie's success neurosis as well. Katherine experiences the fantasy of demonic parents who deliberately torment her by destroying anything good or hopeful. She thus feels a sense of panic and impending doom when things finally turn around for the better.

We do not assume that diverse patients suffer from the same conflict and dynamics just because their symptoms resemble one another superficially. For example, two patients with very different life histories, living in different cultures, with very different personality styles, might both experience shyness with the opposite sex and be unable to flirt. The same is true of success neurosis. There is no single personality structure, attachment style, relational pattern, or any other psychoanalytic designation which has a monopoly on fear of success and achievement. Rather, this phenomenon should be thought of as a relatively common syndrome affecting patients with a diverse range of psychopathologies. The treatment of patients with difficulties pursuing their personal, academic, and professional ambitions must therefore be highly individualised. If there is one generalisation which can be made about this group of patients, it is that they are protecting themselves from the frightening derivatives of unconscious fantasies involving horrible consequences for successful realisation of their goals and ambitions. For each of the patients discussed in this chapter, exploration of the transference was a key element which enabled these fantasies to be elaborated and analysed.

This group of patients suffers from the failure to achieve their potential for satisfaction and success in multiple domains of life. Their stories, over time, involve lost jobs, missed opportunities, and squandered relationships. Therefore, the potential for devastating, lifelong problems in patients who repeatedly sabotage their efforts at achievement cannot be overestimated. With such high stakes on the table, in the face of complex and formidable problems, psychoanalysis should be offered as the first-line treatment of choice whenever possible.

CHAPTER SEVEN

Fear of death

Calvin A. Colarusso

D eath and the fear of death are universal experiences. However, the degree to which any human being, man, woman, or child fears death, and the content of their fears, is highly individual. Further, in a brief article, or in a series of articles for that matter, the infinite variety of experience cannot be approached in any significant way. In this contribution, I provide examples from professional literature, my clinical experience, and literature and film to demonstrate a few ways in which individuals express and deal with this daunting developmental task. I begin, however, with a brief review of what Freud had to say about this matter.

Freud's ideas on the fear of death

Freud (1926d) related the fear of death to the following fears that occur in the course of development during the oral, anal, Oedipal, and latency phases: loss of the object, loss of the object's love, castration, and fear of the superego. The following quote describes the relationship between these early experiences and the fear of death, particularly the effect of the superego.

> The progress which the child makes in its development—its growing independence, the sharper division of its mental apparatus into several agencies, the advent of new needs—cannot fail to exert an influence upon the content of the danger-situation. We have already traced the change of that content from loss of the mother as an object to castration. The next change is caused by the power of the super-ego. With the depersonalization of the parental agency from which castration was feared, the danger becomes less defined. Castration anxiety develops into moral anxiety—social anxiety—and it is not so easy now to know what the anxiety is about. The formula, "separation and expulsion from the horde", only applies to that later portion of the super-ego which has been formed on the basis of social prototypes, not to the nucleus of the super-ego, which corresponds to the introjected parental agency. Putting it more generally, what the ego regards as the danger and responds to with an anxiety-signal is that the super-ego should be angry with it or punish it or cease to love it. *The final transformation which the fear of the super-ego undergoes is, it seems to me, the fear of death (or fear for life) which is a fear of the super-ego projected on to the powers of destiny.* (p. 140, italics mine)

In his paper, "On Transience" (1916a), written during the First World War when death was in the air, Freud was fifty-nine years old and his thoughts were drawn to the idea of loss and impermanence. He described a poet friend's fear of death that interfered with his ability to enjoy the beauty to be found in life.

> The poet admired the beauty of the scene around us but felt no joy in it. He was disturbed by the thought that all this beauty was fated to extinction, that it would vanish when winter came, like all human beauty and all the beauty and splendor that men have created or may create. All that he would otherwise have loved and admired seemed to him to be shorn of its worth by the transience which was its doom. (p. 305)

This eloquent statement contains the essence of the adult struggle with the developmental task of accepting the notion of a personal end. Indeed, there is little in our conscious or unconscious life that does not struggle with the fear of death. In his paper "The Uncanny" (1919h), Freud comments on this universal human struggle.

Two things account for our conservatism: the strength of our original emotional reaction to death and the insufficiency of our scientific knowledge about it. Biology has not yet been able to decide whether death is the inevitable fate of every living being or whether it is only a regular but yet perhaps avoidable event in life. No human being really grasps it [the idea that all men are mortal], and our unconscious has as little use now as it ever had for the idea of its own mortality. (pp. 242–243)

It is interesting to note that Freud, himself, in this statement expresses the wish that somehow science would one day make eternal life a reality, that he, and we, would live forever and no longer need to fear death.

A developmental line of death awareness

We need a baseline before considering the very complex subject of fear of death, a developmental line of death awareness throughout the life cycle. This normative, universal experience in most respects, will allow us to contrast normal and pathologic fears of death.

Early childhood

While infantile annihilation anxiety, called "psychotic anxiety" by Klein (1932) and "unthinkable anxiety" by Winnicott (1962) might, retrospectively, impart a convincing flavour to anxiety about death, such ideational content is not present at its roots. In fact, even through the Oedipal phase, and for many children, through latency, due to cognitive immaturity (Piaget, 1969) there is no conceptualisation of death as final, the end of human existence. For young children who are confronted by the experience of losing a loved one, the person has gone away or is somewhere else, in heaven, for instance (Colarusso, 1975). Sociologist Slater (1964) relates the fear of death to the emergence of separation and individuation.

Fear of death is not at all primitive, elemental or basic. Animals have no such fear, nor do small children. It depends upon the rather advanced and sophisticated awareness of the self as a separate entity, altogether detached from the natural and social environment. For the individual who feels blended with the world and his society, his own death has little meaning. It is only when he comes to view himself as a unique differentiated entity, with an existence which is separable and apart from other men and objects, that he can begin to have anxiety about the termination of that existence. (p. 19)

While this seems true, it is also true that exposure to actual death (usually of older relatives) during childhood can precipitate a premature form of death anxiety, however "unmentalised" it remains at this stage. Take a look at the following brief vignettes.

Clinical vignette: 1

Dave was five years old when his grandfather died. He was taken to a funeral home where his dead grandfather was lying on a bed dressed in pajamas, as though he was asleep. Dave and the other family members repeatedly kissed and hugged the body. After attending an open casket funeral, Dave's grandmother asked if he could stay with her, sleep in her bed, and provide comfort during the acute phase of mourning. When Dave returned to school, his teachers described him as being in a daze. He remained in that daze for many months, fell far behind his peers academically, and never fully recovered emotionally from the traumatic experience. His alcoholism, which began in his teens, could be partly attributed to this very early trauma and his premature death.

Clinical vignette: 2

I had the following experience when I served as a consultant to a Pennsylvania school system (Colarusso, 1975). I was asked to consult with a first grade teacher because the mother of one of her students had died after a long illness. In the months preceding her death, mother had been hospitalised several times. Somewhat used to her absence, Johnny seemed to completely ignore the explanation when told that his mother had died. He cried, and had difficulty sleeping but kept insisting that mother was still in the hospital. When Johnny began berating his father for not visiting mother, the distraught father turned to the school for help, and the school asked for advice on how to handle the situation. Further, the teacher, in her twenties, and the students were also reacting.

As described earlier in this paper, six year olds are not cognitively capable of understanding the finality of death. Dead means being alive somewhere else. In addition to his cognitive inability to understand, Johnny needed his mother. At school, Johnny regressed. Usually outgoing and aggressive, Johnny was easily hurt. He cried frequently and sought special attention, occasionally calling his teacher "mother". The other students reacted, hence the question, "Johnny, did your mother die?" The students asked questions such as "If my mother died, who would take care of me?" Some had difficulty separating from their mothers in the morning. Others sucked their thumbs. Since children express themselves through play, it was not surprising that death became a prominent theme on the playground. A number of students, including Johnny, played "dead". Johnny's confusion and fear were further complicated by a well-meaning family member telling Johnny that his mom was in heaven looking down on him and wanted him to be a good boy. She would always be watching him. This explanation fit his cognitive sense that mother did exist, but for some reason that he could not understand, had decided to leave him. For months Johnny would lay awake at night waiting for his mother to appear. During the day he repeatedly said that he had to be good because his mother was watching him.

While Dave's anguish remained rather "unmentalised", Johnny's concerns were quite intellectually explicit. The reasons for this difference, though unclear, might lie in (i) Johnny being one year older at the time of encountering a death, (ii) Johnny's not being exposed to the open-casket funeral—which could be shocking for a young child, and (iii) Johnny's anticipating ego-preparation for the loss since his mother died after a protracted illness and several hospitalisations.

Adolescence

The cognitive ability to understand the finality of death is present in adolescence but the forward thrust of physical and sexual maturation promotes an internal emphasis on beginnings, not endings, and certainly not a final and irrevocable end. In late adolescence, a clearer sense of the three time modes—past, present, and future—emerges with the realisation that an entire phase of life, childhood and adolescence is in the past and irretrievably lost. Thus, the idea of a personal history that cannot be relived contains the seed of realisation that the self is not safe from a similar fate (Colarusso, 1988). But this dawning realisation is quickly defended against by the false sense of immortality that characterises the risk-taking behaviour of late adolescence and young adulthood. I can picture a young man on a motorcycle going close to 100 miles per hour as he weaves in and out of bumper to bumper lanes of traffic on a crowded freeway (motorway). I've served as an expert witness in many cases of personal injury and seen youths with severe brain damage and amputated limbs. A more sober awareness of the reality of death awaits the passage of time and the aging process in the body which becomes obvious in many in their thirties and certainly in their forties.

Fear of death is not a usual adolescent or young adult experience, but life events often induce fear of death. The increasing frailty and passing away of grandparents especially stirs up such anxiety. The death of peers in road accidents or through excessive drinking is another common trigger for death anxiety during adolescence. Less common, but thrust into public awareness, are suicides and mass shootings of children in schools—the most recent being the mass murder of kindergarten children and teachers at the Sandy Hook Elementary School in Connecticut. Then, certainly, there is war; in contemporary America, two wars in recent years to be exact. The teenagers and young adult men and women who are in combat certainly deal with fears of disfigurement and death. The presence of the World Wide Web and instant communication forces adolescents at home to confront death, and develop fears, with infinitely greater frequency and intensity than ever before.

Midlife

In his classic article, "Death and the Midlife Crisis", Jacques (1965) writes about the need to deny "the two fundamental features of human life—the inevitability of eventual death, and the existence of hate and destructive pessimism" (p. 504). With childhood and youth behind them normal midlife adults are forced to confront the certainty of death as the defences against the acceptance of time limitation and personal death crumble.

In 1979, Nemiroff and I described seven basic hypotheses about the nature of development in adulthood. The seventh one describes the following developmental task: "A central, phase-specific theme of adult development is the normative crisis precipitated by the recognition and acceptance of the finiteness of time and the inevitability of personal death" (Colarusso & Nemiroff, 1979, p. 75). The youthful avoidance of thinking about personal death is impotent before the power of new physical, psychological, and environmental experiences. Stimulated by the aging process in the body, the death of parents and contemporaries, the growth of children into adulthood, grandparenthood, and the approach of retirement, everyone, consciously and unconsciously, face his or her mortality and struggles to accept the painful, unavoidable recognition that the future is limited. They, like their parents and all mankind before and after them, will die and leave behind all that is known and loved.

Engagement of this developmental task has rich emotional rewards. Lifton (1979) powerfully described the growth promoting effect of this recognition on midlife development.

> There is a special quality of life-power available only to those seasoned by struggles of four or more decades. That seasoning includes extensive cultivation of images and forms having to do with love and caring, with teaching and mentorship, with work combinations and professional creativity, with responses to intellectual and artistic images around one, and above all with humor and a sense of the absurd. The seasoned psychic forms are by no means devoid of death imagery. Rather they are characterized by ingenious combinations of death equivalents and immediate affirmations, or melancholic recognition of the fragmentation and threat surrounding all ultimate involvements, along with dogged insistence upon one's own connections beyond the self—one's own relationships to collective modes of symbolic immortality. Like the despair, the life-power of this stage can be especially profound. (p. 5)

Thus, while we will discuss pathological fears of death later in this article, Lipton is describing how an integration of the realisation of a personal end can stimulate a deeper awareness of the human condition and increase the joy of experiencing all that life has to offer. When the acceptance of time limitation and personal death is integrated, the acceptance of death as a natural consequence of aging occurs without shattering the continuity of the intrapsychically perceived life cycle or the integrity of the ego. According to Lieberman and Tobin (1983), in late adulthood, time is measured in distance from death rather than time lived or time left to live. In late adulthood, it is not the inevitability of death that is the issue but rather the timing of death. To quote Neugarten (1979),

> Even death is a normal and expectable event for the old. Death is tragic only when it occurs at too young an age. Even the death of one's spouse, if it occurs on time, does not create a psychiatric crisis for most men or women. (p. 889)

Erikson (1963) suggested that death can be greeted with a sense of equanimity if life has been long and fulfilling and a meaningful quality of life can no longer be maintained, if one is no longer able to contribute significantly to the evolution of society and if one wishes to die with dignity and not be a burden to loved ones.

Old age

As one approaches old age, the awareness of approaching death acquires a sharp edge. Depending upon the libido-aggression balance in the internal economy of the mind, this awareness can induce dread and pain or it can lead to deepening ego synthesis and wisdom. In order to highlight the latter constellation, I have used the unvarnished pain, begrudging acceptance, and wisdom of psychoanalyst Martin Grotjahn (1984) in other presentations and papers. I know of no other words, from a man who studied himself and the human condition, that better express the fear of dying and the ambivalent acceptance of death.

> The assignment of my age is now to achieve wisdom, which is the ability to deal with the unavoidable reality of death. That seems to be the last assignment—and it seems to escape my reach … I did not do badly in the almost eighty years of my life … But now I'm stuck again. I am not ready to die, not ready to say goodbye to this life. I am not ready to say goodbye to myself. That seems the worst; to say goodbye to myself … I know dying is unpleasant, but to be dead is *Nothing*. I like that even less … Fifty-five years of marriage were built with care, study, insight, learning, and patience, and grew to ever deepening love. I am a most impatient person of genuine bad temper, but I worked on myself: I tried to deepen

my insight, to become a better therapist and a better person. And finally, all should turn to ashes? Just because my heart does not want to do its part anymore? One does not need to be a narcissist to find that unacceptable. To say goodbye to myself and vanish into nothingness? Well, it shall be done. Nobody claimed it would be easy. I hope when my time comes to say goodbye to this world and to myself and when I sink into nothingness, I will have enough presence of mind left to say my last words. I would like to say once more and for the last time to my wife: "I love you." (pp. 293, 297, 302)

In the last of a series of articles on the development of time sense throughout the life cycle, I wrote:

> The intense, normative mid-life preoccupation with, and eventual acceptance of, time limitation and personal death is a developmental prerequisite for the benign acceptance of death in old age. When these are engaged and mastered in mid-life, the acceptance of death as a natural consequence of aging occurs without shattering the continuity of the intrapsychically perceived life cycle or the integrity of the ego. (Colarusso, 2010, p. 112)

Awareness, acceptance, and integration of the inevitability of personal death is an essential component of late life maturity.

> Whether viewed as an inevitable consequence of God's grand plan or as an unsolvable mystery, personal death is part of a grander, incomprehensible scheme since all animate and inanimate structure and organization—be it individual human beings, civilization, planets, stars, or galaxies—exist in an unalterable timespace framework, which inevitably moves from birth through maturation to decline and death. The mature, late-life human being must live—and die—with this unsatisfying realization and disquieting ignorance. (p. 127)

Pathological fears of death

In this section, I will describe two different constellations of pathological fear of death: (i) that emanating from a neurotic conflict, and (ii) that leading to a post-traumatic stress disorder-like symptomatology.

Fear of death emanating from a neurotic conflict

Since death has the potential of evoking real and imagined scenarios of separation, loss, narcissistic defeat, punishment, atonement, and castration, it ought not to come as a surprise that neurotic anxieties emanating from various developmental levels can present as (or contribute to) an inordinate fear of death.

Clinical vignette: 3

A very successful, very intelligent businessman, Mr T was married and the father of three adolescent children. He entered analysis because of growing, perplexing feelings of anxiety and depression. The most significant event in his childhood was a parental divorce that occurred in late latency that was followed by maternal de-compensation and paternal abandonment that had a profound effect on his adolescent and adult development.

Six months into the analysis, Mr T turned fifty-four. "What will I do with the rest of my life?" he mused. Gradually his fear of aging and premature death began to emerge. As Mr T approached the end of the first year in analysis, body monitoring became an increasingly prominent theme. After developing a sore back, he remarked, "I'm getting old." Mr T had a sense that there was "no safe haven in life".

A few months into the second year of the analysis, Mr T's associations turned to thoughts of retiring. He had no plans and the subject made him uncomfortable. If he stopped working, he might as well be dead! Death, as an emotionally charged subject, entered the analysis for the first time. In the next session, Mr T began to talk about his parents' deaths. With a sudden awareness and sense of shock, Mr T recognised that he was just a few years younger than his father when he died.

Approximately eighteen months into the analysis, Mr T finally went for a routine medical check-up. Although he was found to be in good health, Mr T's PSA was slightly elevated. A prostate biopsy was negative. With relief and apprehension he commented, "I dodged a bullet but there is more to come." After a precancerous lesion was removed from his face, filled with fear and anxiety, Mr T said, "It looks like it's going to be my face, my prostate, and my bones!" The irrational idea that he might die "soon" was "crushing".

Two years into the analysis, as he turned fifty-five, Mr T continued to resist exercising. I repeated an interpretation that I had made with little effect in the past. "Your resistance to exercise is part of a pattern of avoidance of powerful thoughts and feelings about fears of illness and death." His emotional response, which seemed to erupt from deep inside, took both of us by surprise. "Why should I take care of myself?" he shouted angrily. "I'm going to die in a couple of years just like my father and grandfather." This response was the first indication of what became a central theme in the analysis—a powerful, highly conflicted identification with a father who had abandoned him in childhood. The need to regain the lost object, albeit with feelings of intense rage, was so great that not even death, at the same age that his father died, was too high a price to pay.

The working-through process regarding his expectation of a premature death continued as we approached the end of the third year of analysis. "My father died at fifty-eight, my mother at fifty-six, my grandfather at fifty-eight. What chance do I have? I'm right in the middle of the death zone." Repeated interpretations that his fear of dying prematurely was based on conflicted feelings about his father and not the reality of his health was having an effect. "Death and time have been in my life every day since my parents died. But something is different. Am I starting to believe that I'm going to live beyond fifty-eight?!"

Mr T began to plan in detail for his sixties and seventies. At this point, as he again focused on my age and attitude towards dying, I confirmed that I was sixty-eight years old. If I could be healthy, active, and mentally alert at sixty-eight, so could he. In fact, he could picture me full of life at seventy-five or eighty (I'm seventy-seven years old as I write this). Then, he added, so could he. In the final months of analysis, further evidence of resolution was apparent. "I'm not afraid of death anymore. I was afraid of living. You're not really alive unless you accept the fact that you're going to die."

Fear of death resulting in post-traumatic stress disorder

The criteria required to make a diagnosis of PTSD in DSM IV are divided into four parts. The person must have experienced or witnessed an event or series of events that involved actual or threatened death or serious injury, or a threat to the physical integrity of self or others. Symptoms are divided into three categories—re-experiencing, avoidance, and increased arousal or alertness. The symptoms of PTSD can be understood by using the psychoanalytic concept of the repetition compulsion. When a trauma is too overwhelming to be mastered easily the mind returns to the event or events over and over again during the day and when asleep. Intrusive thoughts, dreams, and flashbacks are examples. At the same time, using the defence mechanism of repression the mind attempts to avoid thoughts or places that are reminders of the trauma. In regard to the symptoms of increased arousal the one that is most relevant to our consideration of the fear of death is hypervigilance. In other words, the fear that one will once again be in mortal danger.

I was in the United States Air Force serving as a psychiatrist during the Vietnam War and served on a triage unit that made initial evaluations and started treatment before sending these psychiatric casualties on to facilities closer to their homes. Some of those individuals who were constantly in actual danger and fearful that they would die for months at a time continue to have symptoms more than forty years after the war ended. Vietnam was a war without boundaries, much like Afghanistan today. There was no place to feel safe. The fear of death was constant and caused profound psychological trauma.

For the past three decades, I have served as an expert witness in civil law suits. Many cases were about the development of PTSD following trauma of various kinds. Among the most extreme cases that resulted in an intense, lasting fear of death are the following two examples.

Clinical vignette: 4

> A *family of five* was spending a weekend at a motel. An intruder, armed with a weapon, tied up the children and the husband and repeatedly raped the wife in front of the family members. He threatened to kill all of them if they screamed. Symptoms of PTSD persisted for decades in all five family members. One of the most predominant, lasting symptoms was the fear that the intruder would return and kill them.

Clinical vignette: 5

> *Fire!* A fifty-two-year-old single woman lived alone in a rural area that was prone to fires. Before going to bed, Ms T could smell

smoke from a fire far in the distance. She slept restlessly because of the intensity of the wind. In the middle of the night, a light went off in the kitchen and then power was lost. Ms T went outside to investigate a weird noise and saw a pillar of fire coming towards her. She immediately called 911. The only way off the property was through the driveway that was blocked by what had become a wall of fire. Hanging up on 911 was difficult because of the sense of being completely alone and in fear for her life. Ms T threw the cat out of the house and got dressed.

As she left the house, Ms T locked the door, thinking "How ridiculous". She felt guilty because she could not warn her neighbours. As the fire continued to grow in size, Ms T heard a siren in the distance. She yelled in the direction of the siren but to no avail. It was dark. Ms T did not see how she could get to the road. Knowing that she could not outrun the fire, Ms T backed up towards a creek that ran behind her house. As embers flew over her head, Ms T knew she had to go into the creek. She tried to put out the embers around her but realised how silly that was. "I said farewell to the house and everything in it." Despite knowing that it was ridiculous, Ms T stomped out embers as she started the climb down to the creek.

The creek water was freezing! Ms T soaked herself and wondered what was going to happen. "I'm glad this happened after my mother died." Knowing that she was in mortal danger and likely to die, Ms T had wishful thoughts that the fire might jump over her and she would survive. She thought about the terrible danger she and her neighbours were in and began to pray, repeating the *Ninety-First Psalm* over and over again. Ms T prayed that the fire would not come to the creek but she knew it would. Would she die from the smoke? She had to wait the fire out. Huge sheets of embers were flying overhead. Breathing was difficult due to the hot smoke. Ms T was terrified and worried that she would pass out and drown. She tried different positions in the water while thinking, "What will happen if I die?" As the fire burned to the edge of the creek, Ms T thought, "This is unsustainable." She reviewed her life. "Who will be affected by my death? I didn't do enough with my intelligence. My father will feel that he failed. My aunt will be terribly grieved. There are internet friends who will feel my loss. I love this place. I spent a lot of my childhood here. I don't want people to think of it as the place where I died."

Breathing became more difficult. Ms T tried to move to a place where she could lie down and still keep her head above water. She left her computer on the bank and found it difficult to plough through the mud. Ms T submerged herself in the water and put her skirt over her head. The smoke was getting thicker. She began to bargain with God: "If I get out of this, I'll do better. I felt ashamed." Ms T covered her eyes with her skirt, hoping to blot out the scene but she could see the fire through her garment. The fire was at the edge of the creek. "I had feelings of horror. There was a wall of fire in front of me."

As the fire died down, Ms T saw a huge red glow. "It was my house." The sounds of the water mimicked people. "I was so lonely. It was wishful thinking. It got agonisingly cold. I had to keep going. For a moment, the warmth from the fire felt good." Sheets of embers continued to rush by overhead. "I should be enjoying this," Ms T joked to herself. She lost a shoe in the mud. After the fire died down, Ms T decided to leave the creek. No one came. She had to find her own way out, but the bank was covered with hot coals and she only had one shoe. Ms T found a blade of a shovel and tried to clear a path through the ashes but burned her foot anyway. Her cat came to the edge of the water. Ms T cried. She thought the cat had died in the fire. The smoke was still heavy. Ms T burned her foot again and got back in the water. She tried a third time to clear a path. At that time, Ms T saw blinking lights on the road and began to yell. The voices answered and came towards her. Four firemen helped her out of the creek so she would not burn her foot. During the flight to the hospital, Ms T felt "a tremendous sense of peace and gratitude". She was alive.

Not surprisingly, Ms T developed classic symptoms of PTSD, and has been in therapy for several years. The most frightening symptoms are the recurrent nightmares and flashbacks that force her to relive the experience over and over again, thinking each time that she will die.

Death awareness and rejuvenation fantasies

The material that follows was taken from an unfortunately rare, wonderful paper about the analysis of a seventy-year-old woman by psychoanalyst Eli Miller (1986). I encourage anyone who is interested in vitality, neurotic conflict, and the ability by older individuals to utilise analysis to resolve conflicts about the past and the late-adult present to read Dr Miller's paper. I will present vignettes from the paper that illustrate how this extraordinary individual dealt with her fears of death and wishes for rejuvenation.

"Eventually themes of dying emerged, and I asked if death was one of the things she had hoped to talk of in analysis. She responded, 'Maybe, but I'm not ready. It's not pinpointed, maybe it's in flux.' I also asked if my younger age inhibited her on this subject [the analyst was in his mid-thirties at the time]. She laughed and said, 'You bring up the quaintest questions! Could I be envious of you? I'm not feeling anything. You could trip on the street and get killed just like that! I might outlive you. One shouldn't go around thinking 'I'll die.' One should be busy. But if you're sixty-nine, like I, it's sort of stupid if you don't know it's coming and not too far away.'"

Dr Miller asked the patient for permission to use her clinical material in a paper on aging. She readily agreed and added, "Aging is simply a process that happens. It's not pleasant. Growing up was hard for me. I'm now watching younger people struggle with reaching another age level. Our forty-four-year-old friend is having leg pains and worrying about it. You're all of thirty-five ... You once told me that some analysts felt that an older person could get depressed in analysis about what they had missed in life, and I said to you, 'I could not have been more depressed than I was when I started.'"

The following paragraph is taken from a section in the paper on the intense erotic transference that had developed on the patient's part towards the analyst. She was as alive sexually as any younger patient of any age. But mixed in with the intense focus on sexuality and rejuvenation were frequent intrusive thoughts about aging and dying.

"Mrs T soon dreamed that someone had given her a handful of spring flowers and that she was giving up her youth. This led to thoughts about old age and seeing the anti-aging drug Gerovital in a store. Feelings about her upcoming seventieth birthday followed: 'I can't believe I'm seventy years old. It sounds like I have a foot in the grave. I can't look in the mirror and believe I'm seventy years old, like it's not me. People who live to be ninety are sweet little old ladies who sit in chairs with their hair parted in the middle, with lots and lots of wrinkles and dimples. Seventy-year-old women wear heavy dark stockings that wrinkle on their legs. The last bit of life is hard to deal with. You can't do anything really big in the last ten years of your life. In some ways it's like going downhill all the way."

"Mrs T reviewed the 'midlife crisis' of her forties when she agonised over the 'meaning of life and death', and now questioned: 'What will I do with the last years of my life? It's not over!' I asked what she wanted to do. 'Play,' she responded. 'I believe in mortality, but putting it off as long as you can!' She added that she had come to analysis to find out what had happened to a 'harmony with the universe' she had experienced many years before and had somehow lost. To her, mortality and the passing of time were linked to this wish for harmony."

"As the analysis progressed, Mrs T continued to allude to aspects of rejuvenation in the context of time passing and reactivated Oedipal wishes. She spoke of wanting a second facelift, and described a recurrent dream of a large door-mounted brass Corinthian clock. Her associations were to limited time: 'A door to step through. Time to step through it. A short set of stairs. Limited time here. It's interesting I say *here*.' By *here* I now assume she was referring both to the analysis and her life on earth."

Some Hollywood movies dealing with death

The fear of death has been a frequent theme in film, none more so than in three classic films, *On Golden Pond* (1981), *Cat on a Hot Tin Roof* (1958), and *Cocoon* (1985). All three address the fear of dying in different ways with different reactions.

On Golden Pond *(IPC Films, directed by M. Rydell, 1981)*

Norman Thayer (Henry Fonda) is turning eighty years old. As the film opens, he and his wife, Ethel, played by Katherine Hepburn, are opening their cottage for the summer. While she is brimming with life and enthusiasm, he is grumpy and depressed. The contrast between them continues as he tells Ethel that she is "old" (in her late sixties) and he is "ancient". He talks of death while she talks of life and wonders about "your fascination with dying". As they open up the cottage, we see Norman look at a family photo from a decade ago and not recognise himself. Ethel prepares to pick strawberries while Norman, totally unrealistically, looks for a job in the newspaper. Ethel lovingly encourages him to join her as she prepares to pick strawberries. He has no time for such nonsense: "I'm living on borrowed time." After she returns, she pushes Norman out the door, pail in hand, to pick berries. As he wanders in the woods, alone and lost, we recognise that he is not just an old, grumpy man who is a little forgetful, he has dementia.

When his daughter, Chelsey (his real life daughter, Jane Fonda) visits, Norman is gradually drawn into a relationship with the thirteen-year-old son of her boyfriend. As they fish together, we see the re-emergence of a softer, loving side of his personality. The man and the boy are determined to catch Walter, the mythical lake trout who has evaded Norman for years. After Billy catches Walter, the struggle between life and death and the wish for immortality is symbolised by Norman and Billy's decision to let the fish live.

Throughout the film, it is clear that Norman's fear of death is greatly influenced by his dementia. College professor that he was, he does not have the presence of higher mental functions to help him face being eighty years old and the prospect of death, and he is consumed by fear and rage. The movie ends as Ethel and Norman close up the house for the winter. Norman keels over. Ethel rushes to his side and asks God not to take him. After all, she must deal with her fear of her husband of many years dying and leaving her. With grace and tenderness, she tells him that if he is planning to die, she would prefer that he didn't. As he recovers, Ethel tells Norman that she could see him dead for the first time.

Cat On a Hot Tin Roof *(MGM production, directed by E. Kazan, 1958)*

In the 1958 film version of Tennessee Williams's Pulitzer Prize-winning play, Big Daddy, played with amazing conviction by Burl Ives, rules his 38,000 acre Mississippi estate with a sense of absolute power and a cold, insensitive iron fist. Nothing, and no one, challenges him until he learns that he is dying. The theme of death and dying is introduced as Big Daddy returns from a famous medical clinic where instead of learning that he was suffering from a fatal illness (which he is), he is told that he is in good health and has colitis. He rejoices at this second chance at life and vows to gratify all of his feelings and desires, without regard for his family's needs or wishes. He rants that he hates his faithful wife of forty years and will find a new, younger woman to satisfy his undimmed sexual desires. Eventually his favourite son, Brick (Paul

Newman) tells him the truth. Big Daddy runs to the basement that is full of valuable antiques that have never been used. They symbolise the worthlessness of possessions as one approaches death. After a tearful confrontation in which father and son work through their estrangement and tell each other that all they wanted was love, Big Daddy comes face to face with his mortality. He takes a drink. "Here's to the last birthday." He boasts of his power and wealth. But as he faces death, he realises that he is powerless. All of his money, land and possessions cannot save him. "One thing you can't buy at a fire sale. You can't buy back your life." But you can try to make amends before you die. He will devote his remaining time to those he should have loved. In this film, in contrast to Henry Fonda's role in *On Golden Pond*, Big Daddy faces death with a clear mind, not in the fog of gradually progressing dementia. In fact, the realisation that he will die soon increases Big Daddy's ability to think and reason, and forces him to come face to face with his impotence and fear of death.

Cocoon *(Twentieth Century Fox production, directed by R. Howard, 1985)*

The fear of dying is reacted to with fantasies of perpetual youth and immortality. Science fiction can be an excellent vehicle for the expression of these wishes because of the fantasy that civilisations from galaxies far, far away may have conquered aging and death. In this 1985 film, director Ron Howard, at that time thirty years of age, raises the question of what happens if rejuvenation and immortality are real choices, as they become for the characters in this film? Would you be willing to fly away on a spaceship and live forever if you had the choice? Could you leave everyone you have ever known, friends, loved ones, grandchildren? Would you choose to leave everything that was familiar that had been the stuff of life for decades to explore the unknown with strange beings? Could you live without the Beetles, Beethoven, Monday night football or the Public Broadcasting Service?

The film opens with a spaceship crashing into the ocean and then shifts to a retirement community where we watch a person die and hear that another is "really limping". Death is in the air. Three eighty-year-old buddies, played wonderfully by Don Ameche, Wilford Brimley, and Hume Cronyn, observe the human wreckage around them as they go off to swim. On the way to a pool on a deserted estate, they bemoan the diminished importance of sex in their lives and ask Cronyn, who has cancer, how he feels. The theme of aging and loss of function continues as we watch Brimley fail an eye test and lose his driver's licence. He covers his car, symbolically burying that phase of his life, while his daughter and grandson, representatives of his genetic immortality, watch.

The ETs, the founders of Atlantis, are returning to retrieve their comrades who have been buried in pods in the ocean for thousands of years. The pods' temporary placement in the deserted pool transforms the waters into the fountain of youth. After the three men dive into the pool containing the pods, they are rejuvenated. They feel "great!", "tremendous!" and walk home with firm erections. They are young again. After seeing their transformation, the entire population of the old age home rushes to the pool and drains it of its life-sustaining energy, causing some of the aliens in the pods to die. The captain of the spaceship, who had met the octogenarians and allowed them to use the pool, cries, "I never experienced the pain of death before. I never lost anyone close to me." Here is the essence of the human condition, namely a life cycle composed of birth, maturation, aging, and death. Without the awareness of death, that is, loss, can the essence of the human condition, the relationship to loved ones, be truly experienced? As the Anterians prepare to leave, the captain offers to take the three men and their friends with them. They would be students, but teachers too. How long would they be gone? "Forever," he answers. "We don't know what forever means," they reply.

The conflict between choosing eternal life and leaving everyone and everything that is familiar is expressed at the end of the film in several ways. Wilford Brimley's character tells his grandson that he is going away and they will never see each other again. No more baseball, hot dogs, or fishing together. His wife painfully says goodbye to her daughter and grandson. There is a price to pay for immortality. "We're cheating Nature." In a fit of mania, Don Ameche empties his bank account and throws the bills at strangers on the street. Hume Cronyn tells his wife that he loves her and wants them to go but if she chooses to stay, he wants "six more months with you over living forever alone". A friend comes to say goodbye. He no longer resents their leaving but says, "This is my home, this is where I belong." The film ends as the spaceship ascends in a bank of fog, hiding those who chose to leave, and their uncertain, endless future.

Concluding remarks

In this contribution, I have surveyed the literature on anxieties pertaining to death and attempted to evolve a "developmental line" (A. Freud, 1981) of such concerns. I have also described certain psychopathological constellations in this realm and commented upon the rejuvenation fantasies that are often associated with encountering death. I have sought to illustrate these phenomena with the help of brief clinical vignettes as well as three Hollywood movies. While I have cast a wide net, two areas have so far eluded my discourse, namely those of religion and culture. Before concluding, therefore, I wish to make some brief comments upon these two areas.

Religion and fear of death

In my opinion, religious belief addresses two very basic human needs by providing a code of conduct for individuals in society and an answer to the unanswerable, namely what if anything comes after death. Western monotheistic religions, to varying degrees, adhere to God-given codes of conduct similar to the Ten Commandments, believe firmly in an afterlife, and relate behaviour during earthly existence to one's place in the afterlife in places such as heaven and hell. The end of life on earth is not to be feared if one has lived a good life according to God's (or his prophets') commandments. Eternal happiness in heaven or earth-like pleasures such as sexual gratification while there, are examples. Death is to be feared if one's fate in the afterlife is eternal suffering and punishment. Eastern religions that believe in reincarnation diminish the fear of death by providing punishment in the afterlife, but more central to our focus, a second chance through incarnation. For agnostics or atheists, beliefs in a personal god and various dogma are nothing more than flights of fantasy ingrained in all cultures across recorded history to deal with the primitive's, and modern man's, inability to tolerate misunderstood natural phenomena such as eclipses and explain the end of individual existence. One of the clearest statements of such thinking was made by Salman Akhtar (2010).

> Anxiety about the limited nature of our existence delivers us to the cushion of handed-down magic as well. We open the windows to religious belief and dreams of heaven, hell, reincarnation, or the continuation of our "souls" one way or the other. Beguiled and

beguiling, we permit ourselves all sorts of illusions and all shades of plea-bargaining in order to save our lives, so to speak. However, such defensive maneuvers do not exhaust the list of our reactions to the thought of our deaths. We are also puzzled and intrigued. Our epistemic instinct exhorts us and we concoct elaborate hypotheses about near-death and after-death phenomena, though slyly we refer to the latter as "after-life" phenomena. We turn our hapless anguish on its head and crack jokes about the "Grim Reaper." We wax poetic about death. We paint scenes of dying, write stories and screenplays, make movies about terminal illness, and stage operas involving death. Injection imagination and pleasure into what seems morbid and frightening allows us a good night's sleep. The horrid witch of mortality becomes the maudlin muse of our creativity. (pp. 1–2)

Acceptance of death as a natural end to life

Psychoanalysts, scientists, philosophers, and many others believe that the full acceptance of personal death leads to diminished or absent fear of death and peace and wisdom at the end of life. The following short quotes from various individuals, from both the West and the East, exemplify this thinking.

Salman Akhtar (2010) describes the thinking of Mirza Asad-Ulla Khan Ghalib (1779–1869), the classic Urdu and Persian poet: the greatest ecstasy for a drop of water is to fall upon a river and become one with it. "Such a sentiment not only accommodates the inevitability of death but ascribes to it a certain sense of desirability and even pleasure ... Ghalib, however, is not content with portraying death as a joyous culmination of a long journey. He adds that without the awareness of its finiteness, life would not be as enjoyable at all" (p. 2). In another couplet expressing the same idea, Ghalib refers to "... the way the beginning sunlight at the time of dawn relieves the candle from the continued necessity to burn, the arrival of death cures all problems of life" (p. 11).

Ilany Kogan (2010) describes a similar conclusion in psychoanalyst Heinz Kohut's thinking:

> Like Freud, Kohut (1977) dichotomizes healthy adaptation and pathological maladaptation along the lines of tranquil acceptance and utter nihilism (pp. 241–242). In his view, the essence

of the achievement of wisdom is the maximal relinquishing of narcissistic delusions, including the acceptance of the inevitability of death, without abandoning cognitive and emotional involvements. The ultimate act of cognition, i.e., the acknowledgment of the limits and the finiteness of the self, is not the result of an isolated intellectual process but is the victorious outcome of the lifework of the total personality in acquiring broadly based knowledge and in transforming archaic modes of narcissism into ideals, humor and a supra-individual participation in the world. (p. 83)

The founder of the Iranian Psychoanalytic Institute, Tooraj Moradi, addresses the similarities and differences between Persian and Western thoughts on death. Referring to Iranian society he writes, "While we traditionally don't run away from mourning, we are also vibrantly alive and value life's *present moments* very much, *while* aware of death" (Moradi, 2010, p. 141).

This brief sample of Western and Eastern thinking on the fear and acceptance of death would not be complete without the frequently quoted words of psychoanalyst Erik Erikson (1963) who suggests the mastery of the fear of death comes from a mystical union with the cosmos: "It is a past-narcissistic love of the human ego—not of the self—as an experience which conveys some world order and spiritual sense ... the acceptance of one's one and only life cycle as something that has to be ... it is a comradeship with the ordering ways of distant times and different pursuits" (p. 268).

EPILOGUE

CHAPTER EIGHT

Fear across the life span

M. Hossein Etezady

Fear, as an innate internal signal, is indispensable for safe and successful conduct of behaviour in the service of survival. Without fear, we would be at the mercy of daily mishaps and ordinary dangers of everyday life. Without fear, one of the greatest virtues of man, courage, daring to risk in the face of peril, might not exist. In man as well as in lower animals, the brain's subcortical and limbic areas, sometimes called the "reptilian brain", scan, register, and diagnose fear, nearly instantly or even before the emerging danger is actually present, as an anticipatory preparation for fight-or-flight response. The subcortical regions then connect their integrated output to the cortex and the orbito-frontal areas for emotional processing and cognitive elaboration. This can lead to immediate, short-term or long-term action measures. Of these some are reflexive, others skill-based or habitual, and still others contingency oriented and more or less subject to reflection and deliberation.

It is generally accepted that while fear is a basic normative affect, it is different from anxiety which is not caused by the presence or probability of actual danger, but is derived from an imaginary danger, independent of any external origin. This may be exemplified by phobias which entail severe anxiety states manifested as misplaced fears. In addition to fear, other stressful emotions can become a source of internal distress and dammed up displeasure. These may be classified in two distinct groups: anxiety and depressive affect. Anxiety is regarded as anticipation of imminent loss or injury, as a consequence of one's own unacceptable wishes, while depressive affect is the displeasure resulting from the notion that such atoning consequence has already occurred as punishment for transgression in pursuit of forbidden wishes.

Fear, when unrelieved or indefinitely extended, can lead to stress-related distress and a chronic state of anxiety. Such chronic anxiety should ordinarily subside once the existing external threat or danger has dissipated. In psychoanalytic metapsychology ever since Freud, we have equated anxiety, as a technical term, with displeasure, requiring psychological action, in order to achieve relief. In addition to damming up of stress or anxiety resulting from intrapsychic conflict, trauma in various ways can also result in anxiety.

According to this theoretical scheme, fears are normal, protective, and adaptive, based on elements of reality. Anxiety and the displeasure of depressive affects, as in the case of neurotic guilt, are based on psychic reality and not on objective external reality. Along with a wish or drive derivative and defensive containment of those unacceptable wishes, anxiety is a component of intrapsychic conflict. In the form of a signal affect, it is an essential ingredient in affect-modulating ego functions, involved in self and interactive regulation. As a neurotic symptom, it is pathological and pathogenic and a hindrance to optimal adaptation and normal development.

In the areas of fear addressed in this volume, a distinction of this kind is essential. Matters such as success and intimacy are generally endowed with desirability and infer an affectively positive tone. Those among our patients who fear success or intimacy experience intrapsychic conflict regarding wish fulfilment and ultimate triumph. This conflict contains unconscious fantasy, unique for, and individually constructed by, each person. It is this unconscious construct that holds and perpetuates the latent meaning of the experience. For each person, the question becomes the uniquely individual and wholly subjective meaning of the object of such fear, in the context of their unique life history and their own individual mode of mentalisation.

In the case of other matters such as death, injury, breakdown, and even being alone, which bear mainly a negative affective tone and represent actual and objective harm, fear may be appropriate and even salutary, unless secondarily entangled in intrapsychic conflict. Fearing death, as an ever-present possibility and an objectively undeniable aspect of external reality, directs our behaviour towards self-preservation, self-protection, and creative adaptation. As an ultimate threat to human life and survival, death maintains the whole possession of all "three calamities of childhood", being loss of the object, loss of the love of the object, and loss of physical integrity (castration anxiety). Although fear of death can lead to anxiety, in itself it is not a neurotic symptom or displeasure encountered as one component of intrapsychic conflict. Such fear, however, may under certain conditions lead to neurotic anxiety and symptom formation, based on distressing excess, trauma, or neurotic conflict.

Fear of success, as an example of contrast to fear of death, is so obviously counter-intuitive and unexpected as to immediately ring of pathology and derailment from the normative path. In either case, whether the objects of fear are dreadful or desirable, internal or external, and adaptive or detrimental, their impact depends on the meaning that each person uniquely and individually has constructed in relation to them. It also depends on whether one is free and able to create one's own mixture of diverse elements of encounter, rather than merely being compelled to rigid confinement to one and divorced from others.

In clinical work with our patients, we discover that neurotic fears are compromise formations resulting from intrapsychic conflict. They represent elements of drive, signal anxiety (or signal shame, guilt, and other signal aversive affects), defence, and compromise formation, each with uniquely personal meaning, contained within the construct of a central unconscious fantasy. Whether oddly counter-intuitive or universally embraced, fears, similar to other emotional states, have their uniquely individual construct based on a personal narrative, within a central unconscious fantasy, formed of compromise formations from developmental or neurotic conflicts.

Humpty Dumpty: fear of breakdown

Unable to do any semblance of justice to the rich content of this wide ranging contribution by Dr Elaine Zickler (Chapter Two of this book), I will confine my focus here to breakdown as implied by Winnicott, by turning to the quandary of the wholeness of things and the integrating unity that holds them, one and all, together. The uncompromising balance that is required for any organism to function depends on innumerable factors and circumstances. This delicate balance supports sequential states of being, evolving, reaching maturity, reproducing, decay, and finally demise. The miracle of life and living is the spectacular manner in which so much is so ceaselessly happening, moving, combining, and taking form, anew or in repetition. Predictably, things happen in an endlessly unpredictable cascade of events and ventures. They combine chaos and disintegration together with order and coalition, of matter and process, over time. Living systems are responsive, accommodating, and vulnerable to external as well as internal influence, impingement, or threat. There are very few and specific combinations of factors and conditions that can support continuation and maintenance of the living dynamics that permit and perpetuate life. An organism is a unitary system which itself is a part of a larger system. These, and still larger systems are tied together by a uniting bond of intricate, purposive, and finely tuned interconnections that hold the totality of all life together. Within one fleeting moment of reality, there is a built-in extension towards the unlimited potentiality of countless future moments.

While the only constant thing is change itself, life and the stability of circumstances that support it are predicated upon continuity, sameness, predictability, and permanence of states. Within and beyond the alternating poles of order and chaos, change and permanence, neo-genesis and demise, all or nothing, and positive versus negative, there exists a reality that is immutable. It is inclusive and permanently prevailing over whatever transpires. Our existence and the experiential register of being alive is but a means, and also a result, of appreciating merely fragmented and disunited manifestations of such reality. It is parcelled out in individually unique slices and versions that constitute our longitudinal sense of being engaged with life and with going on being. Reality determines and dominates our life. Yet we are incapable of knowing or reaching it in the whole. We imagine it, create it in our minds, and put the stamp of our own needs and takes on it. While the whole of reality is beyond the grasp of knowledge, we only have access to aspects or fragments of it. These fragments can be heterogeneous, incompatible, contradictory, and even misleading. As we avoid, deny, distort, and misperceive reality our search for more of the truth can never cease.

Given the infinite complexity and the multitude of elements that enter various systems of substance, connection, and interdependence, and given our limited access only to a small number of resources for their use, the question should be; how do we do it? How do we indeed manage at all to hold it together, as we do, by ourselves, together with others and sometimes in spite of others? How does it happen? What holds all these pieces together, and what organises it all so intelligently, purposefully, irrevocably? Where is it all going and why? Where does this unified movement of time and energy originate and what is the creative source for such compelling narrative, and the producer of the inevitable unfolding of this grand drama? These are simple, naïve, and eternal questions we never stop wondering about. Here questions become increasingly more elementary and the answers ever farther reaching. Of these elemental aspects of reality we know nothing, but we ponder, deliberate and feel fascinated by them. Each of us is content, or otherwise impacted, by our own individual slice of reality of the living present, in our own contextual parcel of time and place. We keep apart what we know from what we believe. For knowledge we need support-ive evidence, but for faith we only need to choose to believe in an illu-sion that manufactures its own conviction regardless of ampleness or lack of any evidence. While the scientific scholar searches for evidential proof of reality, the faithful believer finds solace in the certitude of his own conviction and needs no search. Where the scientist eagerly thrives to slowly and eventually reach, the believer has already arrived and finds himself confidently at home. Our faith-filled confidence in an illu-sion of certitude can eliminate much doubting, fear, and anxiety along with the frightening abyss of dark ignorance. As dark and frightening are uncertainty and ignorance, the certitude born out of faith is com-forting and uplifting. Only humans have the capability of forming an illusion and the choice to believe in their own illusions and self- made creations. This becomes pathological to the extent that such choice is absent or irrelevant.

Illusions, as Winnicott would have it, are created in a transitional space, a no-man's-land, not belonging to in, out, self, object, wish, actu-ality, or true and false. They allow us to have and to consume the object, yet to be free of it, to be with it but without it. In this manner, they serve self cohesion. For the purpose of not losing cohesion, not having a breakdown, and not falling apart, as in fragmentation or annihila-tion, our ego resources, defences, and sublimations are ever vigilant. Winnicott's breakdown speaks of such organismic panic that emanates from the complete absence of maternal availability and total cessation of such auxiliary-ego functions. This is regardless of any connections to sensual, sexual, conflict-based, or developmental considerations. Re-experiencing and mastering this threat is, according to this view, the bedrock of all analyses. Other variations of such fragmentation or dissolution of the self might be seen in the loss of the ego and self boundaries, leading to de-differentiation. Similar regressive retreats may be seen in de-fusion when ambivalence can no longer be tolerated and libido and aggression are split and self and object constancy lost. Self cohesion here requires magical selfobject functions and refuge in archaic states of grandiose self and idealised objects. When the self and ego boundaries are tenuous and symbiotic longings are pressing, the object, via projection of oral-destructive impulses, can represent a devouring and consuming threat experienced as fear of re-engulfment. Projection of one's primitive anal-sadistic impulses may result in experiencing the object as sadistic, persecutory, and bent on domination and destruction of the self, unless the sadistic object is brought under rigid control.

Whether we side with Winnicott's primacy of breakdown regardless of the fate of the drives, or with Freud and Laplanche in inserting libido in any biologically derived physical or mental action, we can find room for both perspectives. Childhood calamities as well as loss of self cohesion or disintegration can, each separately and also together in combination, represent the ultimate fear. Castration anxiety is one such ultimate when viewed as the loss of bodily integrity. Such anxiety can arise from the fear of the object or from its authority internalised in the form of superego dictates. Whatever the nature of the original trauma or deficit, and regardless of the level of the intrapsychic conflict, it is the task of an analytic experience to uncover, reconstruct, rework, and re-establish internal resources that might make it possible for "where the id was there shall the ego be".

Would you be mine? Fear of aloneness

Psychological integrity and a solid sense of self come about in the context of a reliable, loving, and stable relationship with a maternal figure capable of good enough attunement, holding, containment, and mirroring. The formation of the sense of self and the process of differentiation are rooted in the mother's ability to receive, perceive, metabolise, ego-filter, and re-present to the infant his internal experience in a more objective form. Repeated experiences of gratification via maternal availability lead to confident expectation, libidinal object constancy, and the capacity for self-regulation in tandem with interactive regulation and self cohesion. It is the relationship with the primary object that provides these possibilities in the context of the security of such attachment. When the mother is incapable of creating such context then confident expectation, separation-individuation, and identity formation will be accordingly compromised. Mothers whose own early experiences led to insecure attachment are highly likely to have children who suffer from insecure attachments of various types.

Humans are supposed to be "social animals" in that they need each other and depend on the resources of others for physical, emotional, and sociological provisions. Internal models of relationships that govern and determine the course and quality of relationships throughout the life span are internalised early in the course of the day to day interactive encounters with the primary object and available substitutes. Coercive, avoidant, disorganised, or other insecure qualities of early attachment patterns permeate and shape the character of subsequent ties to others. How we experience and conduct ourselves in the presence of an "other" is grounded in the quality of our attachment styles and internal models formed early in life. It all begins with learning to be able to be "alone" in the presence of mother.

We can feel alone yet content in a crowd, or else feel disconnected, insignificant, or alienated, while yearning for recognition, connection, regard, and affirmation. When we feel rejected, discounted, carelessly dismissed, or shunned we feel hurt, angry, anxious, depressed, and perhaps vengeful. We need to see ourselves worthy of care, recognition, and concern by others whom we value and need. Our sense of self and our self worth are greatly influenced and significantly determined by how we think others see us. When we feel we are falling short of the expectations of important others, we can be painfully assaulted by a sense of failure, shame, and humiliation. We need others throughout our life span and we are born to attach to a base of safety and unconditional acceptance. It is therefore not surprising that our deepest and most fundamental anxiety is the loss of the object, which in time evolves developmentally into the loss of the love of the object. For these reasons fear of being alone, when isolation is imposed and solitude is not deliberately sought, can be universal, normative, and developmentally both appropriate as well as enhancing. When we are rejected, left behind, left out, or left to fend for ourselves we feel a vast variety of painful and unsettling emotions that may be difficult to overcome, especially by those with residual vulnerability established early in their object relations due to insufficiency of the holding environment and inadequacy of parental care. Those with pre-Oedipal fixations, insecure attachment, and a shaky or damaged sense of self need others as part-objects to meet their early selfobject needs. Part-objects are void of subjectivity and controlled via omnipotent grandiosity. As Kohut (1977) showed, we need selfobjects for our entire life just as we need oxygen to survive.

In this respect, pathology may be viewed in terms of the level of organisational mastery that has been reached and what level of relatedness is possible, how stable are secondary narcissism and secondary thought processes and whether infantile omnipotence has been relinquished in favour of the depressive position? The archaic infantile selfobjects of a monadic state of relatedness in a paranoid-schizoid position are subjectively composed, far from the realm of objectivity. Selfobject needs for a mature, secure, and productive mother, teacher, grandparent, or a successful leader are object related, intersubjective, and sublimatory. This means young and old, healthy or impaired, male or female, special or ordinary, we all need others. When we choose to, we can be alone even if we do not like it well, especially when we use self isolation as self protection or reprieve, for self reflection, or as an interpersonal strategy.

When isolation is imposed or one is involuntarily cut off from loved ones or abandoned, being alone will be harder to bear. Dreading such a possibility is psycho-physiologically normative, in the best adaptive interest of anyone and is ordinarily not a liability. For those, however, whom Dr Hutson (Chapter Three of this book) describes so clearly and empathically and who are stuck with unresolved pre-Oedipal conflicts of separation-individuation, a sense of control and mastery can only be provided via others as omnipotent selfobjects, in a dyadic and sadomasochistic mode of relatedness where everything stands still and change is not possible. When being alone means the loss and destruction of this tenacious connection to such archaic selfobjects, fear of annihilation and disintegration or panic is the result.

"Soul murder", or the role of parents who habitually or unconsciously, but cruelly, demean and humiliate their children, indicates lack of parental empathy. These are parents who have not succeeded in normally neutralising their own primitive aggression and will likely fail to perform this selfobject function for their child. The child's own un-neutralised aggression will then impede the establishment of positive introjects in order to fuse the drives, heal the vertical split, and render affect modulation and self control possible. The healing of this split is necessary to allow tolerance of ambivalence and to survive losses as it becomes the bedrock for reality processing, the depressive position, object constancy, capacity for being alone, for concern, for empathy, and for triangulation. When mothers' libidinal availability, holding, and containing functions and empathic resources fail, the infant's aggression cannot be sufficiently neutralised to allow the healing of the split and further ego growth.

In a therapeutic relationship the holding, containing, mirroring selfobject functions provided by the analyst, in a context of empathic attunement, can create space for expression and recognition of primary affects and clarification of their connection with behaviour, thought, and fantasy, each in the context of relations in the historical and pre-historical past, in current life circumstances, and particularly in the transference. The analyst's empathic attunement and ability to survive the patient's aggression is crucial in therapeutic healing of the verti-cal split, leading to the possibility of maintaining a stable sense of self, use of affects as signals, and forming the beginnings of libidinal object constancy. With eventual resolution of conflicts of ambivalence and relinquishing infantile omnipotence, transference neurosis and Oedipal resolution in a triangular mode of relatedness become available.

Snuggling porcupines: fear of intimacy

Susan Kavaler-Adler has laid out a broad and well reasoned definition of intimacy in her wide ranging and multifaceted contribution (Chapter Four of this book). Once there is intimacy, getting closer to the other and accessing their subjectivity and internal universe becomes not only pos-sible, but a source of enrichment and enhanced vitality. This goes with-out saying. However, it would be questionable to assume that knowing a lot about one another and having or gaining access to each other's internal world and privacy means intimacy. That could well mean intru-sion, boundary violation, narcissistic exploitation, dissolution of ego boundaries, and the like, not intimacy. In intimacy, we expect openness and mutuality. This openness tolerates and allows for vulnerability and disillusionment. When there is mutuality of care and concern for one another, rather than depleting or exploitative behaviour, the connection is enhancing, self affirming, and empowering. When there is intimacy each side finds and cultivates it and longs for it. Each side contributes to its facilitation and finds it rewarding to grope and to work for it, to take chances, to make sacrifices, and confidently trust in its safety and promise of gratification.

As an ideal state of relatedness this kind of intimacy is the ultimate achievement not everyone has the great fortune to reach. For this the minimum requirement would be optimal or good enough developmental conditions, especially during a childhood free from trauma, with safety, secure attachment, and space for self fulfilment and autonomy. Unresolved Oedipal or pre-Oedipal conflicts impede or obliterate the possibility of such an ideal state. "True intimacy", in the ideal sense described above, would take two remarkably fortunate and unusually intact adults who would be the envy of most ordinary human beings. But we have other kinds and levels of intimacy in which one side may, for example, be a child, the other a mother, immature, emotionally labile, fragile, and needy. There is the "intimacy" that is violently forced and intensified during a sadomasochistic entanglement, or in a battle of the wills between a mother and a "terrible twos" toddler; this sometimes is replicated in the transference. There are different kinds and various levels of intimacy wherein the openness and the fluidity of interpersonal boundaries can be disruptive, intrusive, exploitative, destructive, etc., and certainly not an ideal, mutual, or benign state of relatedness.

One of the achievements of the separation-individuation process is the establishment of optimal distance. Optimal distancing includes both physical/spatial dimensions as well as representational/relational. Optimal distancing is a developmental acquisition that becomes an integral ingredient of "implicit relational knowing" as it determines how close or forthcoming one can be, in whose presence, and in what temporal or actual context. Rapprochement, beginning at about the fifteenth month of life, coincides with the emergence of the verbal "No", Spitz's (1965) third organiser. This is a critical period in establishing boundaries, defining differences, and assertively averting or rejecting what one will. For each person in each relationship, there is an optimal distance. This is a point of closeness or openness that the person will seek at a particular juncture. This distance may be different another time or with another person or the same person in a different context. The calculation and regulation of this distance is a sophisticated and sensitive ego function of self and interactive regulation.

Optimal distance for each side of the intimate connection depends on other factors including the age and developmental acquisitions of each participant. Intimacy between a mother and her child is not necessarily mutual. It is certainly not symmetrical and the individual shares of each side are not equal since the mother carries the lion's share in determining the optimal distance. The same may be said about intimacy within a therapeutic relationship, with respect to the asymmetry and the difference in the role and expectations of each participant in the therapeutic dyad. As in maternal care, attunement, empathy, and fostering a transitional space, as well as the requirements of holding, containing, and mirroring functions during treatment are elements that call for as well as enhance the capacity to tolerate intimacy. When the therapist is caught in the enactment of a parental transference, he may be forced into the need-satisfying intimacy of an idealised wished-for breast/object, thereby losing his own actual identity as a real therapist, meaning being able to be a third party onlooker, witnessing and identifying, but not jumping in, to actually take the place of either one side or the other, of the transference dyad.

But intimacy has many pitfalls. You only hurt those you love most. We find so many broken hearts on the road to intimacy and so many disillusionments before any lasting fulfilment. In fact there are more heartaches, regrets, tribulations, and untold anguish than can be accounted for, from lost or unattainable intimacy. Lost intimacy is always a demanding price to pay for successful termination of a patient who for long occupied such an enormously intimate place in one's subjective universe. It is exactly such intimacy in the course of our daily work that places the greatest burden on each of us, regardless of whether we need it for us, for the patient, or for the sake of the outcome. Porcupines cannot get close without hurting. Our biological endowment of aggression can make porcupines out of all of us, on either side of a relationship, not infrequently. In "true intimacy", there is the possibility of reducing the optimal distance to near zero, yet to maintain or even enhance self affirmation and authentic individuality. In other cases, merger states rather than intimacy are sought. These merger states are narcissistic, represent a symbiotic state of dual unity, and in a primary process fashion they are compelling and not bound by limits or restraints of reality. They seek to undo differentiation and negate or destroy self actualisation and individuality. They also strip the object of any subjective content or existence.

Ordinarily in the last quarter of the first year of life, differentiation begins by delineating self representation from that of the object, heralded by the appearance of stranger anxiety, (Spitz's second organiser). Stern showed that the most momentous event of this subphase is not upright locomotion as Mahler had originally proposed, but the dawn of intersubjectivity. At this stage, the infant has learned that he can influence the internal states of others through his own. He reads these affective states, sorts them, chooses to amplify or dampen them, and elicits or interrupts them. While the identity of a "whole object" includes its subjective components, a "part object" cannot be appreciated for the fullness of its totality with its unique internal make-up. Tolerating the existence and legitimacy of others' subjectivity, in a dyadic accommodation, and later the capacity to tolerate and respect the intersubjective connection between the two other poles of a triad may be impeded. This development is derailed in severe psychopathology where the beginnings of self and object constancy have not been established, thereby rendering mature intimacy implausible.

A realistic fear of intimacy, as a signal affect, regulating optimal distancing and adjusting relational strategy, is an important and necessary contributor to normal adaptation. This appropriate and realistic fear, as other reasonable and common fears, can become entangled in Oedipal or pre-Oedipal conflict and result in a symptomatic compromise formation that represents a central unconscious fantasy, in a uniquely individual narrative. It seeks to perpetuate the past and recreates the un-mastered events of earlier experiences that continue to intrude upon the present. Here, as in other instances addressed in each chapter of the present volume, we find realistic, normal adaptive fear in juxtaposition to anxiety, which is engendered intrapsychically and contrary to the obvious implications of reality.

Intimacy, it should be said, is not all milk and honey, to paraphrase a patient. We have all experienced various states and forms of it, not always painlessly or willingly. We need it, crave it, seek it, and aspire to reach it as we also fear it or feel unsure or conflicted about it. Our existence and humanity is dependent on it as a context for secure attachment, development of the self, and the emergence of meaning, language, abstraction, and mentalisation. Intimacy occurs in different circumstances at different levels and states of relatedness. It is the fertile ground in which humanity and the development of emotional life of humans is cultivated. Challenges of intimacy are indeed great and often grave. Not only joy and triumph but more often loss, pain, and regrets brings us to the understanding of reality on a three dimensional level of self, other, and a third, in an intersubjective field, filled with countless others. It is not until the end of the third year of life when the child is capable of conceiving that others' minds may be, and usually are, different from his own and his version of reality may not coincide with those of others. Until then, knowing the mind of others is not feasible due to neuro-cognitive immaturity and the prevalence of psychic equivalency. Once this neuro-cognitive development is reached, a triadic Oedipal level of conflict resolution can be entered at this point, provided that the course of object relations has not been derailed, blocked, or relegated to defensive regression.

The terrible twos and transition: fear of injury

Jerome Blackman, MD, proposes a fairly detailed developmental perspective on fear of physical injury, in normality and pathology, one's past and present, in the male and the female, the injured and the "not-yet injured", both for individuals as well as across cultures (Chapter Five of this book). His use of pertinent clinical material and the description of his intervention techniques are both illuminating and convincing. These clinical renditions bring into focus important but subtly nuanced elements, whether unconsciously operative, or those that are deliberate, easily recognised, or intuitively obvious. We are rather incidentally presented with a special regard for the vulnerability women feel for being physically weaker than men. We find apparently trite trivia turn into an eye-opening understanding of women's phobic/counterphobic or minimisation/denial strategies in responding to this instinctively compelling fear. Here we see, also, how a signal affect, such as fear of physical injury can, in normal circumstances, help the ego find safe and adaptive solutions, whereas in pathology, in contrast, solutions are symptomatic of unresolved unconscious conflict, manifested in disguise and as compromise formations which are often far from safe or adaptive.

Unresolved pre-Oedipal conflicts can interfere with the formation of signal affects, affect regulation, ego growth, symbolic and secondary process thinking, empathic capacity, mentalisation, ego strength, and superego formation. In other instances, the reality of this innate and gender-based vulnerability is woven into the fabric of a neurotic constellation. On this developmental level, the symptoms or personality traits can be understood symbolically, communicated narratively, and relived and worked through in the transference, using standard analytic technique. We are also made aware that anticipating danger posed by those we treat is a practical and clinical necessity. Dangerous behaviour is shown to be more likely to occur in individuals with a well delineated list of features that clinicians can assess. When there is a history of early trauma, deficit, or deprivation, and pre-Oedipal conflicts remain unresolved, we find impulse control, ego strength, superego functions, empathy, and mentalisation lacking. Traumatic affects related to deficient and painfully failing selfobject experiences are contained as dissociated self states and in disjointed fragments. Projection of one's own aggression in these cases can make others seem dangerous and may therefore necessitate pre-emptive attacks.

Pre-Oedipal relations are based on early oral or anal coercive dyadic modes of relatedness. Being devoured or devouring the object, controlling/destroying or being controlled/destroyed by the sadistic part-objects permeate the quality of these relationships in which boundaries are tenuous, absent, or dysfunctional and the beginning rudiments of self/object constancy not yet reached. As dyadic conflicts remain unresolved, splitting and dissociation, rather than repression, continue to be the main defence mechanisms. We define this as a "vertical split". The "healing of the split" normally occurs during separation-individuation, or roughly in the second and the third year of life. These are, coincidentally, years of transition and transitional phenomena which establish and promote intersubjectivity and "third-ness". During these two years, normally we expect to see a transition from primary to secondary narcissism, from primary process thinking to secondary, and from a dyadic, pre-Oedipal mode of relatedness to a triadic, Oedipal mode, along with representational and abstract mentation. It is not until the beginning of the fourth year when age and phase specific neurodevelopmental maturity and new cognitive tools can accommodate to the requirements of narrative formation, abstraction, and verbal communication. The rapprochement subphase, from sixteen to twenty-four months, is critical for the successful "healing of the split" and for making it past the extreme peaks of ambitendency and the boundary conflicts of "the terrible twos". When this fails, the healing of the split fails. Drive fusion, formation of signal affects, affect modulation, repression, symbolisation, and ego/superego functions falter. Self and object constancy and the depressive position cannot be attained and reality processing remains under the abiding influence of primary narcissism and primary process thinking. Magic, idealisation, vilification, omnipotence, and primitive projections predominate in order to defend against narcissistic vulnerability. Affect modulation, impulse control, empathy, sublimation, and reflective capacity fail, as do other major ego strengths. All this combines with types of attachment that cannot be secure, as self and object representations are split, dissociated, or fragmented, as arrested captives of the overwhelming, un-integrated affective experiences of early relations which keep on repeating in enactments.

Mentalisation, or representational thought process utilised in converting concrete to abstract, somatic to psychic, and the unprocessed content to meaning and reflective capacity, the capacity for narrative formation, and Oedipal level triadic conflict resolution, requires optimal resolution of rapprochement. This is ordinarily supposed to take place during the second half of the second year. Subsequently, from twenty-four to thirty-six months, there is a period of consolidation. This constitutes the last subphase of separation-individuation. It is during the course of this subphase that the mother and the child consolidate what they have managed to learn about being alone in the presence of an "other", now "in a new way", which is intersubjective and tolerates some ambivalence. With fusion of the drives and the healing of the split, primitive aggressive drives can be neutralised so that their neutralised energy may be used for ego growth and expansion. This calls for a surplus of libidinal energy which is ordinarily supplied via maternal care and her libidinal availability. When the mother fails in sufficiently libidinising her interaction with the child, as for example in depression, surplus aggressive energy destroys the good-object representations and leaves an emptiness that hungers for fulfilment and voraciously seeks and destroys the object without being able to "use" it, a la Winnicott.

In this presentation, I am amplifying the underrated and frequently neglected perspective of the separation-individuation process and in particular the critical subphase of rapprochement as a nodal point of transition from a narcissistic/dyadic mode of regulation and relatedness to a triadic/Oedipal mode of conflict resolution in a depressive position. Failure at this nodal point can result in developmental consequences that are ominously pervasive and predominate characterological, symptomatic, and transference manifestations in clinical encounters with severe psychopathology and in those who may pose grave danger to themselves and/or to others. This, I believe, poses profound implications for our understanding of pre-Oedipal pathological formations and their aetiology, as well as for techniques of intervention, prevention, and treatment.

What price? Fear of success

When we think of success, we conjure a sense of accomplishment or achievement, deserved or not, by luck or undaunted persistence, predicated upon meeting a need or fulfilment of a wish. When success is wished and planned for, objectives and goals are invested with one's instinctual as well as honed and targeted drives. These drives aim for the pleasure of meaningful gratification and for the satisfaction of gaining mastery. Or they will be meeting the requirements of higher ambitions and ceaseless demands of obligating duty. In this sense, success may be viewed in one of its manifestations generically, as developmental attainment of organisational mastery. Infancy, toddlerhood, preschool and school ages as well as adolescent and adult life each represent a particular level of organisation that ideally is reached and mastered before the next level of ontogeny and reorganisation calls for new levels of mastery on a higher plane of re-synthesis. Success along this trajectory is normally taken for granted as a regular aspect of the average expectable development.

This level of accomplishment is, however, not easily reached due to a multitude of factors, be they constitutional, acquired, hereditary, or environmental, due to deficit, deprivation, trauma, misfortune, or unresolved neurotic conflict. If the unfolding of developmental levels of higher organisational mastery falters or becomes derailed, success— in terms of fulfilling the promise of one's innate potential—becomes an illusory target with no means to reach it. In another approach to the question, rather than taking the subject of success in broad and sweeping strokes, we might target manifestations of success in circumscribed terms of specific and discrete accomplishments, for example, passing a test, making a deadline, meeting a challenge, or resolving a particular difficulty. Whether in broader terms of developmental acquisition of organisational mastery, or in particular instances of mundane and discrete feats, success can well prove empowering, vitalising, self affirming, and growth promoting as it might also be frightening, overwhelming, challenging, and indeed threatening. Once one has succeeded, one may occupy a place of respect, deference, and social prominence, or on the contrary, become an object of envy, rivalry, and target of hostility. The actual circumstance is usually a combination of both, that is, narcissistic affirmation and pride, together with enduring vulnerability and expectant vigilance.

As sweet as success is reputed to sometimes be, other times it can create fresh challenges, open new horizons of complexity and uncertainty, and bring larger or insurmountable burdens of responsibility and increasing demand. Success usually comes at a price and often involves investment of purpose and hope, drive, persistence, courage, and energy (not to mention good luck, or making one's own good luck). It takes overcoming obstacles and suffering failures, coming to grips with one's own vulnerability and shortcomings as well as with realistic assessment of personally acquired stocks of available resources. The road to success is paved with innumerable pitfalls of disappointment, loss, and failure. We succeed only when we have learned to build our gains on the vestiges of the past losses and when we have weaved our path through assorted gaps of failure, disappointments, and defeat. Success, one might say, comes with great cost and no guarantee. Yes, sweet success at times might make it all worth it, but to be sure, with no pain there can be no gain.

To succeed in arriving at a goal that is ahead, one must decide, plan, execute, and reassess, sometimes move with deliberate intent and other times react reflexively, intuitively, or habitually. Some such reactions, whether reflective or reflexive, may trigger unexpected or costly consequences. Mixed feelings, trepidation, and regrets are not rare in the pursuit of success, where many lessons will be learned "the hard way". It therefore goes without saying that there is much to properly fear on the road to success and still more to face at the final destination. It is sober respect for, and reasonable accommodation to these fears and misgivings that finds the path to a desired end. Fear misjudged, denied, or exaggerated, however, can be of great detriment to success. Here again, if we distinguish fear due to an objective source of present danger, from anxiety caused by intrapsychic disturbance, we can better separate adaptive elements of normal coping from symptomatic pathology.

In Dr Klafter's fascinating clinical material (Chapter Six of this book), we are treated to a series of uncommonly illustrative descriptions and contributions of history, aetiology, psychodynamics, conflicts, symptoms, and analytic process in each of his three cases. We are reminded that fear of success is the most common of fears we encounter clinically. This observation certainly confirms my own personal experience in a large variety of clinical circumstances and treatment settings. Self sabotage before arriving at complete success, and catastrophic collapse or emotional de-compensation following attainment of long cherished life goals are repeatedly encountered in many clinical situations. In these instances, we are not dealing so much with realistic concern or reasonable fear. The culprit is unconscious guilt or anxiety that needs to be looked for, identified, labelled, clarified, and elaborated in terms of the contents of a central unconscious fantasy. It is this construct that enigmatically contains conflicting elements involved in creating and sustaining the symptoms in the final form of a compromise formation. When this symptomatic constellation is the by-product of unresolved Oedipal conflict in an individual with otherwise intact psychological structures and sufficient self reflective capacity, standard psychoanalytic technique can be effectively employed. More often, however, we are dealing with clinical challenges entailed in treating these symptomatic manifestations in victims of biological and constitutional impairment, developmental deficits or conflicts, trauma, abuse, neglect, deprivation, and life's eternally unpredictable vicissitudes and inevitable mishaps. In these instances, psychoanalytic theory can illuminate the field of operation and formulate applied technique, with necessary adaptation and introduction of therapeutic parameters, in allowing for repair, reorganisation, and movement past points of fixation or defensive regression.

Frequently, the initial presentation of the problem seems solidly Oedipal, but this veneer quickly dissolves into dyadic or narcissistic elements that take considerable time and effort before an Oedipal organisation of conflict resolution becomes possible to establish in a stable position that is durable and self-sustaining. In these circumstances, unresolved narcissistic and dyadic conflicts inevitably lead to problems of acting out, re-enactment and perhaps negative therapeutic reaction. The dyadically organised patterns of self and interactive regulation allow no space for loss of control of the object. One side dominates and the other is dominated. Omnipotence reigns and anger leaves nothing standing. Loss cannot be tolerated unless by denial, manic defence, splitting, or dissociation. Repression, representational and abstract thinking, empathy, and capacity for self reflection are not available and sublimation is not possible. What the patient really desires is unconditional gratification of all wishes all the time, through magical accommodation and total surrender by the world, rather than giving up anything in order to accommodate to loss and change. Not the analysand but the analyst is the one to change.

Some of this conflict of rapprochement is omnipresent in any analytic experience as regression in the transference leads to exertion of coercive measures to turn the failing defective mother of separation back into a utopian lost paradise of symbiotic bliss and oceanic dual unity. Whereas in pre-Oedipal pathology, reality principle and repression are not relied on and the narcissistic part object cannot be relinquished or lost, in Oedipal pathology such relinquishment is not problematic as the patient can productively move back and forth between wish and reality and gainfully accommodate to the analytic frame while deeply engaged in living in, "playing" with, and working through the transference. In the latter the emphasis is on resolution of the infantile neurosis and enhancement of autonomy.

In severe cases of pre-Oedipal pathology, until the unresolved conflicts of rapprochement have been sufficiently worked through, few if any, sustainable gains can be expected. In these patients, containment of destructive rage in the negative transference is the means to healing of the split. Without such constancy and containment the vertical split cannot heal, drive fusion is not feasible, and ego development remains stifled, particularly in regard to affect modulation and self and object constancy. In Winnicott's terms the object can be "used", that is, "destroyed" repeatedly and yet survive, if its benevolence and constancy is to be thus internalised. Libidinal object constancy is enhanced while the analyst manages to receive, contain, and metabolise the slings and arrows of disillusionment, without disappearing or retaliating. Normally we see interpersonal dyadic conflicts of ambivalence, power, and autonomy recapitulated in the transference. Issues of a dyadic nature that were not resolved originally or were not further advanced through recapitulation during adolescence can become a significant challenge in treatment, requiring special consideration and close attention. In the case of one my young patients, his self-sabotage and repeated failures were his magical and fail-safe defence of winning by defeating and frustrating the controlling other. The "other" stood for his ambitious and highly productive mother who was the "parentified" child of a distant, demanding, and emotionally unstable mother on whom she could never rely. Lacking the empathic capacity to sense and gauge her son's separation anxiety, she repeatedly left him to his own devices to excel in accordance with his obviously superior intelligence. She would go to any end to rescue him when in need, but would again fail to adequately support him when he needed her for day to day maternal availability. Jim's acting out behaviour resembled the early toddler's "darting" that manages to magically summon the inattentive mother to frantically pursue the heedless darting toddler and sweep him up into her arms and saving him from pending danger.

Jim could be certain to have mother at his side only if he was help-less, defeated, or in danger. As mother continued to impatiently push him on towards autonomy and self-sufficiency, feeling humiliated and disregarded, he retaliated by digging in or dragging his heels when he felt controlled, was pushed ahead, or pulled along. Unbearable anger at mother could not be recognised, processed, and neutralised and there-fore he was unable to relinquish his masochistic tie to sadistic maternal introjects. He routinely externalised his own self-contempt and unbear-able sense of guilt by turning others into demeaning, disapproving, and coercive figures of persecutory authority that he could render helplessly defeated by defiantly failing. In this, there was also identification with the aggressor and turning tables on the sadistic victimiser. I frequently found myself re-enacting or being pulled to react in the role being assigned to me. When aware of this pull I paid attention, played with it, asked questions about it, as sometimes I yielded, other times set limits, and at all times noted the intensity of his passive wishes which he found deeply shameful but unrelenting. Slowly he was feeling stronger, more adventurous, and able to assume and meet responsibility, including the responsibility of seeking fulfilment of his own passive longings for care and loving intimacy. He was doing well, now beginning to embark on a more independent and self-directed course towards success.

The end, as we know it: fear of death

As humans, unlike other sentient beings, we are burdened with the irre-pressible knowledge of the inevitability of our demise, finitude of our life span, and the immutable irreversibility of time. We are inalterably compelled to note that time ceaselessly marches only forward and once lost can never be retrieved. "This too, shall pass" is our stoic consola-tion during hard times, and longingly reaching back for the comforting bliss of the alluring recollections of happier "good old days", long gone, brings us nostalgic relief and rekindled hope for the soothing promise of still more good days, perhaps yet to come. We cannot escape the realisation that our life, contained and organised within the confines and constraints of time, moves only in one direction: inexorably forward, towards death. It is death, the ultimate and the final loss that we fear most, have to face one way or another, and in whose shadow we are forced to live, obliviously distracted or mindfully cognisant. Like an inseparable companion, death is forever lurking at our heels and its ever-present ominous shadow grows and gains in weight as we live and breathe and as we find ourselves traversing milestones. It pursues us as we climb ups and downs, as we delight in the joyful expansion of our new horizons, as we dread the pain of anticipated or unexpected wounds, and as we confront the imagined or unavoidably destined gloom of our future misfortunes. We live with the knowledge of the certainty of an end, to be reached sooner or later, but not comprehended, pondered yet never illuminated, grudgingly conceded but seldom willingly embraced. Those among us who welcome death, prepare to die willingly, or earnestly pursue their own demise comprise exceptional instances or extremity of circumstances and require special and highly unusual considerations regarding elements of reason, motivation, capability, and choice of alternatives. We know about death as we hear descriptions of others passing or having passed, see the fate of those who have reached the end, and indulge in speculative musings and machinations, or adhere to resolute faith as to what may lie beyond the life's end and what it might be like to be deceased. But since death is a state that we cannot personally experience during our actual life, we are unable to reach direct knowledge about, or full understanding of it. While we are living, our knowledge is not capable of entering this realm and once we reach the end our knowledge ceases to exist. Not even the unconscious, with its boundless reach and claim beyond all permutations of possibilities, contradictions, and negations, is capable of fathoming its reality. Yet we fear death above all other threats and the entirety of our physiological and genetic disposition is organised around the lone primacy of avoiding, aborting, and eliminating the remotest indications of its possibility, at any cost.

Psychologically, the outer limits of our conceptual grasp of death is relegated to its mental representation as the far-reaching extensions of the superego and projection of the calamities of childhood, in object loss, loss of love, and the loss of bodily integrity, which unlike death, constitute essential components of our actual existential experience. Our mind and its psychological apparatus fail in coming to grips with death, as do our physical equipment and our somatic resources. We resort to denial, avoidance, rationalisation, fantasies of omnipotence and narcissistic grandiosity, religion, tradition, culture, art, creativity, playfulness, and irony, in our continuing encounter and preoccupation with mortality. In this sense, it might be said that man has tried, known, and created innumerable means and paths of dealing and grappling with the problem of death, but has found no answers to solve it as an enigma or to overcome it as an obstacle even though, undoubtedly in the future as in the past, this quest will not cease.

As clinicians, we are all familiar with the struggles and tribulations of our patients who have faced loss, or are reliving various aspects of it at different levels of experience in the transference. We know about our own encounters, in our own early history and our formative years, or in later times, as well as in various permutations and contexts of transference during our own analysis and in the countertransference, reacting to our patients' internal conflicts and suffering. When such loss consists of death (dying patients or their loved ones), we can most compellingly experience the doom and gloom of its finality and the disarming helplessness that it spells and the upheaval that it creates in the analytic as well as the extra-analytic life on both sides of the couch. When, and if, our empathic capacity can sufficiently endure, we find ourselves at such times more intimately engaged with our patients than almost any other time, and feel most intensely in touch with the exquisite vulnerability that it unveils on both sides of the relationship. These immensely demanding moments challenge our technical, tactical, and personal resources and can exert influences of momentous consequence on the analytic course and process, at times uniquely salutary.

Because of these broad existential, as well as specific clinical reasons, I find Colarusso's multifaceted treatment of this topic (Chapter Seven of this book) cogently rewarding. I regard this effort, similar to his numerous other contributions which address all aspects of the life cycle and cover divergent areas of interest to psychoanalysis, and as we have grown to expect of his writings, high in quality of workmanship, richly informative in content, inclusively thorough in scope, and generously endowed with vivid examples derived not only from metapsychology, clinical experience, and literary sources, but particularly in this case, also from his well-established field of expertise, the cinema. Colarusso's longitudinal perspective on developmental variations on coping with fear of death, in health and pathology, is particularly appealing and easy to resonate with. It follows the natural trajectory of the unfolding of the variations in the subjective sense of the knowledge of one's mortality and its impact on adaptation.

Regarding the capacity of the young child in understanding death, some clarification may be in order. I am thinking of this telling interaction between a six-year-old girl and her nearly four-year-old brother. According to the mother, after the four-year-old boy noticed a dead bird on the lawn, he moved towards it, hesitated and then called out, "A bird! ... a dead bird ... It is dead ..." The sister, quickly moving towards him, yelled, "Wait, let it be, he isn't dead." The boy, now kneeling and looking closely, unconvinced, insisted, "Yes, it is dead, it's a dead bird." Mother was impressed with the fact that during the extended course of this interaction, the sister, who often enjoys misleading and triumphantly confusing her excitable and boastful brother, was unable to deter him from insisting on his firmly held conclusion that the bird was indeed and irrevocably dead. Here we have a four year old who knows dead when he sees it. His conviction is not swayed by authoritarian persuasion and cognitively he is confident about his own observation.

Piaget describes the appearance of "object permanence" as early as the last fourth of the first year. Whereas before that age, a fallen object no longer exists once out of sight, by this time the child follows the trajectory and the sound of the lost object in order to locate it. The object has now achieved permanence, cognitively, even though it has been lost visually. As a permanent object, it can be sought and perhaps found. By the age of four, "the libidinal object", that is, mother's mental representation, as well as self-representations, under optimal conditions, have reached the beginnings of self and object constancy. This means the affectively positive quality of the self and the object representations are no longer as readily lost to upsurges of anger and common instances of frustration. When mother is briefly out of sight, the child's secure attachment and confident expectation of her benevolence and continued availability are not lost. Her soothing image in the child's mind remains intact if her return is not unduly delayed. To maintain self-cohesion, the child needs to know that the mother will return as she has on other occasions. In cases of extended absence, or mother's death, the unbearable reality may lead to regression, magical and primary process thinking, and narcissistic defences. The six-year-old child knows well what it means that his mother is dead, but the notion that she is "really alive somewhere else, loving him and keeping an eye over him", buttresses his magical thinking and narcissistic defences, renders the agonising pain more bearable, and constructs a reasonably coherent narrative to maintain some semblance of self-cohesion, as the loss is being mourned. This is a matter of cognitive elements being mentalised in accordance with the child's developmental acquisitions. When such a narrative is implemented or reinforced by the environment, the defensive fantasy gains a stronger character of "truth" and realness.

The reason older preschoolers and some elementary school beginners hang on to the illusion of fairy tales, tooth fairies, and Santa Claus is, in part, the reinforcing confirmation they are provided by their adult carers. Around this age, children have only recently gained the capacity to juxtapose the pretend mode of thinking with objective reality and have gained some distance from psychic equivalency. Whereas earlier, they took their intrapsychic perception as equivalent of objective reality, by now differentiating the two has become possible. Whereas before this age, reality and pretend mode of thinking were incompatible, they can now be entertained side by side and in combination, if necessary. The child will, however, continue to experience an irresistible pull towards pretend play and a self-made world of comforting and omnipotent fantasy. Adults maintain an intuitive sense of this proclivity in children and are able to take advantage of its influence in their dealing with children, to comfort and sooth, motivate or at times intimidate or manipulate them. As reality processing and cognitive maturity take firm hold, the distinction between the two modes of thinking grow and the individual is able to choose to resort to one or the other or navigate in a transitional realm in-between, where creativity, art, original ideas, and novel solutions may be cultivated. It is this mode of mentation and this transitional realm of experience that we often turn to for answers to questions that are not answerable in terms of objective facts. This is a qualitative capacity that does not discriminate between preschoolers, adolescents, or adults and those in later stages of life. Our mentalisation of death uses this capability, at all ages, differently yet similarly for all of us, with our own unique narratives and the best compromise formations we find ourselves capable of mustering, at various developmental levels.

Legacy of integration

In addressing fears in the context of various life circumstances, the material covered in this volume is impressive in its depth and breadth. It covers various sources of knowledge in a longitudinal perspective as well as across the gaps and links of differing schools of thought. Remarkably notable in this far-reaching excursion is the advent of an increasing inclination towards previously ambiguous and mysteriously inviting procedural acquisitions that take human mentalisation capacity from a monadic, coenaesthetic global experience of primary narcissism, through a period of self and object differentiation. With the dawning of intersubjectivity in a dyadic mode, over a twenty-four-month period of transition, this dyadic organisation evolves into a triadic mode of relatedness. Triangulation rests upon the initial emergence of the beginning germs of self and object constancy. A triadic conflict resolution of an Oedipal nature finally becomes logistically possible after this time. By the age of four, commonly regarded as the entry point into the Oedipal phase of Freud's psychosexual development, neuro-cognitive maturity permits the beginnings of narrative formation, abstract thinking, and reality processing. By this age, we normally expect the beginnings of "the road to self and object constancy" along with the emergence of secondary narcissism, secondary thought process, and theory of mind.

Given average expectable developmental progression, by the age of four we have the differentiated internal structures and their corresponding functions that may be involved in intrapsychic conflict, normally culminating in "the infantile neurosis". By the sixth birthday, the infantile neurosis is expected to be adequately contained and resolved as ego and superego structure are solidified with the waning of the Oedipus complex. The greater portion of recent psychoanalytic research and literature concerns pre-Oedipal and relational matters as two-person psychology and intersubjectivity, for some time now, have occupied centre stage. While the classical stance regards the mind as an identifiable entity to be objectively treated and understood, the intersubjective perspective conceives of the mind not in isolation but as a part component of an interactive field, affecting and being affected by the subjectivity of each participant. The relational or intersubjective view incorporates implications of attachment theory as well as research in the mother/infant relationship. This creates the impression that classical concepts concerning sexuality and gender are no longer relevant.

Here we need to consider that relational matters of the pre-Oedipal period are procedural, not a part of the conscious system of experience and as such they are pre-cognitive, non-verbal or preverbal. Although gender-specific behaviour and discovery of the genitals can be identified as early as the end of the first year, sexuality as a new horizon in subjectivity and object choice gains its prominent place after the age of three. While mother remains attuned to the infant's subjective states— marking, mirroring, amplifying, and elaborating the child's internal states—she leaves the enigmatic, mysterious, and un-integrated sphere of sexuality unattended. Mother will not mark, amplify, or mirror sexuality. In this situation, sexuality is denied, repressed, or negated. This is not the case with affective elements in attachment behaviour, interactive regulation, and/or sensuality in its non-sexual form, as they are intuitive, procedural, pre-representational, dyadic, and not subject to repression.

A classically neurotic individual, presumed to be capable of triangulation and a triadic mode of relatedness or conflict resolution, can reflect upon, pursue, and forge new associations between the past, present, and future while separating transference experience from the reality of the therapeutic frame. Ideally, in this case, we would be dealing with an intrapsychic conflict that can lead to the formation of an analysable transference neurosis and working through of the regressive defences and redirecting emotional life towards new choices of progressive adaptation. In such instances of ideal circumstances, dyadic issues of a relational nature are not central and the patient can gain most from a primary focus on intrapsychic elements from an objectively neutral stance by the analyst. In pre-Oedipal pathology, in contrast, issues of narcissistic relevance and dyadic relatedness with predominantly oral and anal-sadistic derivatives are at the forefront and call for repair, restoration, or resolution before triadic-depressive-Oedipal levels of mentation can be gainfully encountered. For this reason, techniques of intervention and goals in treatment in the two situations are different. In pre-Oedipal pathology much effort and attention needs to be focused on the holding, containing, and mirroring aspects of the relationship, and the therapist has to be vigilant in repair of inevitable disruptions that are frequent and often highly dramatic. Just as in the mother–child relationship, here too, disruptions are routine and par for the course, so that reparative vigilance by the therapist is essential. Concepts of primal scene, negative Oedipus, castration complex, neutrality, frustration, anonymity, abstinence, etc., will always remain of paramount importance in our metapsychology and clinical work. They are not passé, misconceived, or outmoded. They each have simply morphed into the totality of the larger body of current knowledge and stand relevant at different levels of meaning and value at different phases of development, course of treatment, variations of pathology, and styles or technique. Here, we are vulnerable to the pitfall of colluding with our patients, especially children, in remaining entrenched in pre-genital material in our unconscious resistance to the erotic sector of the transference.

Our vast array of theoretical and experience-based data provides a treasure trove of concepts and techniques that makes our field a great deal more capable of directly engaging with an ever-widening scope. This might be a suitable point to endorse the revolutionary contributions of separation-individuation theory in providing a conceptual framework for the development of self and object constancy. Based on the findings of Rene Spitz, the contributions of Winnicott, Anna Freud, object relations theory, and ego psychology, it defines and interconnects the intrapsychic and the interpersonal. It accommodated both to one- as well as two-person psychology and organises the pre-oedipal experience around the universal principles of separation and individuation. This means learning to be alone in the presence of an "other" and to maintain a stable and secure connection in spite of the unavoidable ebbs and flows in the negative affective charge emanating from unexpected disruptions and routine disappointments.

In my comments, I have tried to point out the crucial importance of the rapprochement subphase as the nodal base of the healing of the split and fusion of the drives. It forces the process of transition from primary narcissism and primary process thinking on to secondary. If everything goes well, after a two-year period of this transition which coincides with the ascendance of Winnicott's transitional experience, the road to object constancy can begin. Attainment of self and object constancy only begins a lifelong process here that may never be completed. Triadic relatedness and symbolic thinking available at this juncture allow for entry into an Oedipal organisation of conflict resolution. Without adequate resolution of rapprochement, pre-Oedipal pathology is to be expected. The bitterly poignant resonance of rapprochement reverberates throughout the psychoanalytic treatment of any such patient who wants to destroy the analyst and forge him into an idealised object to match his own grandiose self. Possessing and owning the object to suit you is not the same quality of relatedness as your endless satisfaction in caring for and loving others who have their own unique mind and personhood.

In closing, it is fitting to note the admirable objective pursued by the editor of this collection to bring psychoanalysis to as many unexplored areas of inquiry as possible and to bring and connect to psychoanalysis as many novel entities as he can. This is a legacy of progressive re-synthesis and creative integration that characterise his thinking, teaching, clinical practice, and prolifically gifted authorship. A clinician involved in numerous and often acute or critical circumstances on a daily basis is faced with far more than merely what transpires on a couch, contained in a firm and flexible frame and reliant mainly on empathy, free association, and systematic working through. We need all the tools we can gather in our toolbox to apply, carefully suited to the problem in its native context, eclectically, guided by the ongoing expansion of our multifaceted metapsychology. As a psychoanalyst in practice of general psychiatry, covering all ages and nearly all clinical venues, I appreciate the privilege and opportunity to place my personal views on the subject of this book side by side with the impressive scholarship and refined expertise of such a distinguished group of authors and clinicians as this.

REFERENCES

Abraham, K. (1913a). Restrictions and transformations of scoptophilia in psychoneurotics, with remarks on analogous phenomena of folk psychology. In: *Selected Papers on Psychoanalysis* (pp. 226–234). London: Hogarth Press, 1927.

Abraham, K. (1913b). A constitutional basis of locomotor anxiety. In: *Selected Papers on Psychoanalysis* (pp. 235–249). London: Hogarth Press, 1927.

Abram, J. (1996). *The Language of Winnicott*. London: Karnac.

Akhtar, S. (1984). The syndrome of identity diffusion. *American Journal of Psychiatry, 141*: 1381–1385.

Akhtar, S. (1992). Tethers, orbits, and invisible fences: clinical, developmental, sociocultural, and technical aspects of optimal distance. In: S. Kramer & S. Akhtar (Eds.), *When the Body Speaks: Psychological Meanings in Kinetic Clues* (pp. 21–57). Northvale, NJ: Jason Aronson.

Akhtar, S. (1994). Object constancy and adult psychopathology. *International Journal of Psychoanalysis, 75*: 441–455.

Akhtar, S. (1995). A third individuation: immigration, identity, and the psychoanalytic process. *Journal of the American Psychoanalytic Association, 43*: 1051–1084.

Akhtar, S. (1996). Love and its discontents: a concluding overview. In: S. Akhtar & S. Kramer (Eds.), *Intimacy and Infidelity: Separation-Individuation Perspectives* (pp. 145–178). Northvale, NJ: Jason Aronson.

Akhtar, S. (1999). *Inner Torment: Living Between Conflict and Fragmentation*. New York: Jason Aronson.

Akhtar, S. (2007). From unmentalized xenophobia to messianic sadism: some reflections on the phenomenology of prejudice. In: H. Parens, A. Mahfouz, S. W. Twemlow, & D. E. Scharff (Eds.), *The Future of Prejudice: Psychoanalysis and the Prevention of Prejudice* (pp. 7–19). Lanham, MD: Jason Aronson.

Akhtar, S. (2009a). *Comprehensive Dictionary of Psychoanalysis*. London: Karnac.

Akhtar, S. (2009b). *The Damaged Core*. Lanham, MD: Jason Aronson.

Akhtar, S. (2010). Freud's *Todesangst* and Ghalib's *Ishrat-e-Qatra*: two perspectives on death. In: S. Akhtar (Ed.), *The Wound of Mortality: Fear, Denial, and Acceptance of Death* (pp. 1–20). Lanham, MD: Jason Aronson.

Akhtar, S. (Ed.) (2011). *Unusual Interventions: Alterations of the Frame, Method, and Relationship in Psychotherapy and Psychoanalysis*. London: Karnac.

Akhtar, S. (2013). *Psychoanalytic Listening: Methods, Limits, and Innovations*. London: Karnac.

Akhtar, S., & Brown, J. (2005). Animals in psychiatric symptomatology. In: S. Akhtar & V. Volkan (eds.), *Mental Zoo: Animals in the Human Mind and Its Pathology* (pp. 3–38). Madison, CT: International Universities Press.

Akhtar, S., & Kramer, S. (1997). *The Seasons of Life—Separation Individuation Perspectives*. Northvale, NJ: Jason Aronson.

Arlow, J. (1980). The revenge motive in the primal scene. *Journal of the American Psychoanalytic Association, 28*: 519–541.

Back to the Future (1985). Directed by R. Zemeckis, Universal Pictures production.

Balint, M. (1959). *Thrills and Regressions*. London: Hogarth Press.

Balint, M. (1968). *The Basic Fault: Therapeutic Aspects of Regression*. London: Tavistock.

Bennett-Levy, J., & Marteau, T. (1984). Fear of animals: what is prepared? *British Journal of Psychology, 75*: 37–42.

Bick, E. (1968). The experience of the skin in early object relations. *International Journal of Psychoanalysis, 49*: 484–486.

Bion, W. R. (1962). A theory of thinking. *International Journal of Psychoanalysis, 43*: 306–310.

Bion, W. R. (1967). *Second Thoughts*. London: Heinemann.

Bion, W. R. (1989). *Elements of Psychoanalysis*. London: Karnac.

Birds, The (1963). Directed by A. Hitchcock, Universal Pictures production.

Biswas-Diener, R. (2012). *The Courage Quotient: How Science Can Make You Braver*. San Francisco, CA: Jossey-Bass.

Blackman, J. (1997). Teaching psychodynamic technique during an observed analytic psychotherapy interview. *Academic Psychiatry, 21*: 148–154.

Blackman, J. (2003). *101 Defenses: How the Mind Shields Itself*. New York: Routledge.

Blackman, J. (2010). *Get the Diagnosis Right: Assessment and Treatment Selection for Mental Disorders*. New York: Routledge.

Blackman, J. (2012). *The Therapist's Answer Book: Solutions to 101 Tricky Problems in Psychotherapy*. New York: Routledge.

Blevis, M., & Feher-Gurewich, J. (2003). The jouissance of the other and the prohibition of incest: a Lacanian perspective. *Psychoanalytic Quarterly, 72*: 241–261.

Blos, P. (1966). *On Adolescence*. New York: Free Press.

Blos, P. (1985). *Son and Father*. New York: Free Press.

Blum, H. P. (1977). *Female Psychology: Contemporary Psychoanalytic Views*. New York: International Universities Press.

Blum, H. P. (2003). Repression, transference and reconstruction. *International Journal of Psychoanalysis, 84*: 497–503.

Blum, H. P., & Ross, J. M. (1993). The clinical relevance of the contribution of Winnicott. *Journal of the American Psychoanalytic Association, 41*: 219–235.

Bollas, C. (2013). *Catch Them Before They Fall: The Psychoanalysis of Breakdown*. New York: Routledge.

Bolognini, S. (2011). *Secret Passages: The Theory and Technique of Interpsychic Relations*. London: Routledge.

Bouchard, M., Target, M., Lecours, S., Fonagy, P., Tremblay, L., Schachter, A., & Stein, H. (2008). Mentalization in adult attachment narratives: reflective functioning, mental states, and affect elaboration compared. *Psychoanalytic Psychology, 25*: 47–66.

Bowlby, J. (1940). The influence of early environment in the development of neurosis and neurotic character. *International Journal of Psychoanalysis, 21*: 154–178.

Bowlby, J. (1944a). Forty-four juvenile thieves: their characters and home-life (I). *International Journal of Psychoanalysis, 25*: 19–53.

Bowlby, J. (1944b). Forty-four juvenile thieves: their characters and home-life (II). *International Journal of Psychoanalysis, 25*: 107–128.

Bowlby, J. (1969). *Attachment and Loss, Vol. I: Attachment*. New York: Basic, 1980.

Brenner, C. (1976). *Psychoanalytic Technique and Psychic Conflict*. New York: International Universities Press.

Brenner, C. (1982). *The Mind in Conflict*. Madison, CT: International Universities Press.

Brenner, C. (2006). *Psychoanalysis: Mind and Meaning*. New York: Psychoanalytic Quarterly.

Bretherton, I. (1992). The origins of attachment theory: John Bowlby and Mary Ainsworth. *Developmental Psychology, 28*: 759–775.

Burns, D. (1980). *Feeling Good: the New Mood Therapy*. New York: HarperCollins.

Campbell, J., & Pile, S. (2011). Space travels of the Wolfman: phobia and its worlds. *Psychoanalysis and History, 13*: 69–88.

Card, O. (1994). *Ender's Game*. Tor Science Fiction. http://www.tor.com

Caruth, C. (2001). An interview with Jean Laplanche. http://pmc.iath.virginia.edu/text-onlyissue.101/11.2caruth.txt

Cat on a Hot Tin Roof (1958). Directed by E. Kazan, MGM production.

Chadwick, M. (1929). Notes upon the fear of death. *International Journal of Psychoanalysis, 9*: 321–334.

Clockwork Orange, A (1974). Directed by S. Kubrick, Warner Brothers production.

Cocoon (1985). Directed by R. Howard, Twentieth Century Fox production.

Coen, S. (1981). Sexualization as a predominant mode of defense. *Journal of the American Psychoanalytic Association, 29*: 893–920.

Colarusso, C. A. (1975). Johnny, did your mother die? *Teacher, 92*: 57.

Colarusso, C. A. (1988). The development of time sense in adolescence. *Psychoanalytic Study of the Child, 43*: 179–198.

Colarusso, C. A. (1990). Separation-individuation processes in middle adulthood: the fourth individuation. In: S. Akhtar and S. Kramer (Eds.), *The Seasons of Life: Separation-Individuation Perspectives* (pp. 73–94). Northvale, NJ: Jason Aronson.

Colarusso, C. A. (2010). Living to die and dying to live. In: S. Akhtar (Ed.), *The Wound of Mortality: Fear, Denial, and Acceptance of Death* (pp. 107–123). Lanham, MD: Jason Aronson.

Colarusso, C. A., & Nemiroff, R. A. (1979). Some observations and hypotheses about the psychoanalytic theory of adult development. *International Journal of Psychoanalysis, 60*: 59–71.

Coles, R. (1965). On courage. *Contemporary Psychoanalysis, 1*: 85–98.

Colman, A. (2009). *A Dictionary of Psychology*. London: Oxford University Press.

Cook, M., & Mineka, S. (1987). Second order conditioning and overshadowing in the observational conditioning of fear in monkeys. *Behavior Research and Therapy, 25*: 349–364.

Damasio, A. (1999). *The Feeling of What Happens*. London: Heinemann.

Davey, G. (1992). Characteristics of individuals with fear of spiders. *Anxiety Research, 4*: 299–314.

Davey, G., Forster, L., & Mayhew, G. (1993). Familial resemblances in disgust sensitivity and animal phobias. *Behavior Research and Therapy, 31*: 41–50.

Delprato, D. (1980). Hereditary determinants of fears and phobias: a critical review. *Behavior Therapy, 11*: 79–103.

Deutsch, H. (1929). The genesis of agoraphobia. *International Journal of Psychoanalysis, 10*: 51–69.

Dimbleby, R. (1938). Chamberlain returns from Munich with Anglo-German Agreement. *BBC Video Archive.* http://www.bbc.co.uk/archive/ww2outbreak/7907.shtml

Dorsey, D. (1996). Castration anxiety or feminine genital anxiety? *Journal of the American Psychoanalytic Association, 44S*: 283–302.

DSM-IV-TR (2000). Diagnostic and Statistical Manual of Mental Disorders, Fourth Edition, Text Revision. Arlington, VA: American Psychiatric Association.

Dupont, J. (Ed.) (1988). *The Clinical Diary of Sandor Ferenczi.* Cambridge, MA: Harvard University Press, 1995.

Emanuel, R. (2004). Thalamic fear. *Journal of Child Psychotherapy, 30*(1): 71–87.

Emde, R. N. (1983). The prerepresentational self and its affective core. *Psychoanalytic Study of the Child, 21*: 3–9.

Emde, R. N. (1984). The affective self. In: J. D. Call, E. Galenson, & R. L. Tyson (Eds.), *Frontiers of Infant Psychiatry* (pp. 38–54). New York: Basic.

Epstein, E. (May 24, 2012). Former defense attorney claims serial killer Ted Bundy confessed to 'murdering more than 100 people and his first victim was a MAN'. London: *The Daily Mail.* http://www.dailymail.co.uk/news/article-2149382/ (accessed April 25, 2013).

Erikson, E. H. (1963). *Childhood and Society.* New York: W. W. Norton.

Escoll, P. (1992). Vicissitudes of optimal distance through the life cycle. In: S. Kramer and S. Akhtar (Eds.), *When the Body Speaks: Psychological Meanings in Kinetic Clues* (pp. 59–87). Northvale, NJ: Jason Aronson.

Exorcist, The (1973). Directed by W. Friedkin, Warner Brothers production.

Eysenck, H. J. (1965). *The Causes and Cures of Neurosis.* London: Routledge & Kegan Paul.

Eysenck, H. J. (1976). The conditioning model of neurosis. *Behavior Research and Therapy, 14*: 251–267.

Faimberg, H. (2007). A plea for a broader concept of *Nachtraglichkeit. Psychoanalytic Quarterly, 76*: 1221–1240.

Fairbairn, W. R. D. (1952). *Psychoanalytic Studies of the Personality.* London: Routledge & Kegan Paul.

FBI 100 (2008). The Unabomber. http://www.fbi.gov/news/stories/2008/-april/unabomber_042408 (accessed April 27, 2013).

Fenichel, O. (1945). *The Psychoanalytic Theory of Neurosis.* New York: W. W. Norton.

Ferenczi, S. (1930). The principle of relaxation and neocatharsis. In: *Final Contributions to the Problems and Methods of Psychoanalysis* (pp. 108–125). New York: Basic, 1955.

Ferenczi, S. (1931). Child analysis in the analysis of adults. In: *Final Contributions to the Problems and Methods of Psychoanalysis* (pp. 126–142). New York: Basic, 1955.

Ferenczi, S. (1933). On the confusion of tongues between adults and the child. In: *Final Contributions to the Problems and Methods of Psychoanalysis* (pp. 155–167). New York: Basic, 1955.

Fliess, R. (1942). The metapsychology of the analyst. *Psychoanalytic Quarterly, 11*: 211–227.

Fonagy, P. (1999). Memory and therapeutic action. *International Journal of Psychoanalysis, 80*: 215–223.

Fonagy, P. (2001). *Attachment Theory and Psychoanalysis*. New York: Other Press.

Fonagy, P. (2008). A genuinely developmental theory of sexual enjoyment and its implications for psychoanalytic technique. *Journal of the American Psychoanalytic Association, 56*: 11–36.

Fonagy, P., Gergely, G., Jursit, E., & Target, M. (2002). *Affect Regulation, Mentalization and the Development of the Self*. New York: Other Press.

Fonagy, P., & Target, M. (1997). Attachment and reflective function: their role in self-organization. *Development and Psychopathology, 9*: 679–700.

Freud, A. (1936). *The Ego and the Mechanisms of Defense*. New York: International Universities Press.

Freud, A. (1981). The concept of developmental lines: their diagnostic significance. *Psychoanalytic Study of the Child, 36*: 129–136.

Freud, S. (1897). *The Complete Letters of Sigmund Freud to Wilhelm Fliess, 1887–1904*. J. M. Masson (Ed. & Trans.). Cambridge, MA: Harvard University Press, 1985.

Freud, S. (1899a). Screen memories. *S. E., 3*: 299–322. London: Hogarth.

Freud, S. (1900a). *The Interpretation of Dreams. S. E., 4–5*: 1–626. London: Hogarth.

Freud, S. (1905d). *Three Essays on the Theory of Sexuality. S. E., 7*: 123–246. London: Hogarth.

Freud, S. (1907). Letter from Sigmund Freud to Karl Abraham, July 7, 1907. *The Complete Correspondence of Sigmund Freud and Karl Abraham 1907–1925* (pp. 1–4). London: Hogarth.

Freud, S. (1909b). Analysis of a phobia in a five-year old boy. *S. E., 10*: 5–149. London: Hogarth.

Freud, S. (1914g). Remembering, repeating and working-through (further recommendations on the technique of psycho-analysis, II). *S. E., 12*: 145–156. London: Hogarth.

Freud, S. (1915a). Observations on transference–love (further recommendations on the technique of psycho-analysis, III). *S. E., 12*: 157–171. London: Hogarth.

Freud, S. (1915e). The unconscious. *S. E., 14*: 159–216. London: Hogarth.

Freud, S. (1916a). On transience. *S. E., 14*: 73–102. London: Hogarth.

Freud, S. (1916d). Some character-types met with in psychoanalytic work: (II) those wrecked by success. *S. E., 14*: 316–331. London: Hogarth.

Freud, S. (1918b). From the history of an infantile neurosis. *S. E., 17*: 3–122. London: Hogarth.

Freud, S. (1919h). The uncanny. *S. E., 17*: 217–252. London: Hogarth.

Freud, S. (1920g). *Beyond the Pleasure Principle. S. E., 18*: 1–64. London: Hogarth.

Freud, S. (1923b). *The Ego and the Id. S. E., 19*: 3–66. London: Hogarth.

Freud, S. (1926d). *Inhibitions, Symptoms and Anxiety. S. E., 20*: 75–176. London: Hogarth.

Freud, S. (1937d). Constructions in analysis. *S. E., 23*: 255–270. London: Hogarth.

Freud, S. (1950a). The project for a scientific discovery. *S. E., 1*: 295–343. London: Hogarth.

Freud, S., & Breuer, J. (1895d). *Studies on Hysteria. S. E., 2*: 1–323. London: Hogarth.

Friedman, L. (1983). Reconstruction and the like. *Psychoanalytic Inquiry, 3*: 189–222.

Gellerman, D., & Suddath, R. (2005). Violent fantasy, dangerousness, and the duty to warn and protect. *Journal of the American Academy of Psychiatry and Law, 33*: 484–495.

Gibson, E. J., & Walk, R. D. (1960). The "visual cliff." *Scientific American, 202*: 67–71.

Goldstein, J. (1998). *Why We Watch?: The Attractions of Violent Entertainment.* New York: Oxford University Press.

Good, M. (Ed.) (2005). *The Seduction Theory in Its Second Century: Trauma, Fantasy, and Reality Today.* Madison, CT: International Universities Press.

Grand, S. (2002). *The Reproduction of Evil: A Clinical and Cultural Perspective.* Mahwah, NJ: Analytic Press.

Gray, P. (2005). *The Ego and the Analysis of Defense.* Northvale, NJ: Jason Aronson.

Greenspan, S. (1994). *Playground Politics: Understanding the Emotional Life of Your School-Age Child.* Cambridge, MA: Da Capo Press.

Greenspan, S. (1996). *The Challenging Child: Understanding, Raising, and Enjoying the Five "Difficult" Types of Children.* Cambridge, MA: Da Capo Press.

Greenspan, S., & Lewis, N. (1999). *Building Healthy Minds: The Six Experiences that Create Intelligence and Emotional Growth in Babies and Young Children: A Merloyd Lawrence Book.* Cambridge, MA: Da Capo Press.

Griffore, R. J. (1977). Validation of three measures of fear of success. *Journal of Personality Assessment, 41*: 417–421.

Grotjahn, M. (1984). Being sick and facing eighty: observations of an aging therapist. In: R. A. Nemiroff & C. A. Colarusso (Eds.), *The Race Against Time: Psychotherapy and Psychoanalysis in the Second Half of Life* (pp. 293–302). New York: Plenum Press.

Guarnaccia, P. J., & Rogler, L. H. (1999). Research on culture-bound syndromes: new directions. *American Journal of Psychiatry, 156*: 1322–1327.

Guillaume, K. (accessed April 25, 2013). *The Rape of the Sabine Women*. Painting by Poussin. *Musée de Louvre*. http://www.louvre.fr/en/oeuvre-notices/rape-sabine-women

Guntrip, H. (1969). *Schizoid Phenomena, Object-Relations and the Self*. New York: International Universities Press.

Harley, M., & Sabot, L. M. (1980). Conceptualizing the nature of the therapeutic action of child analysis. *Journal of the American Psychoanalytic Association, 28*: 161–179.

Harrison, B. (July 23, 2003). 'Snake' and playboy had only lust for blood in common: Uday Hussein 1964–2003. *New York Post*. http://www.nypost.com/p/news/item (accessed April 25, 2013).

Herzog, J. (2001). *Father Hunger: Explorations with Adults and Children*. Hillsdale, NJ: Analytic Press.

Hoffer, A. (1985). Toward a definition of psychoanalytic neutrality. *Journal of the American Psychoanalytic Association, 33*: 771–795.

Hoffman, L., Johnson, E., Foster, M., & Wright, J. (2010). What happens when you die? three to four year olds chatting about death. In: S. Akhtar (Ed.), *The Wound of Mortality: Fear, Denial, and Acceptance of Death* (pp. 21–36). Lanham, MD: Jason Aronson.

Holmes, D. E. (2006). The wrecking effects of race and social class on self and success. *Psychoanalytic Quarterly, 75*: 215–235.

Horner, A. (1984). Organizing processes and the genesis of object relations. In: *Object Relations and the Developing Ego in Therapy* (pp. 1–22). Northvale, NJ: Jason Aronson, 2004.

Horner, M. (1968). Sex differences in the achievement, motivation, and performance in competitive and non-competitive situations. [Unpublished doctoral dissertation.] Ann Arbor, MI: University of Michigan.

Hurvich, M. (2003). The place of annihilation anxieties in psychoanalytic theory. *Journal of the American Psychoanalytic Association, 51*: 579–616.

Hutson, P. (1996). *The Envy Complex: Its Recognition and Analysis. Danger and Defense*. Northvale, NJ: Jason Aronson.

Hutson, P., Pulver, S. E., Kilbourne, B., Lansky, M., & Morrison, A. (2003). *Panel on Shame and Intrapsychic Conflict*. American Psychoanalytic Association Meeting, New York City: December.

Ibsen, H. (1886). *Rosmersholm*. J. McFarlane (Trans.). Oxford: Oxford University Press, 1999.

Jacobson, E. (1964). *The Self and the Object World*. New York. International Universities Press.

Jacques, E. (1965). Death and the midlife crisis. *International Journal of Psychoanalysis, 46*: 457–472.

Jaws (1975). Directed by S. Spielberg, Universal Pictures production.

Johnson, A., & Szurek, S. (1952). The genesis of antisocial acting out in children and adults. *Psychoanalytic Quarterly, 21*: 323–343.

Jones, E. (1927). The early development of female sexuality. *International Journal of Psychoanalysis, 8*: 459–472.

Jones, E. (1948). Theory of symbolism. In: *Papers on Psycho-Analysis, 5th Edition* (pp. 116–141). London: Bailliere, Tindall & Cox, 1959.

Jordan, L. (2002). The analyst's uncertainty and fear. *Journal of the American Psychoanalytic Association, 50*: 989–993.

Joseph, D. I. (1990). Preoedipal factors in "Little Hans". *Journal of the American Psychoanalytic Association, 18*: 206–222.

Kafka, H. (1998). Fear in the countertransference and the mutuality of safety. *International Forum of Psychoanalysis, 7*: 97–103.

Kalaidjian, W. (2012). Traversing psychosis: Lacan, topology, and "the jet-propelled couch." *American Imago, 69*: 185–213.

Kanzer, M. (1953). Past and present in the transference. *Journal of the American Psychoanalytic Association, 1*: 144–154.

Kapleau, R., Tisdale, S., & Deshimaru, R. (1998). The encouragement stick. *Tricycle Home Magazine*. http://www.tricycle.com/onpractice/zens-big-stick-the-kyosaku (accessed April 25, 2013).

Karr-Morse, R. (2012). *Scared Sick*. New York: Basic.

Kavaler-Adler, S. (1985). Mirror mirror on the wall. *Journal of Comprehensive Psychotherapy, 5*: 1–38.

Kavaler-Adler, S. (1988). Diane Arbus and the demon lover. *American Journal of Psychoanalysis, 48*: 366–370.

Kavaler-Adler, S. (1989). Anne Sexton and the demon lover. *American Journal of Psychoanalysis, 49*: 105–114.

Kavaler-Adler, S. (1992). Mourning and erotic transference. *International Journal of Psychoanalysis, 73*: 527–539.

Kavaler-Adler, S. (1993a). *The Compulsion to Create: A Psychoanalytic Study of Women Artists*. London: Routledge.

Kavaler-Adler, S. (1993b). Object relations issues in the treatment of the preoedipal character. *American Journal of Psychoanalysis, 53*: 19–34.

Kavaler-Adler, S. (1993c). The conflict and process theory of Melanie Klein. *American Journal of Psychoanalysis, 53*: 187–204.

Kavaler-Adler, S. (1995). Opening up blocked mourning in the preoedipal character. *American Journal of Psychoanalysis, 55*: 145–168.

Kavaler-Adler, S. (1996). *The Creative Mystique: From Red Shoes Frenzy to Love and Creativity*. London: Routledge.

Kavaler-Adler, S. (2003a). *Mourning, Spirituality and Psychic Change: A New Object Relations View of Psychoanalysis*. London: Routledge.

Kavaler-Adler, S. (2003b). Lesbian homoerotic transference in dialectic with developmental mourning: on the way to symbolism from the protosymbolic. *Psychoanalytic Psychology, 20*: 131–152.

Kavaler-Adler, S. (2004). Anatomy of regret: the critical turn towards love and creativity in the transforming schizoid personality. *American Journal of Psychoanalysis, 64*: 39–76.

Kavaler-Adler, S. (2005a). The case of David: nine years on the couch for sixty minutes, once a week. *American Journal of Psychoanalysis, 65*: 103–134.

Kavaler-Adler, S. (2005b). From benign mirror to demon lover: an object relations view of compulsion versus desire. *American Journal of Psychoanalysis, 65*: 31–52.

Kavaler-Adler, S. (2006). My graduation is my mother's funeral: transformation from the paranoid-schizoid to the depressive position in fear of success, and the role of the internal saboteur. *International Forum of Psychoanalysis, 15*: 117–136.

Kavaler-Adler, S. (2007). Pivotal moments of surrender to mourning the parental internal object. *Psychoanalytic Review, 94*: 763–789.

Kavaler-Adler, S. (2010). Seduction, date rape, and aborted surrender. *International Forum of Psychoanalysis, 19*: 15–26.

Kavaler-Adler, S. (2013b). *Klein-Winnicott Dialectic: Transforming Metapsychology and Interactive Clinical Theory*. London: Karnac.

Kernberg, O. F. (1967). Borderline pathology organization. *Journal of the American Psychoanalytic Association, 15*: 641–685.

Kernberg, O. F. (1975). *Borderline Conditions and Pathological Narcissism*. New York: Jason Aronson.

Kernberg, O. F. (1976). *Object Relations Theory and Clinical Psychoanalysis*. New York: Jason Aronson.

Kernberg, O. F. (1980). *Internal World and External Reality: Object Relations Theory Applied*. New York: Jason Aronson.

Kernberg, O. F. (1984). *Severe Personality Disorders: Psychotherapeutic Strategies*. New Haven, CT: Yale University Press.

Kernberg, O. F. (1995). *Love Relations*. New Haven, CT: Yale University Press.

Khan, M. M. R. (1960). Regression and integration in the analytic setting. In: *The Privacy of the Self* (pp. 136–167). New York: International Universities Press, 1974.

Khan, M. M. R. (1963). Ego-ideal, excitement and the threat of annihilation. In: *The Privacy of the Self* (pp. 181–202). New York: International Universities Press, 1974.

Khan, M. M. R. (1972). Dread of surrender to resourceless dependence in the analytic situation. *International Journal of Psychoanalysis, 53*: 225–230.

Khan, M. M. R. (1974). *The Privacy of the Self.* Madison, CT: International Universities Press.

Kidder, R. M. (2006). *Moral Courage.* New York: HarperCollins.

Kilbourne, B. (2002). *Disappearing Persons: Shame and Appearance.* Albany, NY: State University of New York Press.

King and I, The (1956). Directed by W. Lang, produced by Twentieth Century Fox.

Kirkpatrick, D. (January 14, 2013). Morsi's slurs against Jews stir concern. *New York Times.* http://www.nytimes.com/2013/01/15/world/middleeast/egypts-leader-morsi-made-anti-jewish-slurs.html?_r=0

Klein, M. (1932). *The Psychoanalysis of Children.* New York, NY: The Free Press, 1975.

Klein, M. (1940). Mourning and its relation to manic depressive states. In: *Love, Guilt and Reparation and Other Works, 1921–1945.* London: Hogarth, 1975.

Klein, M. (1946). Notes on some schizoid mechanisms. In: *Envy and Gratitude and Other Works, 1946–1963.* London: Hogarth, 1980.

Klein, M. (1957). Envy and gratitude. In: *Envy and Gratitude and Other Works, 1946–1963.* London: Hogarth, 1980.

Knight, R. (2005). The process of attachment and autonomy in latency. *Psychoanalytic Study of the Child, 60*: 178–210.

Kogan, I. (2010). Fear of death: analyst and patient in the same boat. In: S. Akhtar (Ed.), *The Wound of Mortality: Fear, Denial, and Acceptance of Death-* (pp. 79–96). Northvale, NJ: Jason Aronson.

Kohut, H. (1966). Forms and transformations in narcissism. *Journal of the American Psychoanalytic Association, 14*: 243–272.

Kohut, H. (1971). *Analysis of the Self.* New York: International Universities Press.

Kohut, H. (1977). *Restoration of the Self.* New York: International Universities Press.

Kohut, H. (1980). *Self Psychology and the Humanities.* New York: W. W. Norton.

Kramer, S., & Akhtar, S. (1988). The developmental context of internalized preoedipal object relations—clinical applications of Mahler's theory of symbiosis and separation-individuation. *Psychoanalytic Quarterly, 57*: 547–576.

Kulish, N. (1996). A phobia of the couch: a clinical study of psychoanalytic process. *Psychoanalytic Quarterly, 65*: 465–494.

Lacan, J. (1949). The mirror stage as formative of the *I* function. *Ecrits*. B. Fink (Trans.). New York: W. W. Norton, 2002.

Lacan, J. (1953). Variations on the standard treatment. *Ecrits*. B. Fink (Trans.). New York: W. W. Norton, 2002.

Lacan, J. (1953). The function and field of speech and language. *Ecrits* (pp. 30–113). A. Sheridan (Trans.). London: Tavistock, 1977.

Lacan, J. (1958). The direction of treatment and the principles of its power. *Ecrits* (pp. 226–280). A. Sheridan (Trans.). London: Tavistock, 1977.

Lacan, J. (1982). The subjective import of the castration complex. *Feminine Sexuality*. J. Rose (Trans.). New York: W. W. Norton, 1985.

Lamb, M., & Oppenheim, D. (1989). Fatherhood and father-child relationships: five years of research. In: S. Cath, A. Gurwitt, & L. Gunsberg (Eds.), *Fathers and Their Families*. Hillsdale, NJ: Analytic Press.

Lansky, M. (2000). Shame dynamics in the psychotherapy of the patient with PTSD. *Journal of the American Academy of Psychoanalysis and Dynamic Psychiatry, 28*: 133–146.

Lansky, M., & Morrison, A. (1997). *The Widening Scope of Shame*. Hillsdale, NJ: Analytic Press.

Laplanche, J. (1973). *A New Language of Psychoanalysis*. D. Nicholson-Smith (Trans.). London: Hogarth.

Laplanche, J. (1992). Interpretation between determinism and hermeneutics: a restatement of the problem. *International Journal of Psychoanalysis, 73*: 429–445.

Laplanche, J. (2011). *Freud and the Sexual*. New York: International Psycho-analytic Books.

Laplanche, J., & Pontalis, J. -B. (1968). Fantasy and the origins of sexuality. *International Journal of Psychoanalysis, 49*: 1–18.

Ledeen, M. (2007). *The Iranian Time Bomb: The Mullah Zealots' Quest for Destruction*. New York: Truman Talley.

Ledeen, M. (2009). *Accomplice to Evil: Iran and the War Against the West*. New York: Truman Talley.

Leonowens, A. (1870). *The English Governess at the Siamese Court: Being Six Years in the Royal Palace at Bangkok*. Bedford, MA: Applewood.

Lerner, H. (1976). Parental mislabeling of female genitals as a determinant of penis envy and learning inhibitions in women. *Journal of the American Psychoanalytic Association, 24S*: 269–283.

Levy, S. T., Seelig, B. J., & Inderbitzin, L. B. (1995). On those wrecked by success: a clinical inquiry. *Psychoanalytic Quarterly, 64*: 639–665.

Lewin, B. D. (1935). Claustrophobia. *Psychoanalytic Quarterly, 4*: 227–233.

Lewin, B. D. (1952). Phobic symptoms and dream interpretation. *Psychoanalytic Quarterly, 21*: 295–322.

Lewin, K. (1935). *A Dynamic Theory of Personality*. New York: McGraw-Hill.

Lichtenberg, J. D. (1991). Fear, phobia, and panic. *Psychoanalytic Inquiry, 11*: 395–415.

Lieberman, M., & Tobin, S. (1983). *The Experience of Old Age: Stress, Coping, and Survival*. New York: Basic.

Lifton, R. J. (1979). *The Broken Connection*. New York: Simon & Schuster.

Lifton, R. J. (1986). *The Nazi Doctors: Medical Killing and the Psychology of Genocide*. New York: Basic.

Loewenstein, R. M. (1957). Some thoughts on interpretation in the theory and practice of psychoanalysis. *Psychoanalytic Study of the Child, 12*: 127–150.

Lorand, S. (1950). *Clinical Studies in Psychoanalysis*. New York: International Universities Press.

Louis, T. Owens Co., Thailand and England (accessed April 27, 2013). http://www.louist.co.th/index.php/en/about-us#

Mackinnon, R., & Michels, R. (1971). *The Psychiatric Interview in Clinical Practice*. Philadelphia, PA: W. B. Saunders.

Mahler, M. S. (1965). On the significance of the normal separation-individuation phase. In: M. Schur (Ed.), *Drives, Affects, Behavior* (pp. 161–169). New York: International Universities Press.

Mahler, M. S. (1971). A study of the separation-individuation process—and its possible application to borderline phenomena in the psychoanalytic situation. *Psychoanalytic Study of the Child, 26*: 403–424.

Mahler, M. S., Pine, F., & Bergman, A. (1975). *The Psychological Birth of the Human Infant: Symbiosis and Individuation*. New York: Basic.

Maltsberger, J., & Buie, D. (1974). Countertransference hate in the treatment of suicidal patients. *Archives of General Psychiatry, 30*: 625–633.

Marcus, I. (1971). The marriage-separation pendulum: a character disorder associated with early object loss. In: I. Marcus (Ed.), *Currents in Psychoanalysis* (pp. 361–383). New York: International Universities Press.

Marcus, I. (1980). Countertransference and the psychoanalytic process in children and adolescents. *Psychoanalytic Study of the Child, 35*: 285–298.

Marcus, I., & Francis, J. (1975). *Masturbation: From Infancy to Senescence*. New York: International Universities Press.

Markman, H. (2010). The past as resistance, the past as constructed. *International Journal of Psychoanalysis, 91*: 387–390.

Marks, I. (1970a). Classification of phobic disorders. *British Journal of Psychiatry, 116*: 377–386.

Marks, I. M. (1970b). The origins of phobic states. *American Journal of Psychotherapy, 24*: 652–676.

Marks, I. M. (1987). *Fears, Phobias, and Rituals*. New York: Oxford University Press.

Martel, Y. (2001). *The Life of Pi*. Toronto: Random House of Canada.

Maslow, A. (1971). *The Farther Reaches of Human Nature*. New York: Viking Press.

Masson, J. N. (Ed.) (1985). *The Complete Letters of Sigmund Freud to Wilhelm Fliess, 1897–1904*. Cambridge, MA: Harvard University Press.

Masterson, J. F. (1981). *The Narcissistic and Borderline Disorders: An Integrated Developmental Approach*. New York: Routledge.

Matthias, D. (2008). The analyst's fears. *Newsletter of the Psychoanalytic Society of New England East, 20*: 9–12.

McNally, R. J., & Steketee, G. S. (1985). The etiology and maintenance of severe animal phobias. *Behavior Research and Therapy, 23*: 431–435.

Mean Girls (2004). Directed by M. Waters, Paramount Pictures production.

Meers, D. (1970). Contributions of a ghetto culture to symptom formation—psychoanalytic studies of ego anomalies in childhood. *Psychoanalytic Study of the Child, 25*: 209–230.

Meers, D. (1973). Psychoanalytic research and intellectual functioning of ghetto-reared, black children. *Psychoanalytic Study of the Child, 28*: 395–417.

Meers, D. (1974). Traumatic and cultural distortions of psychoneurotic symptoms in a black ghetto. *Annual of Psychoanalysis, 2*: 368–386.

Meltzer, D. (1973). *Sexual States of Mind*. London: Karnac, 2008.

Menaker, E. (1979). Masochism and the emergent ego. In: L. Lerner (Ed.), *Selected Papers of Esther Menaker* (pp. 72–101). New York: Human Sciences Press.

Meth, J. M. (1974). Exotic psychiatric syndromes. In: S. Arieti & E. B. Brody (Eds.), *American Handbook of Psychiatry, 2nd Edition, Vol. III* (pp. 723–739). New York: Basic.

Metropolitan Police The enduring mystery of Jack the Ripper. http://www.met.police.uk/-history/ripper.htm (accessed April 27, 2013).

Military Quotes. http://www.military-quotes.com/Churchill.htm (accessed April 25, 2013).

Miller, E. (1986). The Oedipus complex and rejuvenation fantasies in the analysis of a seventy-year-old woman. *Journal of Geriatric Psychiatry, 20*: 29–51.

Miller, J. R. (1994). Fear of success. *Journal of the American Academy of Psychoanalysis and Dynamic Psychiatry, 22*: 129–136.

Mineka, S., Davidson, M., Cook, M., & Keir, R. (1984). Observational conditioning of snake fear in rhesus monkeys. *Journal of Abnormal Psychology, 93*: 355–372.

Mish, F. C. (Ed.) (1998). *Merriam Webster's Collegiate Dictionary (10th Edition)*. Springfield, MA: Merriam Webster Press.

Mitchell, S. A. (1988). *Relational Concepts in Psychoanalysis: An Integration*. Cambridge, MA: Harvard University Press.

Mitrani, J. (1998). Never before and never again: the compulsion to repeat, the fear of breakdown and the defensive organization. *International Journal of Psychoanalysis, 79*: 301–316.

Mittelmann, B. (1957). Motility in the therapy of children and adults. *Psychoanalytic Study of the Child, 12*: 284–319.

Modell, A. (1963). Primitive object relationships and previous position to schizophrenia. *International Journal of Psychoanalysis, 44*: 282–292.

Moradi, T. (2010). Eastern intersubjectivity: relational homes for frailty and death. In: S. Akhtar (Ed.), *The Wound of Mortality: Fear, Denial and Acceptance of Death* (pp. 135–154). Northvale, NJ: Jason Aronson.

Morrison, A. (1989). *Shame, the Underside of Narcissism*. Hillsdale, NJ: Analytic Press.

Natterson, J., & Knudson, A. (1965). Observations concerning fear of death in fatally ill children and their mothers. In: R. Fulton (Ed.), *Death and Identity* (pp. 235–278). New York: John Wiley.

Neugarten, B. (1979). Time, age and the life cycle. *American Journal of Psychiatry, 136*: 887–894.

Ogden, T. (1986). *The Matrix of the Mind*. New York: Jason Aronson.

Omen, The (1976). Directed by R. Donner, Twentieth Century Fox production.

On Golden Pond (1981). Directed by M. Rydell, produced by IPC Films.

Otto, R. (2000). Assessing and managing violence risk in outpatient settings. *Journal of Clinical Psychology, 56*: 1239–1262.

Ovesey, L. (1963). Fear of vocational success. *Archives of General Psychiatry, 7*: 82–92.

Pally, R. (2000). *The Mind-Brain Relationship*. London: Karnac.

Parens, H. (1980). An exploration of the relations of instinctual drives and the symbiosis/separation-individuation process. *Journal of the American Psychoanalytic Association, 28*: 89–114.

Paskauskas, R. A. (Ed.) (1995). *The Complete Correspondence of Sigmund Freud and Ernest Jones, 1908–1939*. Cambridge, MA: Harvard University Press.

Person, E. S. (1988). *Dreams of Love and Fateful Encounters*. New York: W. W. Norton.

Phillips, A. (1988). *Winnicott*. Boston, MA: Harvard University Press.

Piaget, J. (1969). *The Psychology of the Child*. New York: Basic.

Prall, R. (1996). Separation-individuation-aspects in later life. In: S. Akhtar & S. Kramer (Eds.), *The Seasons of Life: Separation-Individuation Perspectives* (pp. 75–125). Northvale, NJ: Jason Aronson, 1997.

Psycho (1960). Directed by A. Hitchcock, Shamley Productions.

Puppet Masters (1994). Directed by S. Orme, Hollywood Pictures production.

Rangell, L. (1952). The analysis of a doll phobia. *International Journal of Psychoanalysis, 33*: 43–53.

Raphling, D. (1989). Fetishism in a woman. *Journal of the American Psychoanalytic Association, 37*: 465–491.

Raphling, D. (1996). The interpretation of daydreams. *International Journal of Psychoanalysis, 44*: 533–547.

Rodgers, R., & Hammerstein, O. (1951). *The King and I.* http://www.allmusic.com/album/the-king-and-i-original-1951-cast-mw0000690357

Rodman, F. R. (2003). *Winnicott: Life and Work.* Cambridge, MA: Da Capo Press.

Roiphe, H., & Galenson, E. (1972). Early genital activity and the castration complex. *Psychoanalytic Quarterly, 41*: 334–347.

Rosen, J. (1971). Review of "The Complete Psychiatrist: The Achievements of Paul H. Hoch, MD. N. Lewis & M. Strahl (Eds.), Albany, NY State University of New York Press, 1968." *Psychoanalytic Review, 58*: 154–156.

Rosenfeld, H. (1971). Theory of life and death instincts: aggressive aspects of narcissism. *International Journal of Psychoanalysis, 45*: 332–337.

Ross, J. (1996). Male infidelity in long marriages: second adolescences and fourth individuations. In: S. Akhtar & S. Kramer (Eds.), *Intimacy and Infidelity: Separation-Individuation Perspectives* (pp. 109–130). Northvale, NJ: Jason Aronson.

Ruderman, E. G. (2006). Nurturance and self-sabotage: psychoanalytic perspectives on women's fear of success. *International Forum of Psychoanalysis, 15*: 85–95.

Rudnytsky, P. (2012). *Rescuing Psychoanalysis from Freud.* London: Karnac.

Sadock, B., Sadock, V., & Ruiz, P. (Eds.) (2009). *Kaplan and Sadock's Comprehensive Textbook of Psychiatry.* Philadelphia, PA: Lippincott, Williams & Wilkins.

Sandler, A. -M. (1989). Comments on phobic mechanisms in childhood. *Psychoanalytic Study of the Child, 44*: 101–114.

Sandler, J., & Sandler, A. -M. (1998). *Internal Objects Revisited.* London: Karnac.

Sanger, D., & Sang-Hun, C. (January 24, 2013). North Korea issues blunt new threat to United States. *New York Times.* http://www.nytimes.com/2013/01/25/world/ (accessed April 28, 2013).

Scharansky, N., & Dermer, R. (2004). *The Case for Democracy: The Power of Freedom to Overcome Tyranny and Terror.* New York: Public Affairs.

Schur, M. (1966). *The Id and the Regulatory Principles of Mental Functioning.* New York: International Universities Press.

Shakespeare, W. (1606). *Macbeth.* New York: Simon & Schuster, 2003.

Shining, The (1980). Directed by S. Kubrick, Warner Brothers production.

Silberer, H. (1909). Report on method of eliciting and observing certain symbolic hallucination-phenomena. In: D. Rapaport (Ed.), *Organization and Pathology of Thought* (pp. 208–233). New York: Columbia University Press, 1951.

Silverman, M. A. (1980). A fresh look of the case of Little Hans. In: M. Kanzer & J. Glenn (Eds.), *Freud and His Patients* (pp. 96–120). New York: Jason Aronson.

Slater, P. E. (1964). Prolegomena to a psychoanalytic theory of aging and death. In: R. Kastenbaum (Ed.), *New Thoughts on Old Age* (pp. 19–40). New York: Springer.

Solyom, L., Beck, P., Solyom, C., & Hugel, R. (1974). Some etiological factors in phobic neurosis. *Canadian Psychiatric Association Journal, 19*: 69–78.

Spence, J. (1982). *Narrative Truth and Historical Truth.* New York: Basic.

Spitz, R. A. (1965). *The First Year of Life.* New York: International Universities Press.

St. Clair, M. (1996). *Object Relations and Self Psychology—An Introduction.* Pacific Grove, CA: Brooks/Cole Publishing.

Stein, R. (1998). Passion's friends, passion's enemies: commentary on paper by Stephen A. Mitchell. *Psychoanalytic Dialogues, 8*: 547–560.

Stein, R. (2008). The otherness of sexuality: excess. *Journal of the American Psychoanalytic Association, 56*: 43–71.

Steinberg, W. (1987). Fear of success. *Quadrant, 19*: 23–39.

Stone, M. (1980). *The Borderline Syndrome.* New York: McGraw Hill.

Symonds, A. (1985). Separation and loss: significance for women. *American Journal of Psychoanalysis, 45*: 53–58.

Szekely, L. (1960). Success, success neurosis and the self. *British Journal of Medical Psychology, 33*: 45–51.

Texas Chain Saw Massacre, The (1974). Directed by T. Hooper, Vortex Pictures production.

Tyson, R. L. (1978). Notes on the analysis of a prelatency boy with a dog phobia. *Psychoanalytic Study of the Child, 33*: 427–458.

U.S. Census Bureau, Statistical Abstract of the United States (2012). *Table 1103. Motor Vehicle Accidents–Number and Deaths: 1990 to 2009.* http://www.census.gov/compendia/statab/ (accessed April 25, 2013).

Volkan, V. (1976). *Primitive Internalized Object Relations.* New York: International Universities Press.

Volkan, V. (1982). *Linking Objects and Linking Phenomena.* Madison, CT: International Universities Press.

Volkan, V. (1988). *The Need to Have Enemies and Allies.* Northvale, NJ: Jason Aronson.

Volkan, V. (1997). *Bloodlines: From Ethnic Pride to Ethnic Terrorism.* New York: Farrar, Straus and Giroux.

Walcott, D., Cerundolo, J., & Beck, J. (2001). Current analysis of the Tarasoff Duty: an evolution towards the limitation of the duty to protect. *Behavioral Science and the Law, 19*: 325–343. http://users.phhp.ufl.edu/rbauer/Intro%20CLP/ (accessed April 25, 2013).

Wangh, M. (1959). Structural determinants of phobia. *Journal of the American Psychoanalytic Association, 7*: 675–695.

War of the Worlds, The (1953). Directed by J. Carpenter, Paramount Pictures production.

Weinstein, M. (1971). The experience of separation-individuation in infancy and its reverberations through the course of life—1. Infancy and childhood. *Journal of the American Psychoanalytic Association, 21:* 135–154.

Weiss, E. (1964). *Agoraphobia in the Light of Ego Pyschology.* New York: Grune & Stratton.

Winnicott, C. (1980). Fear of breakdown: a clinical example. *International Journal of Psychoanalysis, 61:* 351–357.

Winnicott, D. W. (1958). The capacity to be alone. In: *The Maturational Processes and the Facilitating Environment* (pp. 29–36). London: Hogarth, 1965.

Winnicott, D. W. (1960). Ego distortion in terms of the true and false self. In: *The Maturational Processes and the Facilitating Environment* (pp. 140–152). London: Hogarth, 1965.

Winnicott, D. W. (1962). Ego integration in child development. In: *The Maturational Processes and the Facilitating Environment* (pp. 56–63). New York: International Universities Press, 1965.

Winnicott, D. W. (1963). The development of the capacity for concern. In: *The Maturational Processes and the Facilitating Environment* (pp. 73–82). New York: International Universities Press, 1965.

Winnicott, D. W. (1965). *The Maturational Processes and the Facilitating Environment.* New York: International Universities Press.

Winnicott, D. W. (1969). The use of an object and relating through identifications. In: *Playing and Reality* (pp. 86–94). London: Tavistock.

Winnicott, D. W. (1971). Mirror-role of the mother and family in child development. In: *Playing and Reality* (pp. 111–118). London: Routledge, 1989.

Winnicott, D. W. (1974). Fear of breakdown. In: C. Winnicott, R. Shepherd, & M. Davis (Eds.), *Psychoanalytic Explorations* (pp. 87–95). Cambridge, MA: Harvard University Press, 1989.

Wolf, E. S. (1994). Selfobject experiences: development, psychopathology, treatment. In: S. Kramer & S. Akhtar (Eds.), *Mahler and Kohut: Perspectives on Development, Psychopathology, and Technique* (pp. 65–96). Northvale, NJ: Jason Aronson.

Wolpe, J., & Rachman, R. (1960). Psychoanalytic evidence: a critique based on Freud's case of Little Hans. *Journal of Nervous and Mental Disorders, 131:* 135–148.

Wurmser, L. (1981). *The Mask of Shame.* Baltimore, MD: Johns Hopkins University Press.

Yap, P. M. (1969). Classification of the culture-bound reactive syndromes. *Australian and New Zealand Journal of Psychiatry, 3:* 172–179.

Zilboorg, G. (1943). Fear of death. *Psychoanalytic Quarterly, 12:* 465–475.

INDEX

Stone, M. 14
"success neurosis" 147–148
Suddath, R. 34
symbolism 15
Symonds, A. 4
Szekely, L. 154, 167
Szurek, S. 135

Target, M. 27, 29, 130
terror 4
"terrorism" 18
Thayer, Norman 184
The American Psychoanalytic
    Association 69
The Birds 20
The Exorcist 20
"the ideal gender is male" 72
"the imposter syndrome" 156
"the infantile neurosis" 217
The Interpretation of Dreams 44
The Omen 20
The Shining 20
The Texas Chain Saw Massacre 20
Three Essays 50
Tobin, S. 175
"topophobia" 13
Tremblay, L. 130
Tyson, R. L. 10

"universal fears" 17
"unmentalized xenophobia" 17
"unthinkable anxiety" 8, 171

Volkan, V. 18, 24, 144

Walcott, D. 141
Walk, R. D. 5
Wangh, M. 10
war 60
War of the Worlds 20
Wayne, John 32
Weiss, E. 14
Winnicott, C. 37, 41, 56
Winnicott, D. W. 8, 38–42, 46–49, 55,
    58, 85, 88–92, 94–95, 98–100, 110,
    171, 195, 197–198, 200, 211, 219
Wolf, E. S. 68
Wolpe, J. 11
Wright, J. 6
Wurmser, L. 69

Yap, P. M. 17

Zilboorg, G. 6